SOCIOLOGY AND THE PERIPHERY:
Theories and Issues
Second Revised Edition

Anton L. Allahar
Professor of Sociology,
University of Western Ontario

Garamond Press
Toronto

© Anton L. Allahar 1995

No part of this book may be reproduced or transmitted in any form , by any means, electronic or mechanical, without written permission in writing from the publisher, except by a reviewer who may quote brief passages in a review.

Printed and bound in Canada.

A publication of Garamond Press

Garamond Press,
77 Mowat Ave., Suite 403
Toronto, On.
M6K 3E3

Canadian Cataloguing in Publication Data

Allahar, Anton L. , 1949-
        Sociology and the periphery : theories and issues

2nd rev ed.
Includes bibliographical references and index.
ISBN 0-920059-13-9

1. Sociology.   2. Developing countries - Social
conditions.   I. Title.

HM73.A55 1944   301   C94-932064-1

Contents

Preface   9

CHAPTER ONE   15
The Intellectual Ferment
    Ideology and Science
    Sociology and Science
    Social Structure and the Critical Spirit

CHAPTER TWO   31
The Sociological Tradition
    Positivism
    Positivism and Behaviourism
    Interactionism
    Interactionism and Feminism
    Realism
    Realism and Historical Materialism
    Exploitation and the Question of Value

CHAPTER THREE   53
Social Evolutionism: A European Perspective
    Positivism and Social Evolutionism
    The Law of Three Stages
    Structural Functionalism
    Evolutionism, Functionalism, and Change
    Ideal Types
    The Pattern Variables
    Stages of Economic Growth Thesis
    Politics of Evolutionism

CHAPTER FOUR   79
Modernization: An American View
  Social Psychology and Modernization Theory
  The Latin American Value Structure
  Canadian-U.S. Value Differences
  Modernization, Dualism, and Diffusionism
  Politics of Modernization during the Cold War
  The Post-Cold War Era
  Democracy and Ideology
  Modernization and Social Control

CHAPTER FIVE   105
Dependency: A Third World Approach
  Free Will and Determinism
  Dependency Theory
  Marxism and Dependency
  Dependency and Regionalism in Canada
  Filling the Gaps
  Colonialism and Imperialism
  The Colonial Mode of Production
  From Realism to Revolution

CHAPTER SIX   141
Peasants and Revolution
  Marxism and Revolutionary Classes
  The Peasantry as a Class
  Peasant Social Organization Past and Present
  Power Relations within the Community
  Peasant Revolts and Rebellions
  Peasant Communities in the Age of Imperialism
  Peasants and Revolution
  The Question of Leadership
  The Cuban Experience
  Revolution in the Periphery

| CHAPTER SEVEN | 169 |

Race, Gender, and Development
Racism
History of the Idea of Race
The Ideological Context
Race, Colour, and Christianity
Race, Christianity, and Colonialism
Gender and Colonialism: The Woman of Colour
Women and Development
Women's Economic and Political Responses
Socialism and Feminism: Some Reflections on Cuba
Reflections and Conclusions

| BIBLIOGRAPHY | 201 |

| INDEX | 220 |

List of Tables

Table 5.1   Selected U.S. Corporations in the Caribbean

Table 5.2   Selected Canadian and European Corporations
in the Caribbean

Table 5.3   Commonwealth Caribbean Direction of Trade

Table 5.4   U.S. Military Assistance to the Caribbean Basin
1980-89

Table 5.5   Major Canadian Multinationals in the Caribbean

Table 5.6   Third World External Debt 1982, 1988-1991

Table 5.7   Third World Long-Term Debt

Table 7.1   Changes in Minimum Food Costs and Minimum
Wage, Jamaica 1979-1985

Table 7.2   Indicators of the Rising Cost of Living,
Dominican Republic 1980-1986

For
Anne and Aniisa
you make it so easy for me to do what I do;
and for
Roxanne, Haven, and Kurt,
who continue to honour the memory of our parents
Cynthia I. and Clifton L. Allahar

Acknowledgements

Sociology and the Periphery owes two main debts of gratitude: the first is to my students, who over the years have taught me most of the sociology I know; and the second is to my friends and colleagues in the Caribbean Study Group, who have taught me that intellectual growth is impossible unless one belongs to a community of true scholars. I wish to acknowledge these two groups of teachers, and while I cannot hope to list all the names of those in the first group, I can certainly personalize the members of the second: Percy Anderson, Linda Carty, Rudy "Moscow" Grant, Cecilia Green, Horace Henriques, Odida Quamina, Delroy "Debo" Reid, David Trotman, and Ralston "Wally" Walters. We all share a collective responsibility for the various strengths and weaknesses of the arguments presented here.

In addition, I would also like to thank those colleagues and their students, in Canada, in the periphery, and elsewhere, who used this book in the first edition and made it such a success. I also wish to acknowledge my deepest appreciation to Peter Saunders, Robert Clarke, and the team at Garamond Press for their wonderful encouragement and confidence in this project. I thank you all.

A.L.A., London, Ont., July 1994

Preface

In his sweeping historical survey of slavery in ancient and modern times, Orlando Patterson remarked that the generalist lives in constant fear of the specialist. By this he implied that those whose scientific pursuits are aimed at the acquisition of *nomothetic* knowledge and the discovery of general causal sequences or propositions will often be open to attacks from others who are concerned with generating *idiographic* knowledge from the study of specific, unique events. But this does not imply that idiographic knowledge is to be preferred over nomothetic; or that the nomothetic knowledge is less useful than the idiographic. For as someone who specializes in generalities, the sociologist undertakes comparative research and is of necessity interested in identifying the broad features or patterns held in common by distinct societies or social groupings, and in specifying the conditions under which they are likely to be present.

Sociology and the Periphery is written in the tradition of nomothetic science. It explores in a wide context the social, economic, and political implications of three theories that have addressed the questions of development and underdevelopment in the periphery--that group of countries making up the so-called Third World. The book invites students and teachers alike to look beyond their respective national and regional boundaries and to take account of the different contributions, historical and contemporary, that the periphery has made to the overall formation of the current world system. It also attempts to sensitize us to the shrinking and interdependent nature of the global society by suggesting how such pressing social issues as nationalism and political independence, economic growth, unemployment, poverty, racism, and sexism--issues that occupy so much attention in the countries of the industrialized North, are remarkably similar to the everyday concerns of people in the periphery. In short, the book asks us to think relationally, to view the problems of societal advancement and extreme poverty as two sides of the same coin: the very processes that led to the general accumulation of wealth and a high level of industrial growth in some countries have simultaneously led to deprivation and starkly uneven development in others.

Whether approaching the questions of change and development from a positivistic, interactionist, or realist position, sociologists have been led to speak in generalities. They seek to identify patter n s of social behaviour, economic trends, or tendencies as well as political forms that characterize a given society or set of societies. It is in this spirit that *Sociology and the Periphery* proposes to analyse various theories of development as they apply broadly to the countries of the periphery.

Those countries are by no means identical in human and natural resources, in their social and cultural makeups, or in their belief systems. But it is nevertheless possible to discuss them as a whole, in large part because the so-called "advanced" countries have had such a homogenizing effect on their broad institutional compositions. For it is a fact that as a result of their contact with the industrialized countries, through the processes of colonialism and imperialism, peripheral countries have come increasingly to resemble those Northern countries in terms of selected social, economic, political, and class indicators. Tribal and ethnic *differences* have been converted into tribal and ethnic *divisions*; communally owned property has become privatized; and co-operative working arrangements have given way to competitive and exploitive relations.

Thus, while the life chances and daily pursuits of the general populace in countries such as Mexico, Haiti, and Barbados differ in their details, the general capitalist and imperialist contexts that structure and determine everyday life are strikingly alike. In the societies of the Spanish, French, or British Caribbean the plantation system, for example, has imparted broad structural and institutional similarities, which were reinforced through the imperialist connection and have contributed significantly to the current levels of dependence and underdevelopment.

The idea for this study was born of a common or recurrent complaint that I have heard from students over the past fifteen years. Whether in courses on Introductory Sociology, Social Inequality, Social Change, Political Sociology, or Sociological Theory, students have consistently complained that they "can't see the forest for the trees." While they are usually able to grasp the details of a particular argument, the larger picture seems to escape them. In other words, they experience great difficulty in relating specific analyses and insights to the larger aims and claims of sociological explanation. How, for example, are Durkheim's discussion of social solidarity, Weber's treatment of social meaning, and Marx's concern with worker alienation related to the general questions of social order, social disorder, and social change? Or how does the class structure inherited from the colonial period influence a peripheral country's terms of dependence in the age of imperialism? How does that structure condition the country's potential for development?

One of the main aims of this book, then, is to paint a sharper picture of the "forest," which includes the periphery. For if teachers ignore the periphery in our various sociological lectures and writings, we yield an incomplete picture of social reality, and we deny our students the chance to complete the intellectual journey. Our students must come to understand that the structure of the family, the causes of deviance, the patterns of inequality, or the sources of social change vary greatly from society to society, and are often determined by factors and influences beyond national borders. And this is the sense in which I speak of an increasingly shrinking and interdependent world. The point, then, is to recognize the need for both discrete, country-by-country studies, and more macro, synthetic approaches in our writings and lectures.

Just as importantly, this is a book about sociology and not about the periphery per se. It is not written specifically for students of development, and I make no attempt to offer a detailed and all-encompassing assessment of development processes or projects within peripheral societies. Rather, in examining a number of theoretical and thematic issues of a sociological nature I hope to help correct some of the ethnocentric biases contained in established or metropolitan approaches to sociology. Those approaches, generally speaking, either ignore the periphery altogether or assume that developments within the peripheral societies closely mirror those in the advanced countries. I also hope that the application of such issues to non-traditional intellectual settings will pose new problems, which will in turn call for a re-examination of existing theories and models. The process can only lead to a broadening of the horizons of sociological inquiry and more rigorous thinking on the part of sociologists.

Chapter one seeks to situate the formal beginnings of sociological thinking within the European Enlightenment period and the intellectual ferment of the French Revolution. It addresses the question of method and offers a definition and discussion of the concepts of "ontology" and "epistemology." The chapter also introduces the concept of "social structure," as the key to thinking sociologically. Of major significance here is the treatment of the relationship between science and ideology, which asks that

Preface   11

the various sociological theories and explanations be situated within the practical political contexts of their proponents and adherents.

In chapter two I discuss the three major sociological traditions or schools of thought on development and change and expand the treatment of epistemology, drawing out the ideological and methodological underpinnings associated with these traditions and applying them to concrete examples. Thus, the tradition of positivism is linked with social-behaviourism, while the interactionist school informs a key school of feminism, and theoretical realism is treated as the epistemology that best describes Marxist methodology.

The third chapter deals with one of the earliest approaches to change and development: social-evolutionism. Its roots lie in the classical European tradition, which heavily influenced the thinking of the founding fathers of sociology. As a consequence, positivist methodology is most clearly evidenced in this major sociological school of thought. Some key aspects of social-evolutionism concern its ideological conservatism, its almost total reliance on description as opposed to analysis, its ahistoricism, and its important influence on structural functionalist theorizing.

Chapter four takes up the modernization challenge to evolutionary thinking. For if evolutionary thought sought to minimize the role of human agency in the process of societal change, modernization thinkers wrote human beings squarely into the picture. This school, which clearly belongs to the tradition of interactionist and microsociology, borrows a great deal from psychology and plays down the social-structural and macro-explanations of change. Specifically, modernization theorists see the question of change and development as having more to do with the "internal," psychological make-up of individuals in a given population than with "external," structural factors. Thus, they are also ideologically conservative, although for different reasons than the social evolutionists. The chapter also examines the thorny question of democracy in the post-Cold War era, given the conviction among modernization theorists that liberal democracy is a key element of a modern society.

In the fifth chapter I present the ideologically radical position that draws its theoretical insight and inspiration from Marxism. The theorists who subscribe to this approach are said to belong to the dependency school, given their position that the countries of the periphery became underdeveloped as a direct result of economic dependence on the industrialized countries. Although in its early years the practice tended to be descriptive, dependency theorists later adopted Marxian class analysis and advocated social revolution-

12   Sociology and the Periphery

-a complete breakaway from the world capitalist system--as the only means for true economic and social transformation of the periphery. Because their analyses emphasize factors such as the structures of dependency, exploitation, and class, dependency thinkers can be linked to the tradition of theoretical realism.

Chapter six takes up the issue of revolution in the periphery and analyses various class-structural factors associated with that phenomenon. While Marx's model of revolution in the industrialized capitalist countries had its shortcomings, his method can be utilized to inform an appreciation of just where in the periphery social revolution is likely to occur, who its participants are likely to be, and what types of changes are most likely to be implemented successfully. In this discussion the role of the peasantry and its various fractions merits special attention, because the experience of the twentieth century has seen peasants playing key roles in every major social revolution.

Chapter seven addresses the questions of race and gender in historical and contemporary contexts. As two of the principal dimensions of social inequality and exploitation, racism and sexism are at the heart of major debates in both the highly industrialized and peripheral countries today. This chapter seeks to uncover some of the historical roots of racism and sexism and relate them to questions of politics, ideology, social control, slavery, and the role of women in development. In conclusion, these concerns are related back to the major schools and currents of thought discussed throughout the book.

Preface   13

ι

Chapter One

The Intellectual Ferment

It seems almost a law of human social organization that wherever men and women interact in significant numbers they are divided on questions of preference for things both material and ideational. Perhaps this bears testimony to the freedom of the human spirit and to the fact that as human beings, whether individually or in groups, we are guided by subjective and unique interpretations and evaluations of what is best for us. As individuals, however, our personal preferences and tastes do not always coincide with those of the larger society to which we belong.

Because people tend to join groups and participate in social activities based on their subjective evaluations of their own best interests, a great deal of potential conflict exists not just between individuals in different groups, but also among social groups themselves. Further, this potential conflict is accentuated when social strategists and government planners must perforce make decisions in the interest of wider societal groupings. These groupings include organizations and associations such as big business lobbies, political parties, trade unions, ethnic communities, and unemployed or disabled workers. On any given policy item or social program implemented by a government there are thus bound to be differences and divisions within the population at large. Consider, for example, the issues of constitutional reform, free trade, nuclear disarmament, and legalized abortion.

It is in this context that social scientists tend to employ the terms "radical" and "conservative." By radical they generally mean an orientation that is egalitarian, populist, and democratic in the broad sense. They use conservative in connection with elitist ideas and practices, which are opposed to equality and are generally anti-democratic in their thrust. Here, however, I intend to use these terms in a somewhat broader manner, where, for example, a group of revolutionary socialists can become quite conservative in seeking to protect their political gains, when once they have taken and consolidated power.

Similarly, depending on where individuals or groups stand in relation to the present power structure (status quo), their ideas and views can be either conservative or radical. To put it simply (but without being simplistic), if the group in power espouses policies that are consistent with your interests, you will want to preserve them in power: you will be conservative. Conversely, if that group pursues policies inimical to your interests, you will want to remove them: you will be radical. Of course, it is also possible for the group in power to pursue moderate, middle-of-the-road policies: not too conservative; not too radical. In such a case you will tend to find reform-minded conservatives and radicals--those who want minor reforms, but reforms moving in different directions.

This discussion of subjectively perceived goals and conservative or radical orientations is of prime significance in sociology. In fact, it has become customary to speak of conservative and radical schools in sociological thought in much the same way that one speaks of conservative and radical governments. In his introduction to *Main Currents in Sociological Thought*, Vol. 1, Raymond Aron provides by far the most succinctly stated summary of this division. Aron says that in relation to non-socialist societies, the socialist or Marxist sociology of the type once practised in the Soviet Union was radical, synthetic, and historically grounded. He also terms this practice "progressive" in that Marxist sociology assumes the superiority of the future socialist order over past or current regimes (Aron 1965:9). Because Soviet society had already witnessed its socialist revolution, the "progressive" thrust of that brand of sociology was aimed primarily at bourgeois or capitalist societies. Soviet sociology thus functioned more or less as an official state ideology, which argued that revolutions of a socialist type were necessary to transform the oppressive structures of capitalist society and create a more just and humane social (socialist) order. Hence, while occupying a conservative ideological role relative to socialist society, Marxist sociology has purely radical implications for the non-socialist world, which is yet to undergo "the revolution."

American sociology, by contrast, is fundamentally analytical and empirical. Being less concerned with general laws of history, American sociologists, until the 1960s at least, opted largely for studies dealing with such micro- and social-psychological issues as attitudes towards political parties, motives directing social behaviour, and interaction between teachers and students and classroom settings (Aron 1965:11). Thus the entire tradition of interactionist sociology, which places the individual actor at the centre of the social universe, is distinctively American.

The conservative thrust of this approach lies in its emphasis on the individual as the prime unit of analysis. American sociologists, Aron contends, tend to analyse major social problems such as unemployment, poverty, and racism, for example, from the point of view of individual shortcomings and policy aberrations, rather than by referring to the general nature and structure of capitalist society. In this way they seldom single out for criticism the central institutions of capitalist society, which are portrayed as inherently democratic and open. Like radical sociologists, then, U.S. sociologists in the main also argue that they have already had their revolution, albeit a capitalist one. For this reason, Aron says, American sociology is fundamentally conservative with respect to U.S. society as a whole; and where change is deemed necessary, it is usually conceived of as involving minor reforms and not a radical restructuring of the system:

> American sociologists are more sympathetic than hostile to American society, but their sympathy takes the form of approval of the whole and criticism of the parts.... American sociologists are inclined to be reformists for the whole world.... The adoption of the American sociological method and attitude will lead to the adoption of reformist positions. (Aron 1965:11)

As (social) scientists, then, how do sociologists account for what are in essence subjective orientations towards conservative, radical, or reformist stands on various social, economic, and political issues? For if our preferences for things material and ideational involve ideologies and value judgements, is not our claim to scientific objectivity compromised? Or, as Frank Parkin (1982:32) points out, if our arguments are merely thinly veiled value preferences, it is difficult to see how one of those arguments can claim explanatory superiority over another: "To pit one version of reality against another involves, ultimately, a conflict of moralities." For Max Weber (1949:97), however, there is no necessary contradiction between the subjective value preferences of sociologists and their claims to the pursuit of objective knowledge. Although as humans we are, by definition, subjective beings and thus cannot avoid subjective involvement in our world, it is still possible, cognitively, to distance ourselves from that world and view it in an objective or dispassionate manner. Being subjective does not automatically imply that we are biased. It is, therefore, intellectually healthy to acknowledge our personal subjectivity in order to be able to hold it in abeyance, for only in so doing will we manage to recognize threats to our objectivity.

Thus, in paraphrasing Weber, Barry Hindess notes, "There can be no objective study of social phenomena independent of special and one-sided viewpoints" (1977:32). And as Weber himself insists, the values in question may or may not be shared by the investigator concerned. In principle, he argues, they should play no part in scientific investigation even if "the highest ideals which move us most forcefully are always formed only in the struggle with other ideals which are just as sacred to others as ours are to us" (Weber 1949:57).

The determination of what is true about a given social phenomenon, then, always comes down to the matter of evidence, although, as we will see, the feminist critique of science raises the question of just what constitutes evidence. Regardless of their subjective values and preferences, scientists must always be concerned with the rigour that attends the collection and interpretation of data. For without such concern, ideological considerations may well enter the process of observation and colour the findings. This concern forms a crucial aspect of sociological theories of change and development.

Ideology and Science

Thomas Kuhn's observations that changes in the dominant paradigm "cause scientists to see the world of their research-engagement differently" and that "after a revolution scientists are responding to a different world" are key to the study of ideology and social change (Kuhn 1970:111). For as Mark Hagopian (1974:140) points out, "Scientists are, after all, opinion makers and their views ultimately affect the general state of beliefs in society." He adds, "And it is quite likely that the new world harbours many aspects that are not in keeping with the view of the world associated with the traditional society."

Given the existence of both conservative science and radical scientific revolutions, we can expect each to yield its own ideological justifications and defences for the right to exist. In their theories and descriptions of change, the conservatives argue for the wisdom and correctness of tradition; while in their writings the radicals, who have little or no stake in the existing order, insist on the need for change in a particular direction.

Karl Marx, for instance, views ideology negatively as a set of beliefs that serve to justify and legitimize the rule of the few over the many. He sees beliefs as self-confirming theories whereby any evidence that supports the beliefs in question are emphasized, while evidence that goes against those beliefs is ignored or accorded minimal relevance. Within capitalism, the principal source of ideology for Marx is the economic structure or base of the society. This relates specifically to the system under which commodities produced by workers are appropriated by capitalists, leading ultimately to the development of class conflict between the two. By ideology he means the moral codes, philosophies, art, law, religion, and even literature that comprise a society's "superstructure," the glue that binds together the economic base or "substructure" of that society.

Because Marx gives primacy to economic dealings and to the fact that those activities colour the greater part of all social interactions, and because he links his treatment of ideology with domination and the class structure of society, he underestimates the autonomous role that ideas and ideology can play in everyday life. His use of the term "ideology" is very general, and it was left to other scholars, most notably Max Weber and Karl Mannheim, to attempt a more complete treatment of it. However, neither Weber nor Mannheim manages to divorce ideology completely from class (Gerth and Mills 1958:61-63; Abercrombie, Hill, and Turner 1980:30-36).

From Weber's point of view it is not that Marx is wrong to emphasize the economic basis of domination, for on that score he applauds many of Marx's insights. As Irving M. Zeitlin (1981:128) says, Weber "was not concerned with refuting Marx ... nor did he see himself as having bested Marx. On the contrary, he looked upon Marx's analytical concepts and methodological principles as extraordinarily fruitful." Weber's main quarrel is that Marx does not go far enough and take account of the extra-economic bases of human action. Weber sees human behaviour as informed largely by meanings, subjective perceptions, and personal assessments of goals. Psychological states, he argues, are as important as material interests in guiding that behaviour. This is a central theme in his classic study *The Protestant Ethic and the Spirit of Capitalism* (1958).

Weber, therefore, is concerned with "rounding out" the Marxian thesis; with demonstrating the non-material basis of action and showing how, under certain circumstances, "Ideas become effective forces in history" (Weber 1958:90). According to Hans Gerth and C.W. Mills, "With Marx he shares the sociological approach to ideas: they are powerless in history unless they are fused with material interests" (Gerth and Mills 1958:62). But where Marx emphasizes an almost one-to-one correspondence between ideas and interests, Weber is also eager to recognize possible tensions between them. In other words, although he sees ideas and class interests as often linked, Weber prefers to leave the door open to the possibility of a conflict between ideas and material interests.

Applying the concept of "elective affinity" to the ideas of social and economic change, Weber points out that his argument is not one of cause and effect. In other words, he is not saying that the ideas associated with Protestantism *caused* capitalism; rather, he contends that certain elements in Protestant thinking and practice complemented other elements of early capitalist thinking and behaviour. The relationship was a random one, or one that witnessed an "elective affinity" between one set of religious ideas and another set of economic pursuits. Further, Weber argues that human beings are not total prisoners of social or class structures. They do have some freedom to choose and discard ideas as suits their purposes: "Ideas do gain an affinity with the interests of certain members of special strata; if they do not gain such affinity, they are abandoned" (Weber 1958:63).

Linking the views of Weber and Mannheim on ideology, Nicholas Abercrombie and his co-authors are quick to draw a connection between those views and Marxism. Marx's and Engels's contention that the ruling ideas of every age are the ideas of the ruling class, the so-called dominant ideology thesis, represents their attempt to reduce ideas to concrete economic and political or class interests. But for Weber and Mannheim also, class is a crucial variable:

> The sociology of knowledge tradition of Weber and Mannheim, attempts to show how beliefs can be reduced to social groups.... The sociology of knowledge which tries to develop a non-Marxist theory of ideology in fact arrives at similar class-theoretical conclusions to the dominant ideology tradition with Marxism. (Abercrombie, Hill, and Turner 1980:30)

As far as Mannheim is concerned his sociology of knowledge is firmly rooted in the Marxian tradition: he often acknowledges his intellectual debts to Marx (Mannheim 1936:75-77) and constantly refers to the class (or what he calls "group") origins of ideas and actions. Nowhere is this made more clear than in his discussion of "ideology" and "utopia."

For Mannheim the everyday conditions of existence and the conflicts they generate between various groups and classes lead to two opposing movements of thought or ideas. Such ideas he terms "situationally transcendent" or unreal, for they do not fit into the prevailing order (1936:194). Situationally transcendent ideas are of two types: either "ideological" or "utopian," depending on the social location or perspective from which they are viewed. The rulers, oppressors, or members of the upper strata, who have a vested interest in maintaining the status quo, dismiss the claims of the ruled or oppressed strata as unrealistic, utopian. The oppressed, conversely, see the oppressors' defence of the status quo as ideological: appeals to divine law, the sanctity of tradition, or the natural order of things are deemed ideological, because they are inherently defensive and aimed at conserving the existing order (Hagopian 1974:256).

When we discuss the relationship between ideology and science or ideology and truth, we might say that ideologies are like dogmas. Ideologies claim truth, but do not propose a method to substantiate this claim. Science, on the other hand, pursues knowledge and truth in a demonstrable fashion. Scientific truth can be questioned, tested, refuted, or upheld. As Gustav Bergmann (1951:210) suggests, an ideological statement is "a value judgement disguised as, or mistaken for, a statement of fact." Or, following Garvin McCain and Erwin M. Segal (1969:31-32), who equate ideology with dogma: "One way of contrasting science and dogma is to say that a scientist accepts facts as given and belief systems as tentative, whereas a dogmatist accepts the belief systems as given; facts are irrelevant."

This does not mean that certain scientific truths have not been fashioned into dogma by those who accept them as absolute. Nor does social science only deal with "facts as given." For facts are never free of theory. They are always interpreted and screened subjectively as human beings seek to impart *meaning* to them. Science, too, can also be made into an ideology, as, for example, in the charge that feminists level at traditional (male) science.

By way of definition we can say that an ideology usually consists of five dimensions: the cognitive; affective; evaluative; programmatic; and social (Rejai 1971:3-10). The cognitive dimension refers to the fact that ideologies embody a significant element of myth and make-believe, or willingness to believe, which simplifies a complex social reality. Such simplification is usually accomplished by the use of symbols, such as the crucifix or the swastika, that "package" meanings of, and responses to, reality.

The cognitive and affective dimensions are closely related. To the extent that ideologies elicit emotive responses, they can be embraced blindly and at times passionately. This is clearly evidenced in political, religious, and nationalist ideologies: "One might say, in fact, the most important, latent function of ideology is to tap emotion" (Bell 1960:371). Thus, the affective or emotional elements of the ideologies of feminism or black power, for example, can be seen in the passion that they excite in their adherents.

The evaluative dimension of ideology concerns the question of "the good society." An ideology will either criticize the existing status quo or defend it by appealing to high-sounding moral principles. Especially in political ideology, we often hear explicit references to such things as "regimes" that suppress or support human rights, liberty, equality, and dignity. Ideologies often involve value judgements aimed at discrediting those to whom they are directed. They accomplish this by masking the truth in some cases and magnifying it in others.

Many ideologies also have a programmatic dimension: they call for action that translates specific values, norms, and ideas into practice. Such actions are aimed either at maintaining a given status quo or at transforming it, as in the ideologies of conservatism, nationalism, and racism. As we might expect, the call to action also has a social component. Hence ideologies are associated with social groups and classes whose members represent specific interests, ambitions, hopes, dreams, ideals, or preferences. As the two fundamental units of subjective action in any society, individuals and social groups or classes are creators and carriers of ideology. This is why Daniel Bell (1960:372) refers to ideologies as "mobilized belief systems" that seek to "simplify ideas, establish a claim to truth, and, in the union of the two, demand a commitment to action. Thus not only does ideology transform ideas, it transforms people as well."

As a working definition, then, an ideology is a system of mobilized beliefs that claims to represent the truth and reality, but does not make any provision for assessing the veracity of those claims. To make itself accessible to the majority of the population, ideology simplifies its depiction of truth and reality by using symbols, appeals to emotions, socially accepted values, and high-sounding moral principles. Finally, the values and principles embraced in an ideology usually imply some course of social action if they are to be adhered to, and if they are to successfully represent the interests and ambitions of their promoters.

For Noam Chomsky, ideology is also closely related to propaganda. For him propaganda and ideology are one and the same thing: they both serve the purpose of social control. Significantly, Chomsky (1988) makes a distinction between ideology or propaganda in totalitarian and liberal-democratic societies. Alluding to George Orwell's novel *Nineteen Eighty-Four*, he observes that in a totalitarian society where force is used to keep people in control, propaganda is simply what the state (Ministry of Truth) produces. There is really no need for subtlety. In liberal-democratic societies, where individuals are supposedly free to think whatever they wish, and where it is not as easy to use overt force to control them, propaganda plays a far more important political role. Thus, in a political climate priding itself on the freedom of speech, those in control seek to create the illusion of open debate, of a free press within a population that is free to inquire.

As a specific example Chomsky (1988:79) uses the powerful U.S. media and what he sees as its one-sided coverage of the Vietnam War: "Anyone in the US who thought that our policies in Vietnam were wrong in principle was not admitted to the discussion about the War. The debate was essentially over tactics." What is important, then, is the formula for manufacturing "truth":

> One of the ways to do this is to create political debate that appears to embrace many opinions, but actually stays within very narrow margins. You have to make sure that both sides in the debate accept certain assumptions--and those assumptions are the basis of the propaganda system. As long as everyone accepts the propaganda system, then debate is permissible.

The illusion is that the free debate is narrowly circumscribed to permit discussion on minor issues--but never on larger principles or philosophies of political and moral action.

Sociology and Science

The discussion of "truth," "fact," and "reality" speaks to two key aspects of the scientific enterprise. The first concerns what is called *ontology*, or a statement of truth or fact. For example, to say that on the whole men are smarter than women is to make an ontological claim. The second aspect is closely related to the first and is called an *epistemology*, a theory of knowledge, or a method by which scientists go about collecting data and evidence to justify an ontological claim. Again using the same example, we could take up the method of controlled testing or the assignment of problem-solving tasks to assess whether or not men are indeed smarter than women. In other words, if ontology deals with what is factual or true, epistemology asks the question, "How do we know what is true?"

When sociologists, physicists, geologists, and psychologists refer to themselves as scientists, they are simply claiming to adhere to a specific epistemology or method of pursuing knowledge. Coming from the Latin verb *scire* (to know), science is but one among many different methods that humans have employed throughout history to gain a keener understanding of what is true about themselves and their social and physical environments. The scientific method, whether used in natural or social science, is characterized by the rigorous pursuit of truth and knowledge. This is not to say that such truth or knowledge is absolute, because scientists are always aware of the limitations of the human intellect. Nothing is ever absolutely true for all times and places. Hence the knowledge generated by scientists is always relative to the current state of development of scientific techniques and theoretical insights, and the subjective (ideological) locations of the scientists themselves in society.

The unity of the scientific outlook, however, must not be taken to imply that there is a single scientific method or that all scientists agree on procedures for collecting, analysing, and interpreting data. The process of generating knowledge is as varied as the sources (spiritual, natural, and social) from which that knowledge is generated. Thus, though there may be a general consensus about the aims and objectives of science (the production of ever-increasing knowledge), the basic assumptions made by scientists about their subject matter, and the types of questions they ask, are often very different.

Generally speaking, when we hear the word science we think of natural or physical sciences such as botany, geology, physics, or chemistry. We also think of the scientist as someone making precise and accurate predictions about a certain subject matter. In a sense, the subject matter of natural or physical scientists (plants, rocks, metals, or gases), lends itself neatly to empirical observation, experimentation, testing, weighing, measurement, and manipulation. It is relatively uncomplicated to study such things within controlled laboratory settings, where scientists can observe the behaviour of matter in response to the careful manipulation of specific conditions or variables. This is possible because the subject matter is always compelled to react in very much the same manner when subjected to the same conditions. Water, for example, comes to a boil at 100 degrees centigrade. It cannot *choose* to do otherwise.

The subject matter of social scientists is qualitatively different. It consists of individuals, social groups, and entire societies. Unlike that of physical scientists, the subject matter of sociologists (as representatives of social science) is possessed of consciousness and will. A human being, if punched in the nose today, might *choose* to run away; the same punch tomorrow could elicit the opposite response: he or she might *choose* to punch back.

Because the subject matter of sociologists is composed of rational, thinking beings, with emotions, feelings, sentiments, values, morals, consciousness, and will, its study calls for different methods than those employed by natural scientists. Further, since humans are primarily subjective beings, they interact and communicate through symbols, to *interpret* and *assign* meanings to the multiplicity of phenomena that make up the natural and social universes. This sets them apart not only from rocks and trees but also from lower forms of animal life that do not possess the capacity for abstract thought. Robert A. Nisbet and Robert G. Perrin state the matter succinctly in their book *The Social Bond* (1977). What really serves to differentiate the social from the natural sciences, they say (p.4), is that: "Only individuals assign meanings to the world around them and act in terms of such meanings. The difference between mere water and holy water, or between mere oil and anointing oil, lies in the meaning conferred." Sociology, then, seeks to make sense of those meanings, to uncover what is regular or patterned about them, to identify when and where they can be expected to occur.

As social scientists, sociologists "specialize in generalities," whereas natural scientists specialize in the particular. Sociologists aim not to make precise predictions of how a given individual will react in a given situation; but rather to identify general behaviour patterns within and among groups, explain how and why those patterns emerge, how they persist, why they may break down, and under what conditions new patterns may be established. This social forecasting is never aimed at a one hundred per cent accuracy, for the complex and variable nature of social behaviour does not permit it.

As a social science, sociology recognizes that all individuals are unique, but this is not to say that such uniqueness renders it impossible to make accurate general statements about group behaviour. Paraphrasing Pitrim A. Sorokin, for example, let us assert that all classes of social phenomena have a number of elements, some common and some unique:

economic	a, b, c, n,m, f
political	a, b, c, d, j , l
religious	a, b, c, g, i ,q
domestic	a, b, c, e, r, t
legal	a, b, c, o, z, y

and so on (Sorokin 1969:7-8; Nisbet and Perrin 1977:5).

Whereas sociology's first challenge is to explain those common elements and relationships (a,b,c) in a given social phenomenon, its second challenge is to account for the differences (n,d,g,e,o, etc.). Sociologists are thus concerned both with the parts that make up the whole, and with the whole as a separate entity in and of itself. In this respect sociology distinguishes itself from the other social sciences. While economics, politics, religion, and psychology deal narrowly with *homo economicus, homo politicus, homo religiosus,* and *homo psychologicus, homo socius* of sociology is viewed as a generic and manifold *homo,* simultaneously and inseparably economic, political, religious, ethical and artistic, partly rational and utilitarian, partly non-rational and even irrational, with all these aspects incessantly influencing one another. (Sorokin 1969:7-8).

Therefore, individual uniqueness is not a barrier to sociological explanation. Surely each individual possesses unique qualities and personality traits, but social behaviour never takes place solely on the basis of those qualities and traits that distinguish individuals one from the other. As Margaret Coulson and Carol Riddell (1980:18) state, "There is no incompatibility between a thing being unique and sharing characteristics with others ... an individual does not respond to a situation in terms of one characteristic alone, but as a whole person." Hence, while an individual's total combination of characteristics may make him or her unique, that individual shares many characteristics with others. Those common characteristics make it possible to identify general patterns, and they permit sociological explanation and prediction.

Social Structure and the Critical Spirit

In attempting to unravel the complexities of social living, structuralist sociologists seek to probe beneath the surface appearances of behaviour, to uncover the deeper social structures in which that behaviour is embedded.

The concept of social structure refers to the recurrences, regularities, and stabilities in patterns of relationships:

> Relationships are seen to fall into patterns and the researcher's task is to search for precisely those patterns. The relationships may refer to social or mental phenomena; the ways in which people act or the ways in which they think; they may refer to the arrangement of words in speech or the organization of the written word. (Cashmore and Mullan 1983:130)

These relationships that constitute the patterned or institutionalized ways of behaving are never directly observable. We cannot apprehend them through our senses, nor can they be represented concretely even through the most detailed empirical analyses.

It is the task of the sociologist, then, to abstract from the directly observable and impute an underlying coherence to those relationships and patterns. To illustrate this point more clearly we can refer to the "watch analogy" offered by Coulson and Riddell (1980:34-46). A watch can only provide the time of day if its parts are arranged in a particular manner. If I take a watch apart and hold its pieces in my hands, I won't be able to tell the time from all the screws, springs, wheels, and other bits that are now thrown together in a haphazard fashion. The parts of the watch can only reveal the time when they are placed in a set relationship to each other, when they are structured in a definite manner. While we may be physically unable to see that "structure" or the relationship among the parts, it is nevertheless real.

The same principle applies to social behaviour. Human interaction is never the mere sum of the number of people or behaviours involved, but rather the context and the ways in which individual behaviours are displayed in relation to the whole. Such behaviour is never quite as haphazard as it may sometimes seem. It is patterned, fairly regular, and highly structured; and it is the task of the sociologist to uncover that structure and make sense of it.

Because sociological explanation transcends common sense and attempts to analyse the structural reasons for why people behave as they do, such explanation will tend to ruffle feathers. None of us likes to think that we act unconsciously or that larger social forces beyond our immediate individual control dictate our ways of behaving. This is especially so if those larger forces and social structures impinging on our behaviour appear to be unjust. Take, for example, the argument that an average woman, due to no fault of her own, is likely to receive less education than an average man, and that in all likelihood she will probably never earn as much money as he will. This pattern is bound to create some degree of concern for that woman, particularly if she is told that the gender division of labour in our society, which many of us are so wont to take for granted, is neither inevitable nor natural.

Sociologists who question such things as the origins of social inequality and the social structures that serve to perpetuate it are therefore involved first and foremost in a critical enterprise. For this reason sociology has come to be viewed as an inherently controversial endeavour with distinct subversive qualities (Turner 1985:1-8). This is not to imply that sociologists are in the business of fomenting revolutions and revolts; rather, given the nature of their discipline, their attempts at debunking social myths, questioning sacred beliefs, and analysing the traditional wisdom of long-standing practices, sociologists are often cast in the mould of radical subversives. But as Anthony Giddens (1982:2-3) cautions: "Its subversive or critical character does not carry with it the implication that it is an intellectually disreputable enterprise. On the contrary, it is exactly because sociology deals with problems of such pressing interest to us all, problems which are the objects of major controversies and conflicts in society itself, that it has this character."

Giddens notwithstanding, there are those who will always feel threatened by the aims and claims of sociological research. In the United States, for example, Mike Keen (1992) documents a long history, starting in the 1930s, of FBI surveillance and infiltration of the American Sociological Society and the American Sociological Association. For over three decades, convinced that these organizations were committed to the communist takeover of the country, senior bureaucrats and politicians maintained up-to-date records on the activities of the country's leading sociologists and sought to harass and intimidate others in countless ways.

This critical thrust is not a recent feature of what constitutes the sociological enterprise. The very origins of the discipline reveal clear evidence of an emphasis on constructive social criticism. Indeed, as several prominent social theorists have argued, sociology was born formally out of the turmoil and ferment created by the French Revolution--the age of the Enlightenment and the critical awakening of the human spirit (Nisbet 1966; Zeitlin 1987; Seidman 1983; Collins and Markowsky 1984). As the forerunners of sociological thought, the Philosophes or Enlightenment thinkers of the eighteenth century embraced the critical scientific spirit and subjected all major social institutions and practices to rational ridicule. The Enlightenment period stressed the efficacy of individuals and their ability to comprehend and control the universe through the use of reason and empirical research.

Instead of resorting to intuition, introspection, tradition, authority, and revelation as sources of truth, the Philosophes fought to liberate the human mind from a strictly theological interpretation of the world, from superstition, fear, and manipulation by the "unknown." Denouncing religion as an irrational preoccupation, the forerunners of sociology argued that the natural and social universes were intelligible and that the "laws" governing their operation were not ordained by God (Collins and Markowsky 1984:20-22). Rather, those "laws" could be discovered and manipulated by humans to their own benefit. They criticized the divine right of kings to rule, traditional authority and privilege, and most importantly religion as sources of human bondage.

By appeals to rationality these pioneers of sociological thought, men such as Montesquieu and Rousseau, felt that it was possible for human beings to create a more just and equal order, not just in France, but in all of Europe. Being forever critical, sceptical, and secular, as Zeitlin (1987:1-2) illustrates, they waged constant war against the irrational, using criticism as their major weapon: "They fought what they considered to be superstition, bigotry or intolerance; they struggled against censorship and demanded freedom of thought; they attacked the prerogatives of the feudal classes and their restraints upon the industrial and commercial classes; and, finally, they tried to secularize ethics."

In this way the Philosophes hoped to undermine the *ancien régime* of pre-revolutionary France by destroying its institutional and ideological bases. Concerned as they were with improving the social condition of humanity, they identified and addressed issues that were eminently sociological: social order, social change, inequality, power, religion, ideology, the family, property, and politics--issues that have continued to occupy the central attention of sociologists down to the present.

The Intellectual Ferment   29

Chapter Two

The Sociological Tradition

All the major contemporary currents and theoretical orientations in sociology can trace their roots back to the classical period in which the discipline was born. For history is to sociology as culture is to anthropology. This relationship was abundantly clear to the great sociologically minded poet T.S. Eliot, when he wrote (1944:7) :

> Time present and time past
> Are both perhaps present in time future,
> And time future contained in time past.

In this observation Eliot was in perfect accord with C. Wright Mills, who insisted in *The Sociological Imagination* (1982), "All sociology worthy of the name is historical sociology" (p.146). Mills argued that no social science could presume to transcend history, for what we have today--our ideas, institutions, forms of social organization--are definite products of past experiences and struggles. This makes the relationship between sociology and history an intimate one: "The historical and sociological approaches are both complementary and dependent on one another" (Burke 1980:33). As it is used here the term history comprises the significant ideas, events, and social processes of earlier periods that continue to have an impact on today's world. But, as Charles Tilly (1981:52) points out, to be able to situate those social processes in historical time and place "requires a permanent encounter of sociology and history." Tilly, in short, draws our attention to that quality or state of mind that Mills (1982:6) refers to as the sociological imagination: "The sociological imagination enables us to grasp history and biography and the relations between the two within society.... No social study that does not come back to the problems of biography, of history and of their intersections within a society has completed its intellectual journey."

It is important, therefore, to examine some of the ways in which nineteenth-century intellectual currents have shaped modern sociological thinking.

Positivism

There is perhaps no better point of departure for such an inquiry than the philosophical current of positivism. *Positivism* (or positive science) can be traced back to the ideas of the discipline's founding fathers: Henri de Saint Simon (1760-1825) and Auguste Comte (1798-1857). In its sociological usage the term refers to the intellectual tradition that sought to apply the theories and methods (epistemologies) of the natural sciences to an understanding of the social universe. Its basic or ontological assumption is that societies are subject to influences akin to "natural laws" and could thus be studied by using the same methods employed by natural scientists (Giddens 1982b:68-75).

In other words, positivists see social behaviour as basically "law-like," as tending to follow certain general patterns set by custom or tradition and maintained through the social structures and institutions that people have fashioned in the course of social living. Thus, though not as stable and highly predictable as the subject matter of the physicist, social behaviour can nevertheless be assumed to be governed by "natural social laws." According to this view, the task of sociologists is to discover those laws, which would in turn permit us to predict and ultimately control or modify human behaviour (Bottomore 1983:382-83).

The essential tenets of positivism can be summed up in four broadly related points, based on a general outline provided by John Wilson (1983:11-12):

> · *first*, assuming that no fundamental differences exist between the natural and social sciences, sociology should seek to develop principles that have the same objective status as natural scientific laws or principles;
>
> ·*second*, such laws or principles are to be used as the principal means for explaining social events or phenomena;
>
> ·*third*, social reality is accessible only through empirically observable and measurable data--data that come to us via sensory experience;
>
> ·and *fourth*, science can only concern itself with what is. Science must remain value free, and the scientist, cum scientist, must never speak of what ought to be.

Reacting to the all-pervasive influence of the theological worldview of the seventeenth, eighteenth, and nineteenth centuries, Saint Simon and Comte embraced the idea of progress contained in Enlightenment thought and genuinely felt that society could and should be changed for the better. This was possible, it seemed to them, because if "the physical world was dominated by natural laws, it was likely that the social world was, too" (Ritzer 1992:9). It was the task of the philosopher, then, using reason and empirical research, to discover those social laws and apply them to "the creation of a 'better,' more rational world" (p.9).

At the same time, Saint Simon and Comte cautioned against the potentially destructive consequences that would follow if negative criticism were not tempered with positive and constructive recommendations for rebuilding society (in their case, France). They reasoned that in the new order science could come to play the same role as religion did under the old regime: "Religion, whose essential function had been to provide a coherent view of the universe and of human existence, and thus to unite people on the basis of common truths, would now be replaced by science" (Zeitlin 1987:51-52). For just as a universally accepted belief in God is able to provide a certain measure of spiritual unity among humankind regardless of historical time or geographical place, they felt that scientific truth could come to play a similar role. The main difference was that after unmasking the ideological aspects of religion, the belief in science would come to promote universal intellectual unity among all humankind (meaning Europeans). In other words, realizing that it was not possible to return to the old medieval order in which unity was provided by the church, they argued that the new international principles based on scientific knowledge and fact would be the only means of binding the nations of Europe together. On this basis they developed their ideas concerning a positive philosophy, from which the term positivism is derived.

For Comte, especially--who was more of a conservative than Saint Simon--the positive philosophy was aimed at reconciling two forces previously viewed as contradictory. The principles of order and progress, Comte argued, had to be united at the intellectual level, for only in so doing could stability be restored to the rest of society; and without intellectual unity, society would be devoid of moral authority.

The name that Comte gave to the study that would unite these two forces was social physics, or sociology. Social physics, in turn, comprised the study of (a) social statics or order as it applied to existing social structures, and (b) social dynamics or progress, which results from social change. (These points will be picked up again in chapter three, when we consider Comte's evolutionary theory of change.)

One must not presume that Comte's interest in studying social change meant that he was a radical. Rather, his conservatism and ambivalence about the changes wrought by the Revolution led him to bemoan what was happening in the France of his day, where intellectuals and others had come to be politically divided and had organized themselves into two mutually opposed camps, which he labelled the retrograde party and the anarchical party. The retrograde party stood for order, while the anarchical party represented the forces of progress.

The retrograde party supported the Catholic-feudal or theological interests, which were opposed to the Revolution and the negative philosophy of criticism advocated by the thinkers of the Reformation and the Enlightenment. This party blamed all the terror, anarchy, and corruption in France on the Revolution and its apologists, who had together upset the traditional order and tranquillity of the ancien régime. The anarchical party maintained that the problems being experienced were due to the incompleteness of the revolution. When once the old order was totally destroyed and new institutions were put in place, order and stability would be returned and the society would be able to make progress towards the goals of social development and industrialization (Zeitlin 1987:65-69).

For Comte, however, who viewed order and progress respectively as the static and dynamic aspects of society, both parties had outlived their usefulness. Although appearing to favour the anarchical party more, he felt the time had come for its negative criticism to give way to a more *positive* philosophy and society based on the principles of science and industry. Science thus came to be viewed as the "new religion." In place of priests and feudal lords, scientists and industrialists were to hold sway. Thus Comte could be seen as embodying both Enlightenment and anti-Enlightenment sentiments (Seidman 1983:51).

In contemporary society, both the pronounced drift towards secularization and the belief that scientific truth is superior to all other ways of knowing clearly reflect the influence of earlier positivistic thinking. The positivistic orientation of North American sociology, to which Raymond Aron made reference, is thus merely the continuation of a much older tradition, which treats social reality as consisting of concrete, measurable, and quantifiable processes and events (Mulkay 1977:29).

In their search for universal laws that govern the operation of social groups and organizations, positivists rely heavily on the method of empiricism, which assumes that knowledge of the world comes to us only via observation and sensory experience: seeing, hearing, touching, smelling, and tasting. Positivists dismiss any information that is inaccessible to observation as "metaphysical" and thus not open to scientific analysis. Further, positivists and empiricists are interested in specifying "cause and effect" relationships; they argue that a given effect does not merely follow from a cause, but rather has to follow that cause (Wilson 1983:14). In other words, just as the physicist has been able to identify the law of gravity and use it to explain the behaviour of falling bodies, so too the positivistic-minded sociologists, by identifying one or more universal laws governing a particular social event, deduce that whenever such laws are called into play a certain course of events must result: "An event (B) is explained by reference to some prior event (A), if there is a universal law which states that always, if events of the same type as A occur, then events of the same type as B follow" (Wilson 1983:8).

For the positivist the term *cause* refers to "a necessary part of a combination of conditions which are jointly sufficient to produce an effect" (Benton 1977:59). For example, if we were to find that in the slave-holding colonies of the British West Indies people of African descent were not as highly placed politically as people of Anglo-Saxon descent, the sociologist in search of a "covering law" to explain that situation might deduce that in such societies people of colour were not as politically mobile as whites. As a *general law* the stated relationship between colour and political mobility would be seen to apply only in those British West Indian colonies where the institution of slavery was intact. It would be up to other sociologists, using a scale of political mobility and other empirical data, to falsify that law by finding slave-holding British West Indian colonies where people of colour had either the same degree of political mobility as whites or more political mobility than whites. Positivist sociology, then, as an empirical science, is concerned with developing law-like statements to explain and predict social behaviour, with a view ultimately to controlling that behaviour. From a positivistic standpoint, sociology's aims are not all that different from those of the natural sciences. Anthony Giddens, for example, though highly critical of positivistic assumptions and methodology when applied to an understanding of social phenomena, summarizes the central claim of this tradition as: "Sociology is to strip away the illusions and habitual prejudices that have prevented human beings from understanding the sources of their own behaviour, just as the progress of natural science has eradicated such illusions about the physical world" (Giddens 1982b:74).

There are two other crucial points to add to this. First, the general and pervasive appeal of positivistic thinking, and the rise of sociology as a science with its emphasis on reason, observation, experimentation, and comparison, have meant that a great many sociologists--who would not otherwise see themselves as subscribing to the idea of universal laws and natural science methods in studying social phenomena--have been unwittingly drawn into discussions that reflect positivistic assumptions. This tendency appears to be largely unavoidable given the nature of the scientific enterprise and the precise requirements for the generation of scientific truth and knowledge.

Second, while all positivists may be empiricists, not all empiricists are positivists. Thus non-positivistic scholars such as the team of Charles E. Osgood, P.H. Tannenbaum, and G.J. Suci (1957) could employ empiricist epistemology in "the measurement of meaning" even though meaning as such does not have a physical or material existence of its own. Or Karl Marx, for instance, clearly had positivistic leanings and spoke of laws of capital accumulation or the law of the falling rate of profit. But Marx can be defended against the charge that he was a positivist because he did not intend the "laws" he spoke about to be seen as universal and, further, he saw those laws as always being qualified by the social and historical conditions attendant upon them.

In sum, then, as a major philosophical current, positivism has had a clear influence among strict positivists and non-positivists alike.

Positivism and Behaviourism

The adoption and application of positivistic principles for understanding human behaviour are best exemplified by the behaviouristic thinkers J.B. Watson and B.F. Skinner. Although Watson and Skinner worked formally within the field of psychology, their ideas have had a major impact on other disciplines, most notably sociology.

Arguing against the philosophy of Descartes and other nativists, who held that man's most basic ideas were innate, the behaviourists are committed to a strictly empiricist view of social behaviour. Watson, for example, maintains that human learning has to be understood not by reference to inner cognitive or mental states but rather as the result of conditioning. In other words, human behaviour and learning almost always involve a "stimulus" in the social or natural environment; this stimulus functions to elicit a particular "response." The response or behaviour, then, can be scientifically controlled by identifying the specific stimulus and manipulating it accordingly.

As Raymond E. Fancher (1979:319) states, "Whereas traditional psychologies sought to describe and explain conscious states, Watson's goals were to predict and control overt behaviour." Hence, according to this stimulus-response model, the task of the social scientist is confined to studying "the laws of behaviour, such that, when given the stimulus one can learn to predict the response, or, given the response, one may isolate the effective stimulus" (Watson 1971:433).

The positivistic assumptions of this approach to understanding human behaviour are unmistakable: it uses science in order to know, which in turn enables prediction, which in turn facilitates control. And to carry out this program the positivistic-minded behaviourists deem it totally appropriate "to borrow the perspectives of natural science and see how man looks when standing alongside molecules, plants and so on" (Cashmore and Mullan 1983:60).

Dismissing as irrelevant to the "science of behaviour" such mental phenomena as states of consciousness, motives, will, and subjective intentions, Skinner advanced his ideas concerning operant conditioning and positive and negative reinforcers. Convinced that humans are not active and creative beings, Skinner (1972:202) states: "A person does not act upon the world, the world acts upon him." Assuming the hedonistic principle, according to which people pursue pleasure and avoid pain, Skinner reasons that human beings engage in behaviour that affords pleasure and avoid those things that promise pain. In this model, pleasure acts as a reward (positive reinforcer) and is used to explain the persistence of certain behaviours, while pain is seen as a punishment (negative reinforcer) that leads to the extinction of other behaviours.

Thus, as part of his general program of "social engineering," Skinner maintains that men and women can be shaped or made and remade simply by the manipulation of rewards and punishments. Because human beings are merely passive respondents to their external environments, he argues, because their likes, dislikes, moods, and emotions are all environmentally conditioned, it is possible to study human behaviour scientifically through detached observation without ever having to refer to the existence of "supposed" inner states of mind:

The Sociological Tradition   37

Physics did not advance by looking more closely at the jubilance of a falling body, or biology by looking at the nature of vital spirits, and we do not need to try to discover what personalities, states of mind, feelings, purposes, intentions, or the other prerequisites of autonomous man really are in order to get on with a scientific analysis of behaviour. (Skinner 1972:12-13)

As Giddens (1982b:74) argues, however, the problem with equating sociology and natural or physical science is that the subject matter of each is so qualitatively different that it precludes the possibility of using a single methodology to analyse and understand both. Nevertheless, the full impact of positivism and the problems associated with it will become clear when we discuss the application of positivistic principles to an analysis of social change in the periphery. Its intellectual limitations will also become evident when we look at the interactionist paradigm, which situates subjectivity right at the heart of the scientific enterprise.

Interactionism
As humans we are by definition subjective beings, subjectively involved in our worlds. The starting point of science, then, is subjectivity. As humans, however, we are also given to individual tastes and preferences that can mould and shape our subjectivity. Such tastes and preferences are called biases. But subjectivity and bias are not synonymous. For it is possible to recognize one's bias and hold it aside in arriving at a given (objective) decision. In other words, the scientific concern with achieving objective knowledge and truth may be represented as:

subjectivity - bias = objectivity

If positivists argue that human behaviour can be scientifically studied given its patterned, predictable, almost mechanical nature and its subjection to "social laws," the interactionists are diametrically opposed to this position. As a somewhat more recent perspective in sociology, interactionism pays attention to the active and creative sides of human beings by stressing the inner or phenomenological aspects of their behaviour. Generally referred to as symbolic interactionism, this intellectual tradition maintains that because humans have no instincts to guide their behaviour, they must learn the appropriate ways of behaving. Such learning, they argue, takes place at the level of social and cultural symbols: the fundamental basis of social living is symbolic. Whether discussing language, art, war, literature, marriage, divorce, or any other such process, interactionists contend that the symbolic dimension of social intercourse is paramount. For it is through symbols that we communicate fear, love, anger, or satisfaction. Symbols can take the form of gestures, words, laws, styles of dress, crucifixes, anthems, flags and insignia, cars, membership in certain clubs, and a whole host of other means that human beings take up to choose to express themselves.

To argue that society cannot be understood independently of its symbolic dimension, however, is only one feature of the interactionist approach. A second feature that is absolutely crucial concerns the *interpretation* of symbols (Wallace and Wolf 1986:188-89). For social living to take place in an orderly fashion, the members of a society, group, club, or family must agree on the interpretation of key symbols. Interactionists, therefore, view the establishment of *shared meanings* between and among human beings as the key to the preservation of social order. In a society that respects free enterprise and private property, for example, there will be laws drafted to protect these institutions, which people interpret in the same way and agree to uphold. This makes the study of culture a central feature of interactionist sociology, because culture is made up of shared symbols (including laws and norms) transmitted from one generation to the next, thus enabling the existence of an ordered society. The transmission of culture from generation to generation is nothing but the transmission of meanings and interpretations of common cultural symbols.

But to give primacy to interpretation and the assignment of meaning to symbols is clearly anathema to the positivist, especially one who embraces views as extreme as those of the behaviourist and who is not inclined to grant that human beings have the capacity to evaluate and define social situations. For we are dealing here with phenomena of the mind--mental processes--and the veracity or even the existence of those phenomena is impossible to test or measure empirically. This is the central difference between positivistic and interactionist currents of philosophical debate in sociology. As Ken Menzies (1982:25) puts it, then: "Symbolic interaction is identified as voluntaristic, interpretative description; an approach to sociology that precludes analyses primarily concerned with establishing causal generalizations."

For intellectual parentage, members of this school often lay claim to the ideas of Max Weber and his discussion of *verstehen* or the subjective meanings that people attach to their daily behaviour (Portes 1976:68-69). However, although it would be inaccurate to characterize Weber as a symbolic interactionist and nothing more, it is clear that his writings on "social action" and the meanings (emotional, traditional, rational) that inform such actions provide the basis on which this tradition was built. For Weber the sociological enterprise deals with an interpretive understanding of human social behaviour. To interpret behaviour correctly, he argues, sociologists must realize that human beings are subjective actors who attach meaning to their acts. In fact, interaction is only possible if subjective meanings are shared by the participants in an interaction situation--and this is what makes it specifically social interaction:

> Sociology is a science which attempts the interpretive understanding of social action in order thereby to arrive at a causal explanation of its course and effects. In "action" is included all human behaviour when and insofar as the acting individual attaches a subjective meaning to it.... Action is social insofar as by virtue of the subjective meaning attached to it the acting individual takes account of others and is thereby oriented in its course. (Weber 1964:88)

As a microsociological approach that focuses on individuals as the main unit of analysis, however, symbolic interaction cannot be equated entirely with Weberian sociology. For though emphasizing the importance of *verstehen*, Weber's work was massively informed by a historical and structural appreciation of the manner in which the political and economic interests of social groups and classes served to orient their actions in feudal and capitalist societies. And it is precisely against structuralist views of social action that the major symbolic interactionist thinkers, George Herbert Mead and Herbert Blumer, argue. In fact, members of this school firmly reject anything that smacks of either biological or societal determinism (Haralambos and Heald 1980:546).

For both Mead and Blumer, history is less important than social processes occurring in the present. Because human beings are not prisoners of history, social structure, or instincts, because they are spontaneous and have the ability to interpret, evaluate, and freely choose courses of action,

symbolic interactionists such as Mead do not see the relevance of historically conditioned social action. Thus, in a criticism of Mead, R. Ropers
(1973:50) observes: "The activities that he sees men engaged in are not
historically determined relationships of social and historical continuity; they
are merely episodes, interactions, encounters and situations."

This criticism notwithstanding, symbolic interactionists are convinced
that the basis for co-operative action in society must be understood through
the existence of common symbols and shared interpretations of them. For
to survive, human beings have had to construct and live within a world of
meaning. The identification of common symbols and the interpretation of
their meanings, however, only represent the means by which human
interaction can be accomplished. The key question to be asked concerns the
manner in which such interpretation is effected.

To answer this question we must consider the central concepts in Mead's
social psychology: mind and self. "Human society as we know it could not
exist without minds and selves, since all of its most characteristic features
presuppose the possession of minds and selves by its individual members"
(Mead 1934:227). For Mead, who was greatly influenced by the pragmatist
philosophers William James and John Dewey, the mind is not a passive
spectator of a passing scene, a blank slate, as the positivists would have us
believe. He sees "mind," rather, as an emergent quality that continually
develops out of the interaction between the individual self and its social
environment. What, then, is "the self"? How does it emerge? And how is it
related to the interactionist critique of positivism?

This is the context in which Mead advanced his ideas concerning the
"minding" process of role-taking, which, in essence, implies people
imaginatively putting themselves in the shoes of others with whom they are
interacting. For example: You are walking down the street and suddenly
notice a man running towards you shaking his fist in what appears to be a
menacing fashion. You may interpret this symbolically as an aggressive
gesture, but only after you have imaginatively put yourself in that person's
shoes and concluded (interpreted) that his motives are aggressive. But this
is only one possible interpretation of the situation, for it could well be that the
person is a deaf mute who is trying to tell you that someone is being mugged
in an alley up the street. Nevertheless, you will respond depending on your
assessment of the moment. If it is indeed a show of aggression but you think
that you can physically defend yourself, you will hold your ground. If the
person is bigger and appears stronger than you, you will probably attempt

to run away, to defuse the situation with a joke, to talk it out, and so on. In the meantime, the supposed aggressor is also taking note of your behaviour--taking your role. According to how he interprets your actions (running away, or defiantly holding your ground), he will in turn modify his behaviour. The interaction in which both of you are engaged is thus said to be negotiated: both parties take account of each other and adjust their behaviour to suit the situation.

This example demonstrates how much of our everyday behaviour involves symbols and their interpretations at any given moment; and the mental process of role-taking in which we are constantly engaged is the means by which the self emerges. By placing yourself in the position of another, you are able to look back upon your "self" as an object, a separate entity. The ability to get outside of yourself experientially and view yourself from the standpoint of others is absolutely crucial to the development of self-identity.

For Mead the notion of self is not inborn. It has to be acquired in the process of social interaction. He condenses this process into two principal stages: the play stage and the game stage. The first occurs in early childhood when the young take on the roles of make-believe, in imagining themselves as *significant others*: for example, playing mother, teacher, or doctor. In so doing children look back upon themselves, see themselves from the point of view of a mother or teacher, and thus cognitively separate themselves from other selves. This is what is involved when the little girl, Aniisa, is playing the role of mother and says, "Aniisa, you are being a naughty girl!" Only at this point can it be said that the child has developed some sense of selfhood.

The game stage comes later and involves situations in which children take into account the roles and expectations of *generalized others*. This occurs, for example, in a game of baseball in which individual children play their own roles in relation to the roles of others. Total individuality gives way to team spirit and children learn, for instance, that they can only play first base in relation to others who play second base, third base, catcher, and other positions. By placing themselves in the positions or roles of other players, children come to appreciate their particular role in the game. Their sense of self is thus more firmly established and they learn how to work co-operatively with others. The game stage is thus a rehearsal for social living, because in the wider society they will be called upon to play many roles in relation to the larger whole, perhaps in a team, a family, or a workplace. All of this experience is only possible given the human being's unique capacity to interpret social and cultural symbols and assign meanings to them.

As Mead's most distinguished student, Herbert Blumer rounded out and refined many of his teacher's ideas. A central motif in Blumer's work is the critique of positivistic and empiricist approaches to understanding social action. He felt that non-interactionist sociology painted too bleak a picture of human beings, robbing them of creativity, spontaneity, and free will, while simultaneously portraying them as passive creatures capable only of reacting to external stimuli. Mainstream sociological conceptions of behaviour, he wrote:

> do not regard the social actions of individuals in human society as being created by them through a process of interpretation. Instead, action is treated as a product of factors which play on and through individuals.... The social action of people is treated as an outward flow or expression of forces playing on them rather than as acts which are built up by people through their interpretations of situations in which they are placed. (Blumer 1967:143)

Blumer, then, as a key representative of the symbolic interactionist school, eschews the teachings of positivism and empiricism. Emphasizing the voluntaristic aspects of human behaviour, he and other members of this school take serious issue with the procedure of isolating variables and assuming that one causes the other, with little or no reference to the actor's view of the situation. To gain an accurate understanding of social behaviour, therefore, interactionists begin with actual individuals and attempt to catch the process of interpretation through which they construct their actions (Haralambos and Heald 1980:548). In sum, therefore, if the positivists went overboard in denying people all free will, the interactionists also go overboard in the opposite direction: they invest people with too much free will and play down the influence of social structure on behaviour.

Interactionism and Feminism
In the same way that behaviourism could be used as an example, albeit extreme, of the positivistic approach to knowledge, feminism may be linked to interactionism. Although as an ideology that informs a course of political action, feminism is by no means consensual or homogeneous, for the

purposes of this discussion, I refer generally to postmodernist feminism, which embraces interactionism and places emphasis on subjective meaning and interpretation of social events or phenomena, on the relevance of personal experience and desires, and on individual feeling and sense of identity. According to Jane Flax (1987:625), these ought to be the concerns embodied in the feminist corrective to Enlightenment science: "Feminist notions of the self, knowledge, and truth are too contradictory to those of the Enlightenment to be contained within its categories." While these all fly in the face of objectivist, positivistic science as practised by men such as Skinner and Watson, they form a crucial part of the interactionist approach to knowledge.

Advocating a strategy that is clearly anathema to positivists, Sandra Harding, one of today's leading feminist writers, argues that traditional science "does not encourage us to ask what have been the *meanings* of women's contributions to public life for women" (Harding 1987:4-5). In other words, feminism picks up the subjectivist theme and levels a dual challenge at traditional scientific epistemology. First it accuses such "malestream" science of duplicity in that what it passes off as objective knowledge is really subjectively riddled with male biases and assumptions. The so-called scientific concerns with objectivity, distancing, control, manipulation, and measurement are said to be decidedly male concerns, for even outside of the scientific enterprise it is men, they say, who are interested in logic, control, manipulation, and reason.

The second challenge relates to the first and speaks to the feminist refusal to play the positivistic "game of objectivity." Here feminists insist that researchers acknowledge their subjective involvement with their subjects and projects. Thus Harding (1987:9) cautions that women "need to avoid the 'objectivist' stance that attempts to make the researcher's cultural beliefs and practices invisible.... Introducing this 'subjective' element into the analysis in fact increases the objectivity of the research and decreases the 'objectivism' which hides this kind of evidence from the public."

This is the sense in which feminist *standpoint epistemology* departs from traditional science. It pursues two goals: one is political and the other intellectual. The political goal, or the search for "gender justice" (Flax 1987:627), is aimed at eliminating current male domination of the science and knowledge industries, for therein lies a great deal of the power that resides with men, and which men use to exclude women from key positions in society. Supposedly, therefore, the feminists' critique of what they call the

44   Sociology and the Periphery

androcentrism of traditional epistemologies (Deutchman 1991) is aimed specifically at white, middle-class, middle-aged, males, who for centuries have defined the scientific agenda and have dominated what society at large has accepted as "truth." Their charge is that positivism is a distinctly male undertaking, which uses male researchers to test male assumptions on male subjects with a view to advancing knowledge about males, which is then passed on to society presumably in the interest of all members. This is seen as ideology, not science; for there is absolutely nothing scientific or objective about knowledge thus derived.

Of specific interest here is the ontological claim that power in contemporary society is gendered or, stated differently, that society is structured in a way that gives power to men while simultaneously denying it to women. As a consequence, even the most enlightened and well-intentioned male researchers are not to be trusted, for sexism is so systemic that men are often unaware of their abuse of power over women: "Traditional epistemologies, whether intentionally or unintentionally, systematically exclude the possibility that women could be 'knowers' or agents of knowledge" (Harding 1987:3).

While there is much to support in the political goal of feminism as stated by Harding, its ideological appeal minimizes its potential gains. There is a tendency to view men and women as separate, homogeneous interest groups, which only occasionally break their respective ranks and depart from gendered ways of behaving. Thus, although Harding recognizes that individuals can and often do transcend their racial and class locations, she also implies that transcendence of gender is not as easy or common. She agrees, for instance, that whites could be valued allies of blacks in the anti-apartheid struggle in South Africa, and that Gentiles often risked and lost their lives in the fight against anti-Semitism, but she nonetheless prefers to paint men as virtual enemies, trapped by their deep-seated sexism. On this basis she cautions women "to look especially critically at analyses produced by members of the oppressor group" (Harding 1987:11). To the extent that men can be useful researchers at all, she sees them as being assigned to study "the gendered dimensions of men's thoughts and behaviours," never once indicating that women's thoughts and behaviours could also be gendered. She refers to this as "the phallic critique," which is best conducted by men in those "areas of masculine behaviour and thought" to which they have easier access than women--for example, male locker rooms.

The intellectual goal of feminism is to produce a more objective, more balanced stock of knowledge by utilizing a constructivist epistemology, according to which "reality" is not discoverable in the positivist sense, but rather is socially constructed or invented. As a postmodernist epistemology, constructivism (and deconstructionism) refuses to subscribe to the positivist idea that facts and values are separable for scientific purposes. Thus Rachel T. Hare-Mustin and Jeanne Marecek state, "Whereas positivism asks what are the facts, constructivism asks what are the assumptions; whereas positivism asks what are the answers, constructivism asks what are the questions" (Hare-Mustin and Marecek 1988:456).

Deeply immersed in the world of subjective meaning and the epistemology that accompanies it, constructivist feminists argue that the "real" nature of male and female is impossible to determine, since gender itself is socially constructed. To drive home their point, constructivist feminists take serious issue with other prominent feminists such as Carol Gilligan (1982) and Nancy Chodorow (1978), who unwittingly play into the hands of positivistically minded researchers and think that the genders of males and females are "real," discrete, and discoverable. Thus, where both Gilligan and Chodorow are seen to subscribe to the idea that women are more given to caring than men, and that women are relational while men are instrumental and rational, constructivists such as Hare-Mustin and Marecek view these behaviours as contrived and invented, not as essential.

Using the notion of self-interest, Hare-Mustin and Marecek (1988) argue that the rationality and instrumentalism exhibited by men are to be explained by the fact that such attributes complement the material interests of men, who at this moment in time occupy positions of power. Similarly, women's lack of power via-à-vis men predisposes them to using a strategy of caring, pleasing others, and stressing the importance of relationships. The point is that these are highly variable and adjustable political strategies that are rooted in the structure and distribution of power in society, and are not essential, unchanging attributes of men and women.

It therefore stands to reason that those in power will tend to be conservative and pro status quo, and they will stress such things as rules, discipline, control, rationality, and logic. For these practices were made and put in place by them to serve their interests. Conversely, those without power are usually constrained to focus on communication, relatedness, and compassion. This is precisely why constructivists such as Hare-Mustin and Marecek (1988:459) argue, "In husband-wife conflicts, husbands call on rules and logic, whereas wives call on caring." But when women find themselves in the dominant position, "as in parent-child conflicts, they emphasize rules, whereas children appeal for sympathy and understanding."

Clearly, then, what is "real" or true about men and women, or about social phenomena in general, is best understood as a social construction. Given the elements of standpoint and constructivist epistemology, such reality or truth is bound always to be partial, perspectival, and ideological. Taken by themselves, positivist methods are not enough to help us understand key social processes that necessarily involve subjective considerations of meaning, personal experience, feeling, trust, and powerlessness. This is why feminists who employ the assumptions of the interactionist paradigm are able to "challenge widely shared categories of social meaning and explanation" (Flax 1987:627) and lay claim to a qualitatively different way of knowing; a distinctive approach to science.

Realism

While the ontological and epistemological assumptions of positivism and interactionism appear to reflect diametrically opposing ways of investigating the operations of the social universe, the approach known as theoretical realism probably serves as an effective synthesis of the two (Keat and Urry 1975). Theoretical realism, though subscribing in part to an empirical understanding of social behaviour, nevertheless is distinct from the strict empiricism associated with positivism. This type of realism, according to John Wilson (1983:166), does not restrict scientific analyses exclusively to what is empirically observable, for it seeks often to make claims about the nature and existence of unobservable phenomena. For example, the notion of class consciousness, though not directly observable through the senses, is nevertheless said to exist and to have an influence on human behaviour and social relations.

Thus, while accepting the positivistic assumption that social phenomena can exist and operate independently of human volition, realists reject the notion that such phenomena are only knowable by means of direct sense impressions. As for the interactionist argument, realists agree on the importance of subjective definitions and meanings, but resist the claim that society is nothing but the product of such subjective conceptions. For through its exclusive concern with the self-understandings of social agents, interactionist sociology "is unable to identify the existence of self-misunderstanding, of ideological [false] consciousness. Nor can it recognize the significance of *structural features of society* that operate as unconscious determinants of social phenomena" (Keat 1981:3-4; emphasis added).

Those "structural features of society" relate to the fact that social behaviour, rather than being simply random or haphazard, tends to follow fairly set patterns. Social structures are thus neither visible nor tangible; nevertheless, they are real--they have a definite impact on how human beings relate both to the world of material things and to the world of ideas. The concepts used by theoretical realists, then, are not based on phenomenological categories or things, but rather on the abstract forms or structures that underlie them (Wilson 1983:167; 177).

Take, for example, the racial and ethnic structure of Canadian society, which sees people of Anglo-Saxon descent occupying the leading positions in political, financial, and economic institutions (Hunter 1981:129-40). This social structure comprises a variety of norms, beliefs, social relations, and practices, which, though not directly observable, nonetheless come into play in a definite manner to produce the picture of inequality painted by Alfred Hunter and others. From the standpoint of a realist, therefore, the key to understanding the pattern or distribution of privilege in Canadian society must be sought, at least in part, in the underlying racial and ethnic composition of that society: the social, political, economic, and ideological make-up of its dominant institutions. The specification of the underlying structure, then, is the point of departure for the realist.

Realism and Historical Materialism

According to Russell Keat and John Urry (1975:2), the most "clear-cut example of realism in the social sciences" is Marx's theory of historical materialism. In sketching the overall development of human society, Marx begins with real, active, sensuous human beings (Fromm 1966:8-19), who have variously co-operated with and struggled against the forces of nature in the production of their basic material needs (food, clothing, and shelter, for instance).

Employing the dialectical method of negation and contradiction in arriving at his understanding of societal change and development, Marx traces the interaction between "matter" and "ideas" to show how the material pursuits of human beings conditioned the development of definite ideas about the world, and how those ideas, in turn, informed their dealings with material reality. The starting point, however, is always the production of physical subsistence: "As individuals express their lives, so they are. What they are, therefore, coincides with their production, both with what they produce and how they produce. The nature of individuals thus depends on the material conditions determining their production" (Marx and Engels 1969:7).

In the Marxist schema, "production" is an economic term and refers specifically to the process by which material objects are transformed and made more useful or valuable for human beings. For example, the removal of oil from the ground, its conversion into gasoline, and the use of gasoline to run farming machinery and facilitate the provision of food are clearly parts of a productive process. Such a process is seen to consist of two principal *productive forces*. The first Marx called "means of production," and the second he termed "labour."

Means of production are all the material objects and procedures necessary for a given productive process: raw materials, tools, scientific knowledge, wind, water, land, and any other such factor integral to production. Labour is the element combined with the means of production to harness it and give shape, form, and meaning to the productive process. Without human labour, the means of production cannot enter the productive process.

The realist dimension of historical materialism is found within the analysis of the productive process under capitalism. That dimension was established in the writings of the young Marx, Marx the humanist, who spoke at great length about exploitation, alienation, contradiction, human essence, and social consciousness. In his search for the abstract forms or deeper structures underlying the processes by which human beings produce and reproduce themselves, Marx realizes that they often:

> enter into definite relations, which are independent of their will, namely relations of production.... The mode of production of material life conditions the general process of social, political and intellectual life. It is not the consciousness of men that determines their existence, but their social existence that determines their consciousness. (1970:20-21)

Marx argues here that society's productive forces (the means of production and the labour that human beings provide) will determine or condition virtually all of that society's social relationships: its degree of industrialization and urbanization, its religious outlook and family structure, and even its forms of law and politics, along with most of the particular social arrangements that characterize it. It thus stands to reason that a change in a society's productive forces leads to changes in its social relationships.

The social relations in which human beings engage, however, are not always peaceable and productive. They are often antagonistic and destructive. In fact, for Marx the central motor of social and historical change was class struggle: "The history of all hitherto existing society is the history of class struggle" (Marx and Engels 1955:9). Looking specifically at the dynamics of capitalist society, Marx argues that there are structural contradictions between the principal classes: the bourgeoisie (capitalists) and the proletariat (wage workers). He sees that capitalism, a distinct mode of production, encompasses a unique logic: the logic of accumulation and expansion, which makes the relentless pursuit of profit its sole raison d'être.

Marx uses the term *primitive accumulation* to discuss the transition from feudalism to capitalism. Primitive accumulation encompasses two processes: the separation of direct producers (peasants) from their ownership of the means of production; and their subsequent conversion to wage workers or proletarians. In capitalism, wage labour is crucial to the realization of profit and, as we will see, to the question of value.

In analysing the profit motive, Marx is careful to point out its structural features. It is not that individual capitalists exploit workers purely and simply because they are evil or greedy; rather, as an economic system based on market competition, survival is intimately tied to ever-increasing accumulation, to expansion, and to economic efficiency, with all of these conditions premised upon the exploitation of labour power by capital. The capitalists who are unable to amass profits and expand their operations, who are unable to keep pace and produce commodities as cheaply as their competitors, will be ruined. This is the fundamental logic underlying the system, and which Marx endeavoured to lay bare. In the process of teasing out this logic, Marx (1970:21) crystallizes his ideas concerning exploitation, class struggle, and ultimately revolution: "At a certain stage of development, the material productive forces of society come into conflict with the existing relations of production.... From forms of development of the productive forces these relations turn into their fetters. Then begins an era of social revolution."

The fundamental contradiction between capitalists and proletarians--which, according to this view, will bring about the ultimate demise of the capitalist system as a whole--is thus seen to transcend the individual wills of either of these two classes. That contradiction is structurally engendered by the very logic of the system, which says that capitalists, to be capitalists, must exploit the labour power of proletarians; and in the process they unwittingly increase the class consciousness and potential for rebellion among those same proletarians. The one class cannot exist without the other: a capitalist who does not employ wage labour is not a capitalist; similarly, a worker who does not earn wages is not a proletarian.

> Not only has the bourgeoisie forged the weapons that bring death to itself; it has also called into existence the men who are to wield those weapons--the modern proletariat. In proportion as the bourgeoisie, i.e., capital, is developed, in the same proportion is the proletariat developed--a class of labourers who live only so long as they find work, and who find work only so long as their labour increases capital.... What the bourgeoisie therefore produces, above all, are its own gravediggers. (Marx and Engels 1955:16, 22)

Thus exploitation is a key factor in accentuating class antagonisms and enhancing the likelihood of social revolution.

Exploitation and the Question of Value
In his treatment of exploitation, the labour process, and the creation of value under capitalism, Marx presumes the existence of the wage relationship whereby a worker, in order to survive, is forced to sell labour power to an employer, who owns or controls the means of production. Let us then, like Marx, consider step by step a concrete example of exploitation with a view to clarifying the logic of the exploitive process. We will use a sugarcane plantation that employs wage workers (as opposed to slaves), and for the sake of convenience we will presume that there are ten such workers employed for a one-month period.

Over this time the sugar plantation and its installed sugar mill convert a certain amount of raw cane into refined sugar, which the owner then sells on the market. Following Marx, the price received for the sugar is represented by "P," which consists of three elements: "C" (constant capital), which is the cost paid by the owner to acquire and maintain such factors as the land, buildings, machinery, and other means of production on the plantation; "V" (variable capital), which is the wages paid to the ten workers; and "S" (surplus value), which is created in the process.

The Sociological Tradition   51

Now, let us say that the sugar was sold for a P of $15,000, and that C equals $10,000. This means that something very special occurred in the productive process. The labour power of the workers *created* $5,000 worth of value; but this $5,000 do not belong to the workers. They received a wage of, say, $100 each, for a total variable capital (V) of $1,000. The remainder of the $4,000 is surplus value (S), which belongs to the plantation owner. Marx depicts P as:

$$P = C + V + S$$

To determine the extent to which the workers are being exploited or treated unfairly in this type of case, Marx would look at the proportion or ratio of S to V, or S:V, for exploitation is always expressed as a rate or percentage. Thus we would have 4,000:1,000, or a rate of exploitation of 400 per cent, with the capitalist owner receiving four times more than the workers. This, Marx says, would ultimately produce serious strains in the relation between the capitalist and the workers, especially when the workers become *conscious* or politically aware of the inequality of their situation.

But surplus value is not an undifferentiated phenomenon. There are two types, each corresponding to the level of development of the productive forces in the society, and the rate at which it is possible to exploit labour. In addressing these two types of surplus value, Marx makes the distinction between necessary and surplus labour (*Capital*, Vol. 1, chaps. VII-XI). Necessary labour, quite simply, refers to the actual time expended by workers on the job, the time that is equivalent to the wages they receive. Such wages are necessary to ensure the reproduction of workers on a daily, weekly, or monthly basis. The workers use the wages to pay for the necessary food, clothing, shelter, and other expenses, all of which enables them to survive and continue to show up at work on a continuing basis. To this extent, the workers' necessary labour, as it is represented by their wage, must also cover:

> Time for education, for intellectual development, for the fulfilling of social functions and for social intercourse, for free play of his bodily and mental activity, even the rest time of Sunday.... The value of the labour power includes the value of the commodities necessary for the reproduction of the worker. (*Capital*, Vol. 1:252-53)

Since employers or capitalists are not philanthropists, however; since they do not hire workers out of an exclusive consideration for the employees' well-being, we cannot expect that the wages paid will represent the full value of the commodities produced by workers in a given work period. If such were the case, capitalists, cum capitalists, would not be able to extract surplus value and realize profits, and they would soon be out of business.

It is understood, therefore, that wages paid to workers should represent only part of the value created. It should reflect that part of the value created by their labour, converted into a wage that is sufficient for reproducing them as long as they are in the employ of the capitalist. Marx refers to this as the *necessary labour* of the workers, or that fraction of the working day when they work for themselves. He refers to the rest of the time they work and for which they receive no direct payment as their *surplus labour*. The workers provide this surplus labour for capitalists, and hence the products and the surplus value created also belong to the capitalist employers.

The capitalists, then, are concerned primarily with the extraction of surplus value from workers and try to devise ways of increasing the proportion of surplus labour relative to the necessary labour contributed by the worker. For it is only by thus increasing the *rate of exploitation* that ever more surplus value can be created for the capitalists: "The directing motive, the end aim of capitalist production is to extract the greatest possible amount of surplus value, and consequently to exploit labour power to the greatest possible extent" (*Capital*, Vol.1:313).

But surplus value, remember, is of two types: absolute and relative. Absolute surplus value is the value created during the surplus labour time of the worker and accrues to the capitalist as the owner of the means of production and the purchaser of labour power. To increase the rate of absolute surplus value created by the worker, the prime strategy used by the capitalist is to lengthen the working period or the work day while leaving wages unchanged. If, for example, in an eight-hour work day workers each contribute four hours of necessary labour, the remaining four hours represent their surplus labour, in which they create four hours' worth of surplus value. The rate of surplus value would be 100 per cent, or a ratio of 1:1. If the working day is prolonged, say from eight to ten hours, and the necessary labour remains at four hours, the rate of absolute surplus value would be increased by 50 per cent, or to 150 per cent: a ratio of 2:3.

Because increases in the production of absolute surplus value are premised upon an increase in the length of the working day, and not on improved technological efficiency, such a system would carry with it a built-in limitation or contradiction. Apart from the fact that the duration of the working day is fixed at a maximum of twenty-four hours, there are physical limits imposed by nature on the human body. These limits, when approximated or exceeded, lead to a rapid decline in labour productivity, even to a point of zero.

From the point of view of capitalists, it is crucial, therefore, to find a more reliable and efficient means of extracting surplus value. This is where the question of *relative* surplus value becomes central. To extract relative surplus value from workers, capitalists pursue a different strategy. Rather than seeking merely to prolong the working day, they seek to reduce the time required to produce the worker's necessary labour by relying on the use of more sophisticated, time-saving tools, methods, and techniques. In other words, to return to the earlier example of the eight-hour work day, improved technology would condition a more efficient process of exploitation: instead of a split of four hours necessary and four hours surplus labour, there might be a three-to-five split (three hours necessary, and five hours of surplus labour), or a rate of surplus value of 166 per cent. The enhanced efficiency that accompanies the development of technology and machine production makes possible the reduction of the necessary labour time and the extraction of relative surplus value. It simultaneously overcomes the problems inherent in the biological limitations of the human body and the fact that the working day is fixed at a theoretical maximum of twenty-four hours. In sum, therefore, such modifications to the work process serve to enhance efficiency by promoting technological development and increased machine production.

The logic of the entire system of production, exploitation, and value-creation takes on a life of its own. The decision to exploit the labour power of workers is not left up to individual capitalists. It is systemic. The very structure and make-up of the capitalist mode of production--its laws of survival--impel capitalists to extract as much surplus value as possible from labour. Therein lies the realist dimension of historical materialism. For, although real, exploitation is a technical term that speaks to the process and the *structure* of power and class relations in capitalist society.

Chapter Three

Social Evolutionism:
A European Perspective

Within the social sciences, various disciplines such as anthropology, economics, political science, human geography, and sociology have addressed the question of social change. Indeed, this very question has been a common theme linking all of these fields of intellectual endeavour--although each focuses on a different, albeit related, aspect. All of these disciplines, in the larger, more macro sense, seek to account for how human beings and human societies have been transformed from earliest times to the present.

Sociologists in particular have developed a variety of different theories and explanations to assess the processes of social change. These theories tend to reflect the positivist, interactionist, and realist traditions, and they attempt to explain why some societies have changed more than others. Is it a question of human agency? Or is change a suprahuman phenomenon that occurs independently of human intervention? Or is there some combination of the two?

Generally speaking, many sociologists maintain that the countries making up the periphery or the Third World have changed or "progressed" less than the supposedly "advanced," highly industrialized areas of the globe. Compared to the industrially advanced countries, nations in the periphery experience vastly lower standards of living; they have inadequate medical and educational facilities and fewer social services at their disposal; they offer their people fewer economic options; they are more subject to corrupt and dictatorial governments; and they tend to lag behind in matters of scientific and technological progress.

How do sociologists account for these differences? Do they think that one day the periphery will catch up to the advanced nations? Did the advanced nations suffer similar types of deprivation at some point in their history? Do all countries follow the same paths to economic growth and industrialization?

Within the sociological literature these questions have generated many and varied answers. But regardless of the theoretical position taken, one thing is certain: human economic welfare and societal gains will always be closely bound up with the processes of industrialization and economic development: "It has become common to equate industrialization with economic development, and countries embarking on the path of development have generally assumed that they will have to industrialize" (Kemp 1978:20). Jamaican economist George Beckford describes economic *development* as the process "whereby the material welfare of the people of a nation state (or country) is improved consistently or substantially over long periods of time. The time dimension is important so as to distinguish between development and short-period booms in the level of economic activity" (1975:78). Economic *growth* speaks to a situation in which per capita income is rising. It is to be distinguished from development in that a rise in per capita income may occur simultaneously with the increasing material impoverishment of significantly large groups of people in a given country.

This type of development was the case in many peripheral countries such as Trinidad, Mexico, Nigeria, and Venezuela, where the oil boom of the 1960s and 1970s occasioned massive increases in average per capita earnings but failed to produce local structures ensuring the equitable distribution of those earnings. Given the structure of power at the local level, where the dominant fractions of the national bourgeoisie are firmly aligned with foreign capital, this is not all that surprising. The same may be said of all countries in the periphery where there are abundant supplies of natural resources in great demand on the world market. For in the periphery, as long as the working masses are unable to control and dispose of their resources in a manner consistent with national interests, as long as the local ruling classes, foreign corporations, and international lending agencies continue to exert a determining influence over economic and political directions, economic growth is unlikely to be accompanied by development.

The process of industrial development has to do mainly with machine production and the widespread use of inanimate sources of energy: steam, or hydroelectric and nuclear power. When viewed as a process, nevertheless, industrialization clearly implies a matter of degree. Most countries can be located along a continuum of least industrialized to most industrialized, but even the most "industrially backward" society will be able to boast of some technology, however rudimentary. The same applies to development; in a country such as Canada, one of the most developed in the world, there are still large pockets where people lead traditional, rural lives, have low standards of living, sanitation, health care, and formal education, and few material comforts of life. Examples are the Native reserves, parts of Northern Ontario, the Maritime provinces, and various urban slums in the large cities of Toronto, Montreal, and Vancouver.

Clearly, a society considered to have developed industrially has undergone a very uneven process: not all parts or regions of the society in question exhibit the same levels of industrial advance or development; not all parts have changed to the same degree and at the same pace. But this does not prevent us from saying that Canada is an industrially developed country while Barbados is not. Not only do people in Canada have higher average standards of living and material comforts, but the country also derives a larger proportion of its wealth and Gross National Product (GNP) from industrial operations. Barbados is home to largely traditional, agricultural pursuits, with animal-driven contraptions and labour-intensive occupations predominating.

Positivism and Social Evolutionism
To place these observations in theoretical perspective, let us focus firstly on the school of thought referred to as social evolutionism and examine its links with the positivistic tradition. Comte and the early positivists (see chapter two) thought of social change and development as resulting from an orderly and evolutionary progress through increasingly higher stages of scientific and technological sophistication. Despite criticisms levelled at positivism over the years, many sociologists today view the pronounced positivistic orientation of their discipline as a sign of its increasing maturation. In other words, although sociologists may disagree with some of Comte's early formulations of positivism, they nevertheless agree on the superiority of scientifically and empirically generated knowledge, in comparison to other ways of arriving at truth.

All societies, some sociologists argue, pass through *evolutionary stages* on the road to development. For Sir Henry Sumner Maine (1822-88), for example, the march of civilization followed a series of stages beginning with early forms of social order based on patriarchy and status and culminating with later forms based on freedom and contract (Maine 1885). Lewis Henry Morgan (1818-81), another of the classical evolutionary thinkers, regarded human history as advancing through clearly outlined stages (from savagery through barbarism to civilization) that constituted "a natural as well as a necessary sequence of progress" (Morgan 1963:3). This is the sense in which social-evolutionary thinkers, also known as social Darwinists, borrowed the term "development" from the biological sciences and applied it to society, which they viewed as growing and developing in much the same fashion that human organisms grow and develop. Thus, they argued, societies are like living organisms in that changes within them are seen to be governed by immutable laws, whether social or natural.

This idea, though later systematized by Herbert Spencer (1820-1903) and Emile Durkheim (1858-1917), found earlier expression in the work of none other than Auguste Comte, the "high priest" of positivism (Westby 1991:134-38). In his discussion of "social dynamics," Comte adamantly insisted that societies should be studied as *integrated wholes*. For in the same way that a total appreciation of the human organism cannot be had simply by studying its various parts in isolation from the whole, so too a society, to be fully comprehended, must be approached as a fully functioning, single unit.

This insight gave rise to what is now called the *organic model* or organismic analogy, according to which the arrangement of organs in a living body becomes a blueprint for understanding social phenomena. In other words, just as biological laws govern the development of the biological organism, irrespective of geographical location or historical time (the organism was born, it will grow, mature, become old, and ultimately die), there is no reason to assume that societal change and development are any less subject to (social) laws. On the basis of this model, the evolution and growth of a given society are seen to transcend geography and history. Thus, just as biological organisms can be disturbed or can develop pathologies, so too anything that disturbs or upsets the natural functioning of society (such as a revolution) is said to be pathological. For Comte:

> Pathological analysis consists in the examination of cases, unhappily too common, in which the natural laws, either of harmony or of succession, are disturbed by any causes, special or general, accidental or transient; as in revolutionary times especially; and above all, in our own. These disturbances are, in the social body, exactly analogous to diseases in the individual organism. (1855:477)

Following from this, the positivistic core of Comte's teachings resided in his conviction that the principles of natural science (observation, experimentation, and comparison) and the discovery of those laws that governed society could be applied to the study and comprehension of how societies changed and developed: "The conception of *invariable natural laws*, the foundation of every idea of order, will have the same philosophical efficacy here as elsewhere, as soon as it was sufficiently generalized to be applied to social phenomena, thenceforth referred, like all other phenomena, to such laws" (Comte 1855:433; emphasis added). As E. Ellis Cashmore and Bob Mullan put it, "With positivist sociology, Comte thought he could analyse history and society in exactly the same way as a botanist studies plants or a physicist studies matter" (1983:132). It was in this context, then, that Comte (together with Saint Simon) postulated the "law of three stages" through which knowledge evolved, with each stage corresponding to a different evolutionary stage of society. Each evolutionary stage, he felt, was subject to *determinate* or *invariable laws*. The immutable law of progress, for example, implied that all societies inevitably had to pass through a series of fixed stages on their way to development and improvement. For the succession of social states, instead of being arbitrary, follows natural laws of human development (Comte 1855:465, 483).

While human beings may intervene to retard or accelerate the rate of social change, they can do nothing to reverse the process or skip any stages. This is so because changes within society "are analogous to those of the animal organism" (Comte 1855:470), which follows a natural, irreversible course of growth and development. The law of progress envisioned human societies as growing and developing towards ever higher and better stages. Comte found the proof of this determinate evolutionary sequence in the "superior aptitude for mental combinations, independent of all culture, among highly civilized people; or, what comes to the same thing, an inferior aptitude among nations that are less advanced" (p.468). Abraham Blumberg (1974:vi) offers a capsule summary of the stages of human history according to Comte:

The Law of Three Stages
Comte's quintessentially positivistic "discovery" was the *law of three stages*, through which all human beings and all societies, thought, knowledge, and history *must* pass. It is an ordering of inevitable and immutable evolutionary development. The first stage, the theological, covered roughly the period of classical antiquity right up to European feudalism. It was a period during which the church's authority was more or less final and human beings searched for the meanings of the essential nature of natural and social

Stage of intellectual development	Representatives of legitimate Knowledge	Basic Social Unit	Time Period
Theological	Priests, military Men	family	classical antiquity
Metaphysical	Jurists, church men	state	middle ages, renaissance
Positive	scientists, industrialists	all humanity	late 19th and 20th centuries

phenomena in the religious realm. Theirs was a quest for absolute knowledge, which ended with the postulation of super natural forces or gods as the prime movers of the universe and all within it. Thus, explanation in this stage of human and societal development usually denied the importance of human agency, while it invoked the existence of a God or gods. Military conquest and (ancient) slavery were also defining features.

The second or metaphysical stage coincided with the Middle Ages and the Renaissance, but found its highest expression in the Enlightenment period and the ferment created by the French Revolution (1789). It was characterized by great negative criticism of governmental structures and an unmitigated onslaught against religious authority. The term "metaphysical" was employed in that the main thinkers of the times, or Philosophes, sought and encouraged explanations outside of the physical world. Instead they based their arguments on abstract principles such as justice, liberty, fraternity, and equality, which replaced explanations that invoked the existence of supernatural beings. In addition, as George Ritzer (1992:82-83) points out, for most people vague references such as "an act of nature" or "the will of the people" were sufficient to explain the occurrence of a given natural or social event.

According to Comte, however, the metaphysical stage was a short, transitional period between the earlier theological stage and the third stage, of positivism or positive science. Given his great concern with uniting what was hitherto thought of as two contradictory forces--order and progress--

Comte believed that the first two stages of human, social evolution were fated to be superseded by a higher and more integrative system of thought. Ritzer (1992:85) explains Comte's position as: "Theology offered a system of order but without progress.... Metaphysics offered progress without order." Only with the development of positive science could humans break free (progress) from the social and intellectual stagnation of antiquity and escape the anarchy and intellectual disorder in the Europe of Comte's day. For as the most evolved stage of thinking and societal development, positivism's discovery of the immutable laws that govern a society's functioning would lead to the establishment of universal intellectual order and unity.

In the positive stage, therefore, scientific and industrial pursuits displaced religious speculation and peaceful economic production superseded war-making as the dominant aim of social organization. According to Comte, this stage had already been attained by the countries of Western Europe. It was marked by the clear emphasis on human rationality in everyday dealings and attempted to root all explanations in observation, experimentation, and comparison. A central feature of positivism is its elevation of scientists to the prized positions of prestige in society--positions in keeping with the degree of importance they represent for the progress of the human race as a whole. Scientists (including social scientists) thus come to replace priests as the moral and intellectual leaders of society.

The implications of this model for the nations and people of the periphery are blatantly clear. Not only does Comte, in his cavalier, elitist manner, dismiss people in the periphery as inferior and backward beings, but according to his scheme there is also nothing that they themselves can do to hasten the pace of their own development or advancement. It is all a matter of social evolution, and in the same way that human beings were powerless to arrest or speed up the biological evolution of their own species, they are similarly impotent regarding questions of societal evolution and change (except in the positive stage, when, we are told, some conscious guidance is possible). By viewing "backwardness" as a natural, evolutionary process, this model ideologically diverts attention away from such social phenomena as colonialism and imperialism, and from the roles those forces continue to play in fostering economic deprivation in the periphery.

Social Evolutionism   61

Structural Functionalism

Comte's influence on the development and directions of contemporary sociology, though not often acknowledged, has been marked. As Abraham Blumberg (1974) points out, Comte's ideas concerning social change and evolutionism, social order, the organismic analogy, ideal types, religion and social solidarity, and the division of labour have all found expression in the writings of the classical sociological theorists: Marx, Weber, Durkheim, and Spencer. His greatest impact by far, however, has been on the school of thought known as *structural functionalism*.

Herbert Spencer (1820-1903), one of the first functionalist thinkers, followed Comte's ideas by committing himself to a positivist and empiricist understanding of society. For Spencer, Ritzer (1992:142) notes, sociology was "the study of the evolution of societies," because the universal principle of evolution was to be applied to the "formation of the earth out of a nebular mass, the evolution of species, the embryological growth of an individual animal, or the development of human societies" (Goldthorpe 1969:78). In other words, Spencer saw the process of evolution as the key to understanding *all* phenomena: inorganic, organic, and "superorganic" (society).

Indeed, Spencer first employed the terms "structure" and "function" in ways approximating their present usage by structural functionalist thinkers (Goldthorpe 1969:81). This is not to say, however, that all structural functionalists agree on the definitions of these terms, or that the entire approach can be identified exclusively with any one theorist. Different structural functionalists focus on different aspects or elements of society, ask different questions, and employ different research procedures to answer them. Why, then, are they grouped together in a single school of thought? The answer lies in their *teleological* approach to understanding society: they all seek to analyse social structures and practices by reference to the ends or purposes those structural practices serve.

Structural functional analysis, for example, argues that specific social institutions (marriage, religion) exist *because* they contribute to the overall survival of the social system. Any institutions that do not function towards this end will ultimately disappear. Such reasoning, however, is easily criticized for being circular or tautological. For instance, although the argument appears to represent a scientific, cause-effect type of relation or proposition, this is not quite the case. The statement that the institution of marriage exists, and will only exist as long as it serves a societal need, begs the entire question of cause and effect. In other words, which is correct: marriage exists because it fulfils a social need; or because marriage exists, it fulfils a social need? Which is the cause? Which is the effect? Teleological and tautological statements of this type, which are very common in structural functional analysis, represent one of its most flawed features because they are not open to empirical verification or testing.

Structural functionalism is premised on the notion that society is more than just the sum of its individual parts. For society, like an organism, has a structure of its own, over and above its constituent elements. In the same way that a living organism has *needs* that must be met if it is to survive, so too does society. Hence, according to the *organismic analogy*, society's needs include reproducing the species, regulating the behaviour of individuals, and providing for the physical subsistence of the population.

A number of special terms inform this sociological approach. The adopted strategy of social inquiry treats society as a *system* whose various parts are organized into *structures* or institutions, each of which fulfils some *function* for the system as a whole (Grabb 1984:71). Talcott Parsons (1902-80) is the structural functionalist best known for his use of the concept "social system." For him society or the social system is viewed as "a set of related and interdependent phenomena which have boundaries that are maintained; it exists in a state of equilibrium or balance with its environment and has certain mechanisms for maintaining this state" (Cashmore and Mullan 1983:180). These "mechanisms" are social institutions, which are related to a number of subsystems that in turn are connected to the larger social system. Every social system or subsystem must fulfil four basic needs that are key or vital to its survival: a) adaptation; b) goal attainment; c) integration; and d) pattern maintenance.

At the general level of society these vital system-needs correspond to four subsystems of the larger social system: the economy, the polity, the community, and the fiduciary. As subsystems, however, each of these contributes to the maintenance and survival of the larger whole, which is society. But subsystems are still systems, and as such must also ensure that their respective needs of adaptation, goal attainment, integration, and patterns of maintenance are met. For the social system, then, the economic subsystem that encompasses the economic institutions contributes to adaptation by ensuring the effective production and allocation of disposable resources. The political subsystem and its related institutions set overall goals for the society and provide for their realization. The community functions as an integrative subsystem by promoting a sense of social cohesiveness or solidarity. Finally, the fiduciary is that subsystem concerned with pattern maintenance at the cultural level. It deals with such things as promoting value commitment and shared social goals.

The idea of the social system, then, is one of a social whole in which the various structures or institutions function in harmony to maintain the society in a state of balance or equilibrium. This is how the concept of *structure* becomes relevant to structural functionalism; for structures refer to organized patterns of relationships or practices between parts of a system. Structure also implies that there is some continuity to the pattern--that it is enduring.

Thus if we look at the economic structure of society we see the economic institutions and their specialized tasks or functions in the economic division of labour. In the area of energy, for example, we consider the companies that extract oil from the ground; the processing of oil into gas; the use of gas to power cars; the use of cars in getting people to work; and so on. All of these specialized economic tasks, and the adaptations and interconnections they imply, constitute the *economic structure* of a society. The same patterns apply to the political, juridical, educational, and religious institutions.

To discuss social institutions as structures automatically implies a consideration of the human actors who populate them. For the activities of these actors are themselves "structured" in a hierarchy of statuses that cover a multiplicity of roles. The statuses or positions that individuals occupy in an institution correspond to the goals of the institution, and each individual performs a role with its accompanying rights, duties, and responsibilities. Thus from the micro level of the individual to the macro level of the social system as a whole, we can trace the many links that integrate the society.

This brings us to the last key concept in structural functional analysis: *function*. Here the term refers to the contributions that an institution or structure makes in relation to the whole. In other words, we are told that the "function" of a social institution has to be understood in terms of its contribution to the survival of the social system. The institution of marriage, for instance, functions to ensure orderly procreation and child nurturance, which enable the society to maintain itself from generation to generation.

But as Robert K. Merton, himself a structural functionalist, points out, this view is conservatively biased in favour of a strict, orderly view of society. It leaves little room for considerations of change and conflict. If all institutions function positively to promote system survival, how does change come about? Thus, while Merton (1957) acknowledges the fact that a given social structure may be functional for some, he also recognizes that it will not necessarily be functional for all. In his analysis of the political machine he came to appreciate the existence of conflicts between competing interest groups in society, though he never says how they can be eliminated. In addressing the conservative bias, however, Merton introduces the notions of "functions" and "dysfunctions" of social structures: the structures that help the system adapt to its environment are said to be functional; those that impede such adaptation are labelled dysfunctional.

Although Merton recognizes that the same structure could have both functional and dysfunctional consequences, he and other structural functionalists usually assume that a given pattern or institution would not survive unless its functions outweighed its dysfunctions (Wilson 1983:76). To this he adds one further refinement. The functions and dysfunctions of an institution can be *manifest* or *latent*: if they are intended and recognized by members of society, they are manifest; if they are unintended and unrecognized, they are latent. For example, the institution of religion has the manifest function of giving the individual spiritual support and comfort, while it functions latently to maintain group solidarity.(Cashmore and Mullan 1983:152).

Evolutionism, Functionalism, and Change

While they are silent on the question of social revolution, structural functionalists have not totally failed to deal with the question of social change. Rather, the problem is that they have done so in an unsatisfactory manner. Concerned as it is with forces promoting social equilibrium and system survival (Smelser 1968:216-21), structural functional analysis appears unduly biased in favour of a strict orderly view of society. As structural functionalist Wilbert E. Moore (1963:73) puts it, "A social system depends for its existence on the maintenance of order--on predictable conduct and conformity with norms of conduct and values."

Although Moore argues elsewhere (1964:337) that he prefers to view society "as a tension-management system rather than a self-equilibrating one," this hardly exonerates him. For the very term "tension-management" serves to deflect attention away from sources of dissidence, deviation, controversy, and conflict in society. At the very least it minimizes the potentially disruptive consequences of such sources of disaffection.

When structural functionalists do address change, their arguments are almost exclusively related to the *internal* adjustments and "discontinuities" experienced by social systems in coping with their natural and social environments. They either ignore or mention only in passing external sources and causes of change: for example, colonialism and imperialism. Using classical evolutionary theory as their point of departure, they account for "backwardness" in peripheral countries in suprasocietal terms: they do not see change and development as resulting from the purposive actions of individuals, but instead as the working out of some grand force that lies beyond the realm of human agency. Thus they conclude that economic growth in the peripheral countries will occur in due course when the universal law of evolution gradually moves those states to the next higher stage. Development does not take *place*; it takes *time*. For in the same way that humans could not intervene to accelerate or retard the process of evolution of the species, they cannot affect the evolution of societies. Evolutionary change is both inexorable and immanent.

As S.N. Eisenstadt points out, this view has major defects, two of them absolutely crucial. The first concerns the assertion that the development of human societies is unilinear and follows universal stages. The second speaks to the approach's failure to specify the characteristics of evolving societies and the mechanisms by which they change and develop (Eisenstadt 1964:375).

But while criticizing the classical evolutionary approach to social change, structural functionalists such as S.N. Eisenstadt, Neil Smelser, and Moore have not quite managed to free themselves from its influence. In fact the notion of evolution is built into their theory. Key concepts such as "specialization" and "complexity," which were used by the older evolutionary thinkers (for instance, Spencer 1897) to describe the various developmental stages of society, were adopted later by leading structural functionalists such as Eisenstadt himself (1964, 1966), Moore (1963, 1964), Smelser (1968), and Parsons (1964). Very often when the more recent theorists claim to have transcended the earlier evolutionary perspective on social change, it turns out that they had merely changed the form of the argument while leaving the substance largely intact.

Spencer, like Durkheim after him, preferred to regard societies as evolving from simple, primitive forms towards complex, industrial entities. His evolutionary sequence involved simple, compound, doubly compound, and trebly compound societies in which the major motors of change were the twin processes of "integration" and "complexity." He argues: "The states of compounding and recompounding have to be passed through in succession. No tribe becomes a nation by simple growth; and no great society is formed by the direct union of the smaller societies" (1897:555). For Spencer, integration or "augmentation of mass" implied growth and assumed two distinct forms: first, "increase by simple multiplication of units, causing enlargement of the group," for example, population expansion; second, through the "union of groups, and again by union of groups of groups," for example, the joining of tribes, cities, or states into a common political unit (pp.449, 465).

Accompanying this process of growth or integration is the progressive *differentiation* of the various structures in society. As Smelser (1968:243-44) points out, the consolidation of small, dispersed groups into larger political units leads to increasing political complexity as kings, chieftains, councils of elders, and various local rulers begin to exert their authority. As structures are increasingly differentiated, so too are activities or the "functions" among structures. This gives rise to a greater need for integration and co-ordination of mutually dependent parts of the social system in order to maintain harmony and equilibrium. Thus, underlining once again the organismic analogy, Spencer (1897:462) states: "The mutually dependent parts, living by and for one another, form an aggregate constituted on the same general principle as an individual organism."

Increasing complexity and differentiation lead to greater *specialization* of functions within the social organism. In the simplest societies such specialization tends to occur around: a) matters of defence and offence against external enemies (human or animal, real or imagined); and b) questions of general sustenance--provision of food. This process establishes the differentiation between warriors, cultivators, hunters, fishers, priests, and so on. But, in addition, warriors must eat and cultivators must be protected. So, as the society grows and evolves, further specialization takes place in the development of "distribution" functions that facilitate economic exchanges among the differentiated parts of the system. These distribution functions include occasional meetings for local barter activities, more complex market transactions, and even the creation of money and credit systems. In his discussion Spencer (1897:510) once again makes a direct reference to the organismic analogy as he describes blood vessels in the organism and roads in the society as analogous "channels which carry, in the one case blood corpuscles and serum, and in the other case men and commodities."

Finally, to complete the picture, the society gradually sets in place a system of regulation, which might best be thought of in terms of political functions. Designed also to enable co-operation among differentiated parts of the society, the regulating system speaks to the appearance of leaders and law-makers who determine the rules that govern the general polity on matters of both internal and external concern. Thus Ritzer (1992:122) writes that, for Spencer: "The regulative system takes the form of the neuro-muscular system in organisms and the government-military apparatus in social systems."

While Spencer recognizes the difficulty of empirically specifying the boundaries between simple and more compound societies, he nevertheless speaks in broad terms of two contrasting types of society: the militant (less evolved) and the industrial (highly evolved). According to Smelser's interpretation, "The former is based on a predominance of structures for carrying on conflict with other societies, whereas the latter is based on a predominance of structures for carrying on sustenation" (1968:145). Thus, considering the evolution from simple to complex or militant to industrial societies, Spencer argues that the simple or militant is premised on coercive or compulsory co-operation, while the complex or industrial entails voluntary co-operation. It is largely on the basis of this type of ideological schema that he would explain the social and political instability in so many of the present-day peripheral societies, and, by contrast, the marked degree of stability that supposedly attends social and political life in the industrial nations. Politically speaking, he would be at great pains to explain the massive military build-up in the United States today, although he might have some ideological defence of it.

There are, then, broad similarities between Spencer and Durkheim. Both subscribed to the tenets of evolutionism; both employed the organismic analogy in their descriptions of social structures; and both were equally concerned with describing the processes of transition from simple to complex social forms. Where Spencer spoke of the need for "co-operation" in society, Durkheim emphasized the concept of social "solidarity." For Durkheim the principal question guiding his work was "how is society possible?" In attempting to answer this basic query he was led to formulate some of his central sociological ideas, which have remained influential among structural functionalists down to the present.

Beginning with the concept of "solidarity," Durkheim tries to explain how, in spite of all the tensions and conflicts in society, human beings are nevertheless bound together in stable and enduring relationships.

For Durkheim, depending on the society in question, solidarity or social cohesiveness is of two types: *mechanical* and *organic*.

He associates mechanical solidarity with primitive societies. It is a solidarity based on "likeness" or "sameness," for in societies in which people are organized into clans, tribes, extended families, and other such units, the members all share basic similarities. For example, they are self-sufficient, employ simple tools, and are deeply religious. What particularly binds these separate groups together, what gives them solidarity, is a "collective conscience--a totality of beliefs and sentiments common to average citizens of the same society" (Durkheim 1933:79). Further, Durkheim says, the collective conscience, which embodies the moral rules that make solidarity possible in primitive society, is rooted in religion. For early religion "contains in a confused mass, besides beliefs properly religious, morality, law, the principles of political organization, and even science" (p.135). He thus argues that law is essentially religious in its origin and that legal or judicial rules gradually grow out of the collective conscience through the influence of religious beliefs. When there is a close correspondence between the laws and the collective conscience of a society, that society is a moral one (Grabb 1984:75).

Durkheim links organic solidarity with modern societies. For him, the principal motor in the transition from primitive to modern society was the increasing specialization of tasks and activities associated with the division of labour. As opposed to primitive society in which most people worked at similar tasks, held similar beliefs, or possessed similar amounts and types of knowledge, modern society is characterized by social *dissimilarity*, the rise of individualism, and a corresponding variety of values and norms to suit the new circumstances.

Hence, the forces of modern society gradually undermine mechanical solidarity, and the growth of a "personal conscience" erodes the collective conscience. For this change to occur, Durkheim says, people must be freed from the pervasive hold that the collective conscience has on them in primitive society. He states: "The individual personality must have become a much more important element in the life of society, and in order for it to have acquired this importance, it is not enough for the personal conscience of each to have grown in absolute value, but also to have grown more than the common conscience" (Durkheim 1933:167). The decline of mechanical solidarity, then, is accompanied by "a growing multitude of individual differences" (p.172); and in order that society not directly fall apart, "another solidarity must slowly come in to take the place of that which has gone" (p.173).

Durkheim calls the new form of solidarity "organic." Stemming from the division of labour, organic solidarity refers to the fact that society, like a living organism, is made up of distinct parts that must be integrated if the whole is to survive. This task of integration falls to the division of labour, which promotes the interdependence of the parts and replaces the collective conscience as the glue of society (p.181).

From the standpoint of the later structural functionalist thinkers, Eisenstadt (1964:376) argues that the terms "specialization" and "complexity" have been largely displaced from accounts of social change in favour of the concept "differentiation." But for Spencer and Durkheim, increasing social differentiation was a key factor in descriptions of change. Nor does Eisenstadt himself completely dispense with specialization and complexity. He writes: "At each more advanced level or stage of differentiation, the increased autonomy of each sphere creates more *complex* problems of integrating these *specialized* activities into one systemic framework" (p.377; emphasis added). Making explicit the link with Durkheim, he continues: "The degree of differentiation refers mainly to the 'division of labour' in any social system. It denotes the extent to which a society has been transformed from something approximating Durkheim's 'mechanical' model to a potentially more 'organic' one" (p.378).

For his part, Smelser sees social change and development as a "contrapuntal interplay between differentiation and integration" (1968:138). Whereas differentiation serves to divide or fracture established society, integration reunites differentiated structures on a new and higher basis. Smelser sees "simple kinds of economic organization, like subsistence agriculture or household industry," as being characterized by "*unspecialized* activities." But, "as the social systems grow more *complex*," greater specialization results. This, in turn, leads to the development of more sophisticated structures of integration (pp.138-140).

In attempting to make his theoretical discussion more concrete, Smelser turns to the underdeveloped countries of the periphery, and in the process betrays his adherence to the unilinear thinking of classical social evolutionists. He approvingly cites the work of J.H. Boeke, who envisages peripheral societies as developing through several "points on the continuum from structural fusion to structural differentiation" (Boeke

1942:90). Talking about the separation of production from consumption units and the growing differentiation within kin and village communities, Smelser focuses on the introduction of money crops and wage labour as important moments in the transition (evolution) from tribal and primitive groupings to modern social forms.

This transition proceeds from subsistence agriculture through household and cottage industry and handicraft production, culminating in manufacturing and the expanded factory system. After tracing this series of evolutionary sequences Smelser concludes with the categorical statement: "Empirically, underdeveloped economies may be classified according to the respective distances they have moved along this line of differentiation" (1968:131). Implicit in the argument is Smelser's view of all societies as developing along a single path and following set or universal stages. He was thus not very successful in distancing himself from one of the chief defects of classical evolutionary theory, as pointed out by Eisenstadt. However, in an earlier work he also states, "The causes, courses, and consequences of economic development must be expected to vary widely from nation to nation" (Smelser 1967:717).

In his discussion of "evolutionary universals in society," Talcott Parsons seeks to account for social change in terms remarkably similar to those used by the classical social evolutionists. In fact, Parsons uses the concepts *evolutionary* and *universal* to describe "any organizational development sufficiently important to further evolution that, rather than emerging only once, is likely to be 'hit upon' by various systems operating under different conditions" (1964:339). For primitive societies to move towards higher stages of modernity, certain "inventions" are absolutely essential: for example, social stratification, bureaucratic organization, money and market relations, and the democratic association. As evolutionary universals these "inventions" emerge slowly over long periods of time, and they tend to be present in all societies that have attained the stage of modernization.

In outlining his position on social change, Parsons, like the other structural functionalists, also subscribes to the notions of specialization, complexity, and differentiation. In addition he makes direct and more explicit use of the organismic analogy, likening the evolutionary universals in society to biologically based evolutionary universals such as vision and the brain in the human organism. For example, just as the molluscs, insects, and vertebrates have evolved visual organs that aid in their adaptability to their environments, and even though those organs are anatomically different,

Social Evolutionism   71

"There is no evidence that it [vision] was not independently 'hit upon' three times" (Parsons 1964:340). He thus concludes that an evolutionary universal in society is similar to that in a biological organism because it "is a complex of structures and associated processes, the development of which so increases the long-run adaptive capacity of living systems, that only systems that develop the complex can attain higher levels of general adaptive capacity" (pp.340-41).

Thus, in accounting for the various degrees of social and economic "backwardness" in the periphery, Parsons places major emphasis on the fact that those people have not yet invented or adopted the major evolutionary universals so crucial to human social progress and advancement. The very language and concepts Parsons employs leave no doubt as to his intellectual parentage. Although they are careful to provide detailed descriptions of social change, Parsons and the other structural functionalists fail to explain adequately just how and why change comes about (or does not come about). Once again, ideologically, their descriptions of the political, economic, and living conditions of the periphery are in no way linked to the factor of historical and contemporary interference from the outside.

Ideal Types
In seeking to account for the differences between pre-industrial and industrial societies, many social-evolutionary theorists have adopted the "ideal-type" approach. This involves selecting certain features of given societies and classifying them as either pre-industrial or industrial, either backward or advanced. These theorists clearly see the pre-industrial societies as having evolved less than the industrial. As a consequence, there is an explicit value judgement in their approach, similar to the theories of the social Darwinists; for, following the principle of natural selection, they see the more highly evolved societies as being somehow "more fit" or better than the others. Ritzer writes, for example, of Spencer's "belief in a sociological version of survival of the fittest," even to the point of him seeing superior moral behaviour in certain societies as the result of "natural selection" (Ritzer 1992:107, 109).

Accepting the basic ideas and assumptions of evolutionism, which means "improved capability to adapt to environmental pressures or changes" (Wilson 1983:95), a great many sociologists have sought to marry it to the ideal-type or bipolar view of how societies change. Among these, Ferdinand Toennies's "community" versus "society" and Emile Durkheim's "mechanical" and "organic" solidarity are perhaps the best known (Toennies 1957; Durkheim 1933). For Toennies, "community" represents a simple, even rural way of life, in which spontaneity and intimacy characterize the interaction between and among people. He sees social relations within "society" as more complex, impersonal, and formal. Durkheim, too, in talking about "mechanical" solidarity or society, posits a fundamental "likeness" or similarity among people, based upon a common "collective conscience" and morality. Organic solidarity, conversely, describes contemporary society based on an intricate division of labour and increasing social dissimilarity, differentiation, or complexity. The move in both cases--from community to society, and from mechanical to organic solidarity--implies evolutionary changes from one ideal type to another.

As Alejandro Portes (1976:62) points out, a whole host of other social-evolutionary writings on this theme emerged. Charles Horton Cooley (1962), for example, describes "primary" and "secondary" social attachments in a way that echoes the thoughts of Toennies: primary, face-to-face social encounters apply in those societies where little social differentiation had taken place; and secondary, impersonal, even superficial relations prevail in advanced societies. Portes also mentions Henry Maine (1907), who distinguishes between societies based on "status" and those based on "contract"; the famous anthropologist Robert Redfield (1965), who opposes "folk" to "urban" cultures; and Howard Becker, who examines the differences between "sacred" and "secular" social orders. In this context, Portes states, "The contemporary distinction between 'tradition' and 'modernity' can be easily conceptualized as a latter-day counterpart of a theme present since the beginnings of sociological thought" (1976:62).

The Pattern Variables

To give more concrete content to the ideal-typical features of traditional and modern societies, several social-evolutionary theorists seized upon the "pattern variable scheme" developed by Talcott Parsons (1954). Although Parsons himself did not initially conceive of the pattern variables in this context, they were adopted by theorists such as Berthold Hoselitz (1960) and Szymon Chodak (1973) in their descriptions and explanations of social change. As a central feature of both the social-evolutionary and the "value orientation" theories of change, the pattern variable scheme has coloured much of the work in the sociology of development.

The idea of the pattern variables came to Parsons during a study of the doctor-patient relationship. He observed that in such a highly specialized relationship, the doctor's behaviour towards the patient is guided by the same principles that inform the patient's behaviour towards the doctor: their interaction is patterned. The patient expects the same degree of concern, dedication, and professionalism from the doctor as the doctor in turn affords to all other patients. No favouritism or prejudice should come into play. The doctor, at the same time, expects to be judged on the basis of competence and according to the same universalistic criteria by which all other doctors are judged. No exceptions or personal considerations should enter the picture.

It occurred to Parsons that our patterns of social interaction in modern society increasingly reflect the highly specialized conditions under which we live. Not only the doctor-patient relationship, but also teacher-student, employer-employee, and many other contacts occur in institutional and bureaucratic settings that more than anything else serve to define contemporary living. In the public domain we expect, and are expected by others, to act in certain specific and patterned ways as established by social convention or traditional practice. This was the context in which Parsons identified, among people, four *variable sets of interaction patterns*, known in sociology as the pattern variables.

Briefly stated, the four sets of pattern variables or the four sets of continua along which our social behaviour tends to vary are: a) particularism-universalism; b) ascription-achievement; c) diffuseness-specificity; and d) affectivity-affective neutrality. In contemporary society our *formal, public* behaviour, for example, at work or at school, resembles more closely the universalistic, achievement-oriented, specific, and affectively neutral types. This means we expect, and are expected by others, to be judged according to impersonal criteria that are equally applicable to all other members of society; we expect, and are expected by others, to move ahead on the basis of merit and knowledge or skills acquired in fair competition with all co-competitors; we expect, and are expected by others, to interrelate on the basis of specific roles such as doctor, student, or employee; and finally, we expect, and are expected by others, to interact, not merely on the basis of emotion, but according to reason, following our "heads" rather than our "hearts."

Conversely, our *informal, private* behaviour, for example, within the family or peer group, follows more particularistic, ascriptive, diffuse, and affective lines. We do not expect our mothers to treat us like our teachers

74   Sociology and the Periphery

or bosses do. Parents or friends usually take into account the particular attributes of individuals and respond on a more personal level. Furthermore, our status within the family is ascribed: we occupy diffuse roles such as daughter, brother, cousin, or parent, and we are sensitive to the emotions and moods of other family members. Moreover, homes are supposed to exude love and warmth in a way that offices and schools are not.

The pattern variables were quickly adopted by several sociologists and applied to the study of social change. For Hoselitz (1960), for example, they represented the "sociological aspects of economic growth" (the title of his book). In that study, Portes (1976:62) argues, Hoselitz portrays the underdeveloped, traditional, or backward societies as having roles that are ascribed, functionally diffuse, and oriented towards narrow, particularistic goals. Hoselitz sees the developed, modern, or advanced societies, however, as characterized by clearly delineated specific roles, acquired through achievement criteria and oriented towards universal norms. Ideologically, then, the pattern variables encourage a very simplistic, distorted, and even static view of change and development in both peripheral and advanced countries.

Stages of Economic Growth Thesis

W.W. Rostow presents an interesting variant on the theme of evolutionism in his classic study *The Stages of Economic Growth* (1962). Introduced as a necessary corrective to the prevailing bipolar or two-stage view of change, Rostow's study tries to fill in the gaps, positing a series of intermediate evolutionary stages in the passage from backwardness to advancement. From the perspectives of Hoselitz (1960) and Rostow, underdevelopment becomes the original state of society: the starting point from which all change begins.

Hence, in basic agreement with the ideal-typical approach, at least as far as the first stage of traditionalism is concerned, Rostow proceeds to identify four other stages of economic growth. The second stage occurs when the preconditions for economic "take-off" emerge. This usually happens as a result of scientific and technological diffusion, when a more developed country comes into contact with a traditional one. In Rostow's third stage, actual take-off is experienced through increased manufacturing, trade, and commerce. The fourth stage, "the drive to maturity," witnesses the increased application of modern technology to the bulk of the society's resources, leading ultimately to the fifth stage of "high mass consumption," as evidenced in the leading countries of Western Europe and North America at the time of writing.

Although appealing as a descriptive schema, Rostow's stages of economic growth, like other evolutionary views, suffer from two general shortcomings. Firstly, they cannot explain the changes observed. Although Rostow presents descriptions of the various stages, he makes no attempt to specify exactly what causes the move from one stage to the other. In fact, as Andre Gunder Frank points out in a very telling critique of this entire school of thought, "No underdeveloped country has ever managed to take off out of its underdevelopment by following Rostow's stages" (Gunder Frank 1973:24).

The second general problem inherent in Rostow's approach concerns its lack of sensitivity to historical process. To say all societies begin from a condition of original underdevelopment and proceed along the same path to development ignores the infinite variety of history. The paths to development followed by Britain, the United States, and Japan, for example, were greatly dissimilar: Britain was a colonial power; the United States was a colonial possession; and Japan was never colonized by any foreign power--yet they all became major, industrial, capitalist countries. Further, the assertion that underdevelopment is the original stage of all societies directly implies that those which have become developed have had a history, the history of their development; while those that are still underdeveloped, have never moved: they have had no history because they are still in the original underdeveloped stage (Gunder Frank 1973:19).

Following Gunder Frank's line of argument, then, here I intend to utilize a critical and materialist understanding of the term *underdevelopment*. And along with the historical-structural factors associated with the development of underdevelopment, I will also presume the existence of those chronic conditions that routinely accompany it: "famine and malnutrition, displacement and homelessness, unemployment and underemployment, disease and mortality, the destruction of the environment, and political repression and violence" (Acosta-Belén and Bose 1990:301).

The Politics of Evolutionism
As Portes explains, theories of social evolution borrow the concept of "development" from the biological sciences and seek to apply it to the continuous transformations experienced by human societies. Such societies are seen as growing organisms that pass through a series of ordered and inevitable stages, which "culminate in the highest levels of societal complex-

ity, represented by the advanced European nations" (Portes 1976:61) and, I might add, the United States. Thus, following the key idea of "survival of the fittest" as enunciated by Darwin and embraced by evolutionary thinkers generally, the ideological implication is that the present-day developed nations were able to attain their high levels of development on the basis of being more fit or better equipped than the nations of the periphery to respond to the challenges posed by their environments.

But even more important for our consideration of ideology is the assumption on the part of the social-evolutionary theories that underdevelopment and development are unrelated stages in the *universal* and *unilinear* path to advancement. They are viewed as *natural* and sequential stages through which all countries must pass. The theories make no reference to colonialism and imperialism and to the consequences of those processes for the making of underdevelopment; nor is there any hint at the fact that human beings can and do alter the course of history. The message is clear: there is no need for the people in today's underdeveloped countries to become alarmed about their "backward" conditions, for "in time" they too will progress and advance to higher stages of development. If these people can be made to understand that underdevelopment is a natural condition or state, then revolution and other forms of social protest are inconsequential--as social processes they cannot serve to hasten or alter a natural fact.

Rostow's model of stages of economic growth has been criticized for being incorrect primarily because it does not correspond to the past or present realities of the peripheral countries whose future development it is supposed to mirror. In other words, the costs of confusing past and present are far higher in economics and politics than in grammar, and this is why it is important to draw a distinction between "undeveloped" and "underdeveloped." Although the countries of Western Europe and North America were once undeveloped, they were never underdeveloped. To be undeveloped is a natural state; to be underdeveloped is a social product. Confusion of the two terms will lead to a distortion and misreading of the history of world development. Ideologically speaking, those who were instrumental in creating the squalid social and economic conditions that prevail in various parts of the world today, especially the periphery, and those who claim to be promoting modernization and development, are freed from accepting responsibility for their actions. They see underdevelopment

Social Evolutionism 77

simply as a fact of nature. When this type of explanation is accepted by those who live in the underdeveloped countries, then, the "developers," the multinational corporations, and the industrial magnates can continue to reap handsome profits in those countries, secure in the knowledge that their presence and their investments are viewed in favourable light.

This ideologically conservative social-evolutionary school thus ultimately brands any attempts to experiment with alternative models of political and economic development as "communist" or "socialist," and as presenting a threat to the security of the Western world. This school of thought came to play in the political situation of Brazil, Cuba, the Dominican Republic, and Vietnam in the 1960s, in Chile, Angola, and Mozambique in the 1970s, and in Grenada and Nicaragua in the 1980s. As an approach it is also at the root of the U.S. government's ongoing opposition to popular struggles in countries such as Guatemala, Puerto Rico, Panamá, and El Salvador in the 1990s. In the post-Cold War era, given the so-called New World Order and the dismantling of socialism in what was once the U.S.S.R. and in Eastern Europe, it should be interesting, therefore, to witness the emergence of new "evolutionary" explanations of traditional societies in that part of the world and elsewhere.

Chapter Four

Modernization:
An American View

The debate over the theory of social change and development did not end with the demise of the classical evolutionary school. Nor were the structural functionalists, who adopted and built on many of the central concepts of that school, able to answer certain vexing questions concerning the actual dynamics of change. Limiting themselves largely to the level of description, the structural functionalists for the most part ignored questions of explanation and analysis. They never quite said just how change is put into effect.

Another group of theorists, responding to various shortcomings in classical evolutionary and structural functionalist thought, suggested a different approach to the problems of change and development. These theorists--members of what is usually called the "modernization school"-- concerned themselves with the processes by which societies become "modern." For them a modern society includes, among other things: a commitment to scientific rationality; the widespread use of inanimate sources of energy; significant levels of industrialization; abundant food and material goods; bureaucratic and political structures run in an impersonal and meritocratic way; people "freed" from kin and community obligations; and secular and rational religion.

Departing radically from the largely mechanical, positivistic, and suprasocietal view of change and development that was propounded by the social-evolutionary thinkers, modernization theorists have more in common with the interactionist tradition. From that tradition they take the idea that human beings are the subjective creators of their own worlds: people fashion their own cultures, symbols, and institutions, investing them with *social* meaning. As rational actors, people are capable of defining and assessing social situations, assigning significance to those situations, and judging for themselves what is in their best interests. According to this view, individuals are rationally able not only to calculate the outcomes of their actions but also to choose the most appropriate means for pursuing certain desired goals or ends (Weber 1978:63-75).

For Max Weber, the ends towards which social action is directed are infinite and cannot be determined by the so-called "functional needs of society." Human beings, nevertheless, do seek, through the imposition of subjective definitions, "to create a finite segment of meaning from the meaningless infinity of the world process" (Weber, as quoted in Ashley and Orenstein 1985:205). In other words, social reality, which encompasses questions of change and development, is the product of active interactions and exchanges between and among social actors.

In the hands of modernization theorists, this voluntaristic conception of the human being, though microsociological in origin, is applied to the larger, cultural, and macrosocietal levels. In so doing members of this school see themselves as being aligned with the Weberian tradition of idealism, and they reject the deterministic current evident in evolutionary and structuralist thinking: "All analogies with the 'organism' and other similar biological concepts are condemned to sterility" (Weber 1978:1377). For, to realize the main aims of social science, to penetrate the subjective understandings of the individual actor, the assumptions and methods of natural science are totally inappropriate.

Thus, paying special attention to the subjective dimension of social actions and Weber's treatment of the role of ideas in history, modernization theorists look to the sphere of value orientations as the key to understanding why some societies and countries supposedly advance while others remain backward. As Alejandro Portes writes, "The value approach to the problem of development lays claim to, and often labels itself as a direct continuation of, the thesis Weber developed in *The Protestant Ethic and the Spirit of Capitalism*" (1976:68). Indeed, what Portes refers to as the "value approach" goes to the core of Weber's writings on social change and the development of modern capitalism. For if premodern society valued tradition more than anything else, modern society places a high premium on goal-oriented, rational behaviour: "Weber's emphasis on 'rationalization,' on the key importance of being able to predict institutional responses and of calculability more generally is the linchpin of the approach. Increased 'rationality' is the definition of the movement towards modernity, or more crudely put, of progress" (Evans and Stephens 1988:741). People, it is understood, give expression to their basic value commitments in the conduct of their daily lives. Their orientations to the world are thus guided by *culturally sanctioned norms and values* that variously reflect traditional, affective, formally (instrumental) rational, and substantively (value) rational understandings.

In attempting to fuse Weber's ideas on social action with the approach stressing the role of cultural attributes in the process of change and development, David Ashley and David Michael Orenstein draw attention to the fact that in many traditional societies individuals live highly routinized and structured lives, wherein everyday ceremonies are generally seen as ends in themselves: "This type of action is very different from the action of modern individuals who have to adopt a great many highly specific roles that require them constantly to shift perceptions and allegiances" (Ashley and Orenstein 1985:205).

Thus, merely *describing* the behaviour of individuals in traditional and modern societies is not enough; the main point is that such behaviour is informed and guided largely by the wider cultural context, which embraces the overall value system of a given society. To get to the *explanatory* dimension of the modernization approach, we must further explore the link between culture, values, and social psychology.

Social Psychology and Modernization Theory

In contrast with the social-evolutionary thinkers, modernization theorists are less concerned with detailed descriptions of traditional or modern social structures. Rather, they place more stress on the actual *character and personality* of the individuals who live in particular societies. Their aim is to assess in social-psychological terms how those individuals' actions are informed, and how those actions serve either to bring about or to retard change. As Myron Weiner observes, modernization theorists believe, "Attitudinal and value changes are prerequisites to creating a modern society, economy and political system" (1966:9).

According to this perspective, questions of change, development, or industrialization cannot be separated from a consideration of the values that underlie those social processes. Hence, as Szymon Chodak points out: "Instead of asking 'what is development?' or 'what happens in its course?', modernization theorists ask *why* it happened, and what specifically *caused* the breakthrough from traditional into modern societies. Thus such theories start with the question 'what are the causes of industrialization?'" (1973:11; emphasis added). In positing their answers to such queries, modernization theorists emphasize the importance of value orientations within specific cultures. Adopting more of an analytical approach than the earlier evolutionary school, they reason that it is possible to identify certain factors. When present, those factors lead to development and industrialization; when absent, they result in stagnation.

The main factors singled out for attention are related to the *values* and *attitudes* held by members of a given society and their willingness to embrace education as a means of promoting a meritocratic and individualist ethos in society (Ballantine 1989:301). Implicitly, therefore, the countries of Western Europe (and more recently North America) were able to develop and advance on the basis of their value-structures and attitudinal structures, while in the countries of the periphery, the people are somehow devoid of similarly "progressive" values and attitudes. The ideological message inherent in this type of cultural chauvinism is clear. For rather than discussing the historical and structural antecedents of deprivation (for example, colonialism and imperialism), this approach seeks to lay blame for the socioeconomic and political problems of the periphery within the periphery itself, and specifically in the social-psychological make-up of its inhabitants.

Nevertheless, this school is more analytical than descriptive in its approach, because it does attempt to answer the question "why." Unlike the social-evolutionary school, it does not content itself with a mere description of traditional and modern society, but tries to explain why some remain backward and why others are able to advance. As David McClelland, one of the leading representatives of this school, argues, too much attention has been paid to the *external* causes of development--such as favourable trade opportunities, abundant natural resource endowment, and conquest of markets. In opposition to any approach that seeks to identify and emphasize external reasons for backwardness, McClelland says, "I am interested in the internal factors--in the values and motives men have that lead them to exploit opportunities, to take advantage of favourable trade conditions; in short, to shape their own destiny" (1964:179-80).

According to the modernization school, then, the mere existence of objective trade opportunities or natural resources is not sufficient for development to occur. Key ingredients, or the catalyst that can turn such objective conditions to advantage, are found in the values and motives held by members of the society. For there is "the growing conviction among social scientists that it is values, motives or psychological forces that determine ultimately the rate of economic and social development" (McClelland 1963:17). In referring also to "men shaping their own destinies," McClelland runs counter to the positivistic conception of the human being

82   Sociology and the Periphery

as a wholly passive creature, while endorsing the general interactionist view of man as an active, rational utility maximizer. Thus the cliché "where there's a will there's a way" appears to be an apt summary of McClelland's thinking on change and development.

McClelland examines two related factors that are supposed to lead to development: a need for achievement (n'Ach); and entrepreneurship. Societies in which people demonstrate a high need for achievement are more likely to be developed than those in which traditional values and non-progressive attitudes and orientations prevail. The need for achievement is a psychological factor that promotes modernization, and McClelland defines this factor as a desire to do well, not so much for the sake of social recognition, but to attain an inner feeling of personal accomplishment or self-satisfaction. It is thus like an internal force that drives individuals "to work harder at certain tasks; to learn faster; to do their best work when it counts for the record, and not when special incentives like money prizes are introduced; to choose experts over friends as working partners etc." (McClelland 1964:180-81).

Arguing that people who have a high n'Ach usually make the most successful entrepreneurs, McClelland goes on to show how those societies that encourage entrepreneurial behaviour and competitiveness among their members tend to be more developed than those in which people tend to "act very traditionally on economic matters" (McClelland 1964:183). For him, then, entrepreneurs are possessed of the "strategic mental virus" that leads to the establishment of businesses, economic rationality, and market innovativeness that are so crucial to the development of any society. He almost totally disregards the wider social and structural contexts within which such matters as business rationality and market innovativeness actually take place.

Building more or less on these same assumptions, another modernization theorist, Daniel Lerner, speaks of *The Passing of Traditional Society*. Lerner views Western culture as one in which people have become "habituated to the sense of change and attuned to its various rhythms" (1965:47). Hence, "Whereas traditional man tended to reject innovation by saying 'It has never been thus,' the contemporary Westerner is likely to ask 'Does it work?' and try the new way without further ado" (p.49). According to Lerner, a key factor in the promotion of modernization is what he calls the development of a "mobile personality endowed with instrumental rationality." It involves the ability of individuals to exercise personal freedom of choice in seeking their own versions of a better life, and also their willingness to embrace a "system of values that sees social change as normal.... Personal mobility is itself a first-order value" (p.48).

Generally speaking, therefore, the modernization of any society would entail "great characterological transformations," for "Whereas the isolated communities of traditional society functioned well on the basis of a highly constrictive personality, the interdependent sectors of modern society require widespread participation" (p.51). Thus, for Lerner, modern man and Western man are one and the same. Among those features that make Western people modern are their mental adaptability to change, their rationality, their ability to make independent choices regarding their individual destiny, and their disposition to forming and holding political opinions that may be at variance with those of their immediate family, kin, or community groups.

In similar vein, Alex Inkeles (1973:345) more or less duplicates Lerner's list of the attributes of modern man by pointing to a number of traits: openness to new experience, self-assertiveness, a belief in the efficacy of science and medicine, a strong interest in political affairs, and ambition for oneself and one's children. Like McClelland and Lerner, Inkeles is concerned with the social-psychological import of values and attitudes, and the roles that those values and attitudes play in "making men modern" (the title of his study) and in the promotion of a meritocratic, market society. To this end he constructed a questionnaire "intended to measure the range of attitudes, values and behaviours conceived as relevant to understanding the individual's participation in the roles typical for a modern industrial society" (p.343). On the basis of that questionnaire, Lerner asserts: "Evidently the modern man is not just a construct in the mind of sociological theorists. He exists and can be identified with fair reliability within any population which can take our test" (p.345).

There are obvious shortcomings associated with these views and their underlying assumptions. First, the ideal of meritocracy has proved elusive the world over. Very significantly, in the United States for example, Tadeusz Krauze and Kazimierz Slomcyznski (1985:637) have analysed labour force statistics, educational levels, and status and income differentials and have convincingly concluded that society "is far from meritocratic." Jeanne Ballantine, too, studying the situation in certain formerly non-market societies of Eastern Europe (Poland, Hungary, Czechoslovakia, and the U.S.S.R.), has found that those societies were closer to the meritocratic ideal than several Western European societies, including France, Sweden, Switzerland, Britain, and West Germany. Further, she agrees with Krauze and Slomcyznski and contends that "contrary to widespread beliefs, Japan and the United States are very far from ideal meritocracy--much further than some less developed countries" (Ballantine 1989:302).

A second criticism that can be levelled at the modernization thinkers concerns the ethnocentrism of their model. Their assumption that all countries in the world will follow or even want to follow the path taken by Western countries is not warranted. Finally, there is a criticism relating to the assumption that, unlike peripheral societies, modern societies are progressive and stable. But among the Western nations recurrent crises have led to war, serious economic displacement, deep political discontent, and widespread alienation in some social sectors, for example, youth (Côté and Allahar 1993). Nevertheless, as José Nun (1991:8) observes, even in the contemporary period, some thirty years after the initial emergence of modernization thinking, there are those who continue to view modernization in unproblematic terms as the principal solution to the ills of countries in the periphery.

The Latin American Value Structure

Based on his study "Values, Education and Entrepreneurship," Seymour Martin Lipset (1967) placed himself squarely in the camp of modernization theory. In seeking to account for the general underdevelopment of the periphery, and of the Latin American region in particular, Lipset sought to combine Parsons's pattern variable scheme with the value orientation approach of McClelland and others. Focusing on culture as the embodiment of societal values, Lipset begins his study with the observation that whereas "structural conditions make development possible; cultural factors determine whether the possibility becomes an actuality" (1967:3).

Lipset finds that particularism and ascriptive criteria are emphasized in the context of Latin America and concludes that underdevelopment is the natural result. He thus focuses on the type of value systems that have come to predominate in the region and have fostered behaviour antithetical to the systematic accumulation of capital. In the United States, by contrast, the pattern variables of "universalism" and "achievement orientation" are the norm. This specific combination is "most favourable to the emergence of an industrial society since it encourages respect or deference toward others on the basis of merit and places an emphasis on achievement" (p.6). Therefore, in social systems that are united around themes such as kinship and local community, one does not tend to find people who exhibit or display those characteristics associated with "modern man." Power and authority are decentralized, roles remain diffuse, expressive rather than instrumental behaviour is common, and traditional values are perpetuated. These precise value orientations, Lipset argues, are symptomatic of backwardness and underdevelopment. They do not foster the development of mobile personalities, nor do they recognize the importance of change itself as a vehicle for progress. The observations of Carlos Fuentes, the celebrated Mexican novelist, former cabinet minister, and ex-ambassador to France, written two decades after Lipset's study, show where those in high places are not immune to the ideology of modernization:

> The United States was born in perfect consonance with the values of modernity: the wedlock of religion and economics; free enterprise; free inquiry; self government; scepticism; criticism; division of powers; federalism....

> Latin America was born in perfect discord with these same values: dogmatism; royal absolutism; the refusal of modernity; centralism; the decision to prolong the Holy Roman Order; the divorce between religious man and economic man. (Fuentes 1985:10-11)

What Fuentes leaves out of his description is a consideration of power. The United States is rich and powerful enough to enjoy free enterprise, self-government, free inquiry, and so on, and powerful enough to prevent others from doing the same if it so chooses. Eduardo Galeano captures this point most succinctly when he speaks of Latin America's foreign debt and the harsh conditions imposed on the region by the IMF and compares this to the situation of the United States: "The United States, which owes much more than all of Latin America put together, doesn't accept conditions, it imposes them." In the same piece he reflects on the common pretext (protecting American lives) used by the United States to invade weaker countries, and muses: "Imagine the Mexican army invading Los Angeles to protect Mexican people during the recent riots" (Galeano 1992:213).

Still, Lipset is explicit in trying to account for the origins of the supposedly deficient ideas and values among Latin Americans. He argues, for example,

86   Sociology and the Periphery

that we can trace the ideas and values back to the very institutions and norms that the Spaniards and Portuguese took to Latin America during the period of colonial rule. At the time of the colonial conquest, he reminds us, both Spain and Portugal were engaged in a long struggle to expel the Moors, who were Moslems, and the Jews, who had occupied parts of the Iberian peninsula for centuries. Apart from being non-Christians, the Moors and the Jews were also engaged in economic activities that at the time were seriously frowned upon by the Catholic Church. They monopolized commerce and banking, and their role in banking especially was viewed as sinful because it represented institutionalized usury and a crass preoccupation with material possessions.

During the colonial period, Lipset observes, the roles of soldier and priest came to be glorified by the Spaniards, while commercial and business pursuits were denigrated (Lipset 1967:8). As a result the dominant culture and value systems that emerged in Latin America were "not supportive of entrepreneurial activity" (p.23), which the modernization theorists view as the cornerstone of economic development. Because the leading political and economic institutions in the society did not encourage pragmatism, materialism, and rational business dealings, there was little or no opportunity for the emergence of modern people with modern ideas directing the development of a modern society.

On this score, Lipset also examines the structure and content of school curricula and the pattern of landholding, with a view to assessing the types of values they inculcated and reflected. Here he finds that at both the secondary school and university levels the content of education continued to mirror the values of an aristocratic, landed upper class, with its inherent "disdain for practical work" (p.19). Rather than manual skills the society placed its emphasis on the acquisition of intellectual skills, which yielded well-cultivated minds that were not directly productive from the economic point of view. In landholding patterns, huge estates or *latifundia* were the norm. The comparatively small class of aristocratic landowners lived like feudal lords or patrons, commanding the labour services of masses of peasants and peons who did the actual farming of their lands. The prevalence of feudal or semi-feudal relations between rich patrons and impoverished clients thus contributed to further economic stagnation and actively militated against the development of a modern capitalist society.

Again, this approach to understanding underdevelopment is almost totally devoid of any attempt to examine the wider context of relations between and among countries. It is one thing to say that certain non-progressive values and attitudes prevail in a given situation, and quite another matter to historically analyse the institutional mechanisms and class forces that created and continue to perpetuate those values and attitudes. Values and attitudes, after all, do not just fall from the sky.

Canadian-U.S. Value Differences

In addition to his study of Latin America, Lipset also applied the "value question" and pattern variables to an analysis of the cultural differences between two developed countries, Canada and the United States (Lipset 1985). He begins his comparison with the American Revolution and goes on to discuss differences in the religious, political, legal, socioeconomic, and ecological spheres of both societies. Unlike the U.S. citizens who embraced the liberal-democratic traditions of the French Revolution, Canadians, he says, opted for continued colonial dependence on Britain. As a result Canadian society and institutions came to exhibit a European bias, complete with a conservative political orientation and a healthy respect for the established European churches (Roman Catholic and Anglican). In the United States, conversely, there was a greater emphasis on the separation of church and state and the growth of non-conformist Protestant sects opposing organized state religions.

Lipset maintains that Canadians and Americans differ greatly politically and philosophically. Canadians tend to be more elitist and resigned to accepting governmental intervention in their lives; while Americans are more strongly committed to egalitarian thinking and are clearly concerned about limiting state interference in their private lives. Canadian conservatism contrasts sharply with U.S. liberalism and individualism. In economic matters these differences are crucial. Reflecting the classic biases of modernization theorists, Lipset argues: "The United States, born modern, without a feudal elitist, corporatist tradition, could create ... the purest example of a bourgeois society. Canada, as we have seen, was somewhat different, and that difference affected the way her citizens have done business" (1985:42).

Describing Canadian capitalism as "public enterprise" (as opposed to "private enterprise" U.S. capitalism), Lipset implicitly criticizes public or state ownership of parts of the Canadian economy. Because Canada has not experienced "a pure laissez-faire market capitalism," he affirms, Canadian capitalists have grown dependent on government for precisely those things that make U.S. capitalists strong. Canadian capitalists, in comparison to their U.S. counterparts, are less aggressive, less innovative, and less willing to take risks. These are exactly the same terms McClelland and Lipset himself used to describe underdevelopment in Latin America.

Such a situation, we are told, is clearly related to the fact that Canada lags behind the United States in developing a modern society. According to the model of pattern variables, Canadians are more elitist, ascriptive, and particularistic, whereas Americans are more committed to egalitarianism, achievement orientation, and universalism: "Canada's economic backwardness relative to the United States is primarily a function of her value system" (Lipset 1985:15).

The important question is: if Canadian value orientations are so similar to those of the Latin American (and Caribbean) periphery, why does economic development in Canada more closely mirror that of the United States than that of Latin America? Clearly, the answer must involve some explanation other than mere cultural values and attitudes, or personality and character traits.

Modernization, Dualism, and Diffusionism

Two additional concepts are important to the central premises of modernization thinking. The first, economic dualism, describes the countries of the periphery not as integrated economic wholes but as disarticulated or fractured societies with radically distinct traditional and modern sectors. Thus, just as these countries appear to be backward or traditional in comparison to the nations of the industrialized world, so too within them one can find both traditional and modern sectors. In the traditional sectors particularistic relations or kinship obligations tend to predominate, while in the modern sectors, which develop as a result of outside penetration and investment, modern ideas, values, and structures are widely embraced. The challenge of development or modernization, then, is to bring these two sectors together.

The second concept, diffusionism, picks up that challenge. It points to the fact that modernization can and will be effected when and if the appropriate values, attitudes, institutions, and technology from the modern sector are passed on (diffused) to the traditional sector.

Dualism

Sociological and economic theories of dualism are the products of earlier work done by anthropologists such as Robert Redfield (1941, 1947), who spoke of folk-urban or rural-urban differences between and within societies. Given the view that the ideal-typical or bipolar approaches to understanding social change were rooted in a fundamental dichotomy that saw development or modernization as the passage from traditional to modern forms of social organization, the countries of the periphery then came to be seen as consisting of separate traditional and modern sectors with few structural links between them. The traditional sector is characterized by predominantly feudal, agricultural pursuits, using rudimentary technology. Productivity is low and agriculture is generally subsistence-based, producing little surplus that can be marketed. These agriculturalists are thus largely outside of and not caught up in the fast-paced world of business and high finance. The members of the modernization school portray these people, then, as holding non-progressive values and attitudes. According to this perspective, therefore, as Norman Long critically points out, backwardness results from the fact that the people of the agrarian sector display "a high preference for leisure and little interest in profit maximization" (Long 1977:39).

The modern sector is capitalist. The bulk of its people are employed in industrial settings, are rational and market-oriented, and hence are supposedly more receptive to change than their agrarian counterparts. Thus, whereas output in the rural sector is a simple function of the relationship between land and labour, the urban-manufacturing sector views the relationship between capital and labour as the key to its prosperity and advancement.

To the extent that there are any links between the two sectors in this model, the connections concern the question of labour transfers. Because large numbers of people live in the rural areas of the peripheral countries, we are told, those areas experience a great deal of underemployment and unemployment. In time, as people begin to move to the urban areas in search of work, pronounced labour shortages will tend to occur in the countryside. These shortages, in turn, will serve to "trigger off a process of rapid economic modernization which is achieved through the more efficient use of a modern technology and through changed economic attitudes and incentives" (Long 1977:40).

As persuasive and appealing as this argument may be, it is seriously flawed. Experience has shown that the type of labour attracted away from the countryside is predominantly that of young males (and females to a lesser extent), who seldom return to their villages. This has major consequences for the stability of family life, for community cohesion and continuity, for the survival of subsistence agriculture, and for general development. Depending on the actual resources a specific sector has to offer (agricultural, mining, or labour), no "efficient modern technology" might ever find its way there. For as often happens in cases in which labour resources are the main attraction, a rural sector can be reduced to a mere reserve labour pool that responds almost exclusively to the demands for labour in the urban capitalist sector. The village itself is thus left to languish in poverty and its remaining older and weaker members come to depend on small remittances from those who have migrated to the urban centres. Two clear cases of this process have been documented by Y. Michal Bodemann and Anton L. Allahar (1980) for Central Sardinia and Nii-k Plange (1980) for Northern Ghana.

Seemingly oblivious to these sorts of critiques, theories of social and economic dualism persist. W. Arthur Lewis, for example, a prominent Caribbean and international economist, argued that dual economies represent a necessary *transition phase* between a purely traditional society and a wholly modern one. Hence in a given peripheral country: "Economic growth does not begin throughout the economy simultaneously. Here some corporation opens a mine, employing 500 people. Somewhere else a port is built. Somewhere else a merchant begins to buy a commodity for export.... *Ultimately, the developing sectors will grow until they embrace the whole economy*" (Lewis 1983:626-27; emphasis added). From the straight economic point of view, therefore, these theorists do not see the transition to modernity as problematic. Echoing many of the sentiments associated with the social-evolutionary school, they see it as a phase through which all countries must pass.

This perspective sees only one potential problem, albeit a short-term one, that has to be guarded against. This is what economists and sociologists such as W. Arthur Lewis and Wilbert Moore, among many others, call the "revolution of rising expectations." For due to the climate of hope that the modernization process creates among large masses of impoverished people, and the general social, economic, and political dislocations that attend the transition to modernity, "Trouble may be expected" (Lewis 1983:626). This "trouble" concerns the increasingly visible polarization between the immediate beneficiaries of modernization and those who live and work in the depressed sectors that are not yet touched by the process.

The polarization has the effect of exacerbating the potential for revolution. According to Moore (1964:338):

> Revolution is not the normal consequence of modernization, though under certain combinations of circumstances it is not unknown. The spread of sharp rises in aspirations, combined with relative slowness in economic improvements, greatly increases the probability of revolution in "new nations." Polarization, then, is a key indicator of incipient revolution.

In essence, then, Moore argues that because polarization is a key indicator of revolution, and because revolution is not the normal consequence of modernization, then polarization also is not the normal consequence of modernization. Where, therefore, does this leave the whole dualistic thesis that is premised upon the dichotomy between backward and modern sectors?

Nevertheless, failing to consider this logical contradiction in their argument, modernization theorists who address the question of revolution in the periphery focus on the growing polarization between the "haves" and the "have-nots" and contend that such major social upheavals are neither necessary nor inevitable. For by *accelerating* the process of modernization, quickening the transition, the people who live in the traditional sectors can be reached earlier and shown the benefits of modern living before their disaffection grows too great. Hence, according to this model, social strife is viewed largely in inter-sectorial terms, while intra-sectorial conflicts of a class or political nature, for example, receive scant attention (Hunter 1969:3-29).

Diffusionism

As a central concept of modernization theory, diffusionism is intimately linked with the assumptions of dualistic thinking, as well as with the ideas of Rostow and the structural functionalists. Diffusionists see the solution to the problems of traditional societies as coming from outside those societies. This solution involves the spread of skill, technology, capital, values, institutions, and knowledge from modern countries to backward countries or from the modern sectors of a given country to its backward sectors (Nash 1963:5).

According to this view, because development consists of the diffusion of certain economic, organizational, and cultural practices from the advanced to the backward countries, underdevelopment can only be explained by the presence of certain obstacles or resistance to such diffusion (Gunder Frank 1973:27). One clear obstacle that the diffusionists identify is poverty, defined as the lack of investment capital. Unable to invest, people in backward sectors are unable to develop and consequently unable to escape their poverty. The tautological reasoning aside, the solution to this problem, the diffusionists argue, must be sought in the diffusion of capital from the advanced to the backward nations. This view, persuasive as it is simplistic, has been vigorously criticized by writers such as Paul Baran (1957), Andre Gunder Frank (1967), Ivar Oxaal and his colleagues (1975), Daniel Chirot (1977), and Gavin Kitching (1982), among many others.

Their criticisms examine the central assumptions of diffusionism. Are the developed countries net exporters of capital to the underdeveloped ones? It would appear not. For using the U.S.-based multinational corporations (MNCs) as a case in point, researchers found that in the 1960s returns on MNC investments in peripheral countries such as Mexico, Brazil, India, and Pakistan exceeded the initial amounts invested by several billions of dollars (Magdoff 1966; Griffin and French-Davis 1964; Alavi 1963; Frondizi 1967; and Jalée 1968, 1969).

During the 1970s and 1980s this trend continued. For example, Tom Barry, Beth Wood, and Deb Preusch (1983:10) discovered that in 1970 the Central American region had a trade deficit of $369 million with the United States; by 1980 that deficit had grown seven times to $2.6 billion. These authors state:

> Central America has received an ever increasing infusion of foreign investment and capital without an accompanying redistribution of the wealth. The multinational corporations, with their superior control of capital, technology, and marketing, have relegated the nations of Central America to roles of producers of unprocessed commodities and providers of cheap labour. (p.7)

In another study, this time of the Caribbean region, the same team of researchers found: "The rate of return from U.S. investments in the Caribbean is substantially higher than in other regions. In 1980 the rate of return in the Caribbean was 30.5 percent, considerably higher than either the international average of 14.3 percent or the Latin American average of 15.8 percent" (Barry, Wood, and Preusch 1984:19).

It would appear, therefore, that the poverty of the peripheral countries and their existing value structures are no obstacle to the accumulation of capital. It is not the fact that these countries do not have much initial investment capital that causes them to be poor. It is important, rather, to examine the process by which the capital generated in those countries is siphoned off by the multinational corporations and their various agents. That capital flows out to the developed countries, where it is then employed to create jobs, to stimulate industry, and to further development there. The developed countries, then, are not net exporters of capital to the underdeveloped countries, because the largest part of the capital they own in the periphery is acquired locally (Gunder Frank 1973:29).

Politics of Modernization during the Cold War

Given that "modernization" is a perspective that came to enjoy wider acceptance than social-evolutionary thinking, its practitioners cannot be seen as mere academicians. They have served as advisors to governments and international agencies in the peripheral countries, as planners and developers, and as teachers of planners and developers (Weiner 1966:v-vi, 1-14). Their analyses and recommendations, therefore, became immediately pertinent to the situation of the peripheral countries and to their relations with the developed world.

In the so-called development decade of the 1960s, problems of inflation, recession, war, and unemployment were on the minds of many people. More than ever before various national governments and international bodies became preoccupied with the challenges posed by vast economic inequalities, political instability, and opposing ideological orientations. By the 1970s the differences between North and South or East and West, and the claims by newly developing nations to a "fair" share of the world's wealth, threatened to upset the traditionally constituted international order and division of labour.

This served to condition the Cold War climate between the two superpowers. Along with a deterioration in relations between the United States and the Soviet Union, and the jeopardizing of peace talks, came realistic fears of a nuclear holocaust. In addition, everything from economic and trade deals to cultural and sporting links were either curtailed or vastly reduced at one time or another. Given this major rift between the superpowers, most other countries in the world found themselves in the unenviable position of having to choose sides. In the meantime, the superpowers saw the populations of the least developed countries as integral to their respective continued dominance. Those populations had to be courted, cajoled, and manipulated, for they held the key to the balance of world power, both economically and geopolitically. The superpowers realized the strategic importance of the Third World and sought to secure "friendly" relations with various peripheral states in their continuing battle for world hegemony.

In political terms, almost three decades ago, C.B. Macpherson traced the roots of the crisis back to the period immediately after the end of World War II: "The Soviet Union is no longer considered unviable: its achievements during the war and its subsequent technological advances have made this clear.... Liberal-democratic nations can no longer expect to run the world, nor can they expect that the world will run to them" (Macpherson 1965:3).

Accompanying this bifurcation in the centre of world power, the United States and the Soviet Union set about the task of "securing allies" and delineating their respective spheres of influence. They did this through the outright invasion of less powerful states, by resorting to various forms of economic blackmail and coercion, or by taking up more subtle ideological guises. In the realm of the ideological, which most directly concerns us here, the term "democracy" came to assume vital importance, especially for the United States and its Western allies. The so-called democratic countries saw themselves as making up the Free World; they saw the citizens of the Soviet Union and its "satellites" (as opposed to its allies) as living "behind the iron curtain."

For the U.S. government, the newly developing countries in South America, Central America, and the Caribbean were especially crucial to its hegemonic interests. To control populations that were potentially vulnerable (to Soviet advances) and to maintain friendly relations with them, U.S. administrations saw the importance of convincing those peoples of the evils of communism--as a destructive ideology that is particularly appealing to those who live in the poorer countries (Millikan and Rostow 1957:1-23). Given the geopolitical importance and economic significance (mainly as sources of raw materials and as export markets) of the so-called Caribbean Basin and surrounding territories, the United States became determined not to lose them to the Soviet camp.

Invoking the terms of the 1823 Monroe Doctrine, by which the United States gave itself the right to intervene in the affairs of these countries, various U.S. administrations stated their preparedness to use force, if necessary, to prevent any "foreign" interference in its "backyard." Still, overt force was supposed to be employed merely as a last resort. In the meantime, the United States would use economic and ideological means to control the government and citizens of those countries, to keep them in line and in the process safeguard its own legitimacy. This is where the ideologies of modernization and democracy as mechanisms of social control come into play (Allahar 1986).

As Daniel Chirot points out, beginning in the 1950s the U.S. government and its agencies became deeply involved in the internal affairs of most countries of the underdeveloped world, and the main official reason given for such involvement revolved around a concern with stopping the spread of communism. But Chirot questions this pious intention:

> Was it really a defensive strategy against Soviet aggression, or was it an aggressive plan to encircle the Soviet Union? Was it primarily a military strategy, or was it designed mainly to protect raw-material sources and export markets for the American economy? Was the policy idealistic and designed to help the world, or was it imperialistic and designed to help the U.S. at the expense of the poorer societies? (1977:2)

Successive U.S. administrations portrayed communism as a disease that afflicted the poor countries in the early stages of development when blocked individual and social mobility contradicted the promises of modernization, and when communist teachings identified class inequality as the main source of the problem. It thus became the major task of the rich countries such as the United States to "assist" poor nations to pass through the early stages as quickly as possible.

The various "assistance packages" provided by the U.S. government, I argue, are ideological and serve the purpose of social control, because they seek to paint a picture of underdevelopment and its causes in a manner not consistent with the available empirical evidence. They are ideological because they *mask* key aspects of social reality and propose courses of political and economic action tailored to preserve precisely those conditions and structures they purport to oppose. The ideology of modernization, therefore, serves the purpose of social control by co-opting potentially disruptive segments of society, by providing them with less accurate but more palatable explanations of their problems, and by thus distracting them from the real causes of their problems.

For example, various foreign aid programs, whether intentionally or unintentionally, serve only to deepen the conditions of economic malaise and stagnation in the recipient countries. This foreign aid is usually "tied aid," which means it is not to be used in just any way that the recipient sees fit, but rather is often accompanied by strict instructions about how it must be used. The stipulated uses are usually designed to complement or enhance the political and economic interests of the donor country. Political interests are served, for instance, through various military aid packages. Economic interests are served via an insistence on aid being spent on promoting certain specific industries linked to parent companies in the donor country; to develop infrastructure (roads, railroads, or ports, for example) that support the extraction and removal of raw materials from the recipient country; or, viewing the recipient country as a market outlet, or encouraging economic activities that bind the recipient to the donor for technology transfers, spare parts, patents, expertise, or equipment. To emulate the core countries, then, the countries of the periphery are made to surrender a great deal of their political and economic independence or autonomy. On the ideological level this is portrayed as a "joint partnership" or as a matter of "friendly relations."

The Post-Cold War Era
While many observers agree that Japan and Korea won the Cold War between the United States and the Soviet Union, U.S. political leaders and other spokespersons are keen on continuing the fiction that they are the true victors. Thus, in a speech during his losing campaign for re-election in 1992, U.S. president George Bush proclaimed that they (the government and the American people) had been able to "punch communism squarely in the gut and send it tumbling down the back stairs of history." In Bush's mind he had been able to fulfil the wish of his predecessor (Ronald Reagan), who, referring to the Soviet Union as an "evil empire," vowed "to reduce Marxism-Leninism to the ash heap of history."

When the "victory" over communism in the U.S.S.R. and Eastern Europe is placed alongside the "victory" over Saddam Hussein in the Persian Gulf and the general acquiescence of other adversaries in the Middle East (Arafat and the PLO, Gadhafi in Libya, Assad in Syria, and Rafsanjani who replaced the Ayatollah Khomeini in Iran), it does indeed seem that the New World Order is well on its way to becoming entrenched. For in America's own backyard, "upstart" governments in Grenada and Nicaragua have been removed, while rumblings in Panamá have been decisively silenced. This leaves Cuba as the only real "unfinished business" in the Western hemisphere. But not wishing to provoke a major war on its doorstep, and remembering the lessons of Vietnam, which taught them that entrances to far-flung political quagmires are much easier to find than exits, the U.S. government has restricted itself for the moment mainly to covert operations there. Thus the popular refrain in certain Washington political circles after the invasion of Panamá and the defeat of the Sandinista government in Nicaragua: yesterday Manuel, today Daniel, tomorrow Fidel!

Given the current winds of change that are sweeping the world economically in the direction of market society and politically in the direction of Western-style democracy, it stands to reason that modernization thinking would enjoy something of a revival or a return to its popularity of the 1970s. For this reason it is instructive to consider the fairly recent views of Lawrence Harrison, a researcher and member of the prestigious Harvard Center for International Affairs, and a senior consultant with the U.S. Agency for International Development, where he acted as an advisor to Latin American governments for twenty years (1962-82). Because he is such a perfect representative of modernization thinking, I will treat him in detail.

Harrison's ideological commitment to the interactionist-modernization approach is evident in the very title of his book: *Underdevelopment Is a State of Mind* (1985), and his political position is apparent from the outset. On the second page he states categorically that those who wish to explain economic underdevelopment in the Third World in terms of the processes of colonialism and imperialism are engaged in "a paralysing and self-defeating mythology." This mythology, he explains, is Marxist-Leninist doctrine. Invoking all the arguments and images of the modernization school, Harrison unequivocally dismisses as idle talk the argument holding "that the rich countries are rich because the poor countries are poor" (1985:1-2).

Taking his cue from McClelland (1964), who spoke of the need to focus on the *internal* factors responsible for promoting development, Harrison notes that he "looks inward rather than outward to explain a society's condition" (p.2); and also appearing to copy Lipset (1967), who saw cultural factors as the key to explaining change and development, Harrison submits, "It is culture that explains why some countries develop more rapidly and equitably than others" (p.xvi). Defining culture exclusively in terms of values and attitudes, and virtually ignoring historical and structural variables, he goes on to speak of "progress-prone cultures as better places for human beings to live, than traditional, static cultures" (p.xvii).

To the extent that Harrison focuses on external (non-psychological) factors at all, he identifies such factors as resource endowment, soil quality, geography, and even climate. He explains that climate can be very important, for apart from the fact that rainfall, sunlight, and temperature can directly affect agriculture, everyone knows that "temperature may affect human motivation. That most poor countries are found in tropical climates cannot be ignored" (p.xvii). What can be ignored are the vast quantities of wealth produced in such tropical regions of the world as India, Africa, the Caribbean, and South America. Also to be ignored are the viable and flourishing cultures that existed in those regions prior to European conquest--and that continue to exist despite economic deprivation--and their significant contributions to world scientific and mathematical knowledge.

Such deficiencies in theory and deliberate factual omissions in presentation are not only ideological but also intellectually dishonest and morally inexcusable. This is especially so when the person responsible has the formal title of advisor to governments and is able to design and implement development programs that will have an impact on the lives of millions of people. But Harrison apparently never gives this a second thought, for like presidents Reagan and Bush (among many other political and economic leaders in the West), he is committed to a singular view: "The most progressive cultures that humankind has thus far evolved follow the democratic model of the West" (p.xvii).

Democracy and Ideology

"... for those who profess to love sausage and democracy should be present at the making of neither."

The democratic model that Harrison refers to is liberal democracy. It is the political system most common in the principal Western capitalist societies, and the one that the leaders of those societies *claim* to prefer for all countries, including those of the periphery, and which they also claim is a prerequisite to modernization (Evans and Stephens 1988:751-54). I say "claim" because it is the case that while pursuing the establishment of democratic institutions at home, those same leaders have often been directly responsible for the installation of dictatorships abroad: the Somozas in Nicaragua, Amin in Uganda, Pinochet in Chile, Hussein in Iraq, Marcos in the Philippines, the Shah in Iran, Noriega in Panamá, and the Duvaliers in Haiti are merely a few of the most recent cases. At the same time, the tolerant, hands-off attitude long displayed by Western leaders towards the fascist dictatorship in South Africa has been matched only by their silence concerning the absence of democratic and human rights for the Palestinian peoples.

There are many historical and ideological confusions about just what liberal democracy is. One thing is certain: it is not an unmitigated blessing the world over; and like modernization, it is not the natural, inevitable, automatic choice of all peoples at all times. For throughout history human beings have shown themselves to be remarkably versatile and diverse in their preferences for political institutions, types of leaders, and the processes of recruitment to leadership positions.

There is perhaps no clearer introduction to the historical and political dimensions of this question than C.B. Macpherson's *The Real World of Democracy* (1965). As Macpherson points out, liberal democracy as a system of government was liberal for a long time, in some cases for well over one hundred years, before it became democratic. What this means is that in the transition from feudalism to capitalism in Europe, *economic* change preceded political change, and economic change brought the establishment of a capitalist or market society before the addition of the democratic franchise. For unlike feudal society, in which markets were either small or non-existent, and where people were more inclined to think of themselves as belonging to communities or collectivities governed by custom and tradition, capitalist society was premised on the spread of impersonal market or exchange relations.

In the process individuals were swept into the free market, and all their former personal, face-to-face, informal dealings were swiftly converted to impersonal, superficial, and formal exchanges in the marketplace. They became more mobile than before and were theoretically freer: "Before democracy came to the Western world there came the society and politics of choice, the society and politics of competition, and the society and politics of the market. This was the liberal society and state" (Macpherson 1965:6). In other words, the establishment of capitalism required a total revolution in social relations whereby individual freedom of choice, free competition, and open markets would define the day.

But make no mistake: the liberal society was not then, and is not now, an equal society. For premised as it is on capitalist principles, according to which some own the major means of production and others do not, the system can never include structured equality. Rather, according to Macpherson (1965:7), the liberal system "involves inequality in freedom of choice: all are free but some are freer than others." In its early days, all the talk of freedom and choice in the liberal society did not extend to slaves, women, those on poor relief, and even wage-earners. Although they made up as much as two-thirds of the population, such people, the reasoning went, "were dependent on others, and so not entitled to a political voice" (p.6).

To give coherence to the market society and make it work, it was necessary to entrust its daily operations to a group of men who had its interests at heart and would agree to represent their fellow human beings. This is the original idea of representative government, whereby prominent individuals who owned property and who, as a consequence, had a stake in the market economy agreed to a set of rules by which the system was to be run. One of the important rules adopted was that each person from the ranks of the property owners would have one vote regarding relevant issues. Still at this time the system was not democratic. As Macpherson puts it, "The electorate did not need to be a democratic one, and as a general rule was not; all that was needed was an electorate consisting of men of substance, so that the government would be responsive to their choices" (p.8).

In time, therefore, as economic and political interests sorted individuals into distinct groups and classes, the political process was expanded to encompass a variety of liberal freedoms that remain with us today, including freedom of association, of speech and publication, and of movement. The liberal state was born, and before long non-propertied groups and classes came to use these same freedoms to claim a political say. But it was not an overnight process, because in promoting the liberal society, the guardians of the liberal state were quite aware that to maintain their positions the society could be neither democratic nor equal. This is why writer José Nun prefers the term "democratic liberalism" over "liberal democracy" to describe the political system in question, because "in this fashion the customary ideological displacement of the adjective which transforms 'liberal democracy' into 'democracy' tout court could be avoided" (Nun 1991:1).

What Nun alludes to is the ideological use of the term liberal democracy by contemporary Western politicians and other commentators (such as Lawrence Harrison) as being synonymous with equality. He agrees that

Western capitalist societies are fully liberal, but they are democratic only in the limited sense of "one person, one vote." Therefore it is more appropriate to use the term "democracy" as an adjective to describe the (unequal) liberal society, rather than as a noun that takes for granted, or as unproblematic, its egalitarian nature. Stated in this way, the internal, structural inequalities of these societies, and the support of their leaders for non-democratic governments in the periphery (and elsewhere), is not inconsistent with the history of the development of this system, nor with its designation as one of democratic liberalism. For consistent with the protection of its class interests from the beginning, any *unsanctioned* departures from the liberal state and economy today are viewed as threats that are to be speedily arrested and reversed.

On this score, the honesty and realism of a former U.S. secretary of state, John Foster Dulles, ought to be applauded. "The United States does not have friends," he declared, "it has interests" (quoted in Fuentes 1985:56). This is a key insight that every single modernization theorist has missed.

Modernization and Social Control

Like social-evolutionary thinkers, modernization theorists do not seek to make the link between underdevelopment and the processes of colonialism and imperialism. Whether focusing on McClelland's notion of "need for achievement" or Lipset's concern for the lack of entrepreneurial talents in the peripheral countries, they see underdevelopment as issuing from an outmoded, traditional, defective value structure that can and must be changed. Once people who live in the underdeveloped countries accept this definition of the situation, once they come to see their "small piece of the pie" as their just and fair deserve, that is, as owing to their natural state, they will mount programs of social, political, and economic modernization patterned along lines suggested by the developed countries. They will be firmly committed to the acquisition of those "modern" values and attitudes that promise an escape from poverty and misery. They will police and control themselves, while remaining squarely within the sphere of influence of the developed countries.

We know, however, that such modernization programs are premised upon false assumptions and an incorrect reading or appreciation of history. As Paul Baran observed almost forty years ago in reference to those who bewailed the lack of entrepreneurial talent in the Third World: "In all parts of the world and at all times in history, there have been ambitious, ruthless,

102   Sociology and the Periphery

enterprising men who had an opportunity and were willing to `innovate,' to move to the fore, to seize power, and exercise authority" (Baran 1957:235).

The point, then, is to explain why and under what specific conditions entrepreneurship is rewarded. Why, for example, has a country such as India, whose methods of production and of commercial and industrial organization could stand comparison with those in vogue in any other part of the world, a country that has manufactured and exported the finest muslins and other luxurious fabrics and articles, failed to become a thriving, industrial metropole? Baran's answer is that the failure was not "something accidental or due to some peculiar inaptitude of the Indian race. It was caused by the elaborate, ruthless, systematic despoliation of India by British capital from the very onset of British rule" (pp.144-45).

To see present-day backwardness and underdevelopment in India as stemming from any local, psychological, or character defects is to have a distorted view of India's history; and to consciously portray or depict present conditions as having arisen owing to that distorted history is ideological. In one of his articles Marx (1972b:85) quotes an observation made by George Campbell, a senior English administrator in India from 1843 to 1874: "The great mass of the Indian people possess a great industrial energy, is well fitted to accumulate capital, and remarkable for a mathematical clearness of head and talent for figures and exact sciences. Their intellects are excellent."

The social-evolutionary and modernization schools, then, serve to complement one another. They both represent conservative views of change and progress and explicitly assume that there is a single path to development and industrialization, a path all societies are fated to follow. Their policy formula for the poor countries is thus straightforward: "You subtract the ideal typical features or indices of underdevelopment from those of development, and the remainder is your development program" (Gunder Frank 1973:5).

This line of thought pays no attention to how organizations such as the International Monetary Fund (IMF) and the World Bank, along with government foreign-aid agencies, actually shape the patterns of development in peripheral countries by making financial arrangements dependent on the elimination of social welfare programs, the devaluation of currency, or the holding down of wages, among other measures. It focuses no attention on the banks, business corporations, and investment firms that are the true recipients of aid--given their control over the supplies of patents, technology, machinery, capital, expertise, and other key ingredients of the development process. For example, when a government in a peripheral country receives foreign aid or a loan to build a dam or a harbour, the actual business contracts for the project go to the corporations, firms, and agencies located in the developed countries. The various banks and development corporations, then, have no real stake in remedying the problems of underdevelopment. As far as they are concerned, underdevelopment is good for business--so long as they can also secure the means of repressing dissent if the need arises. Finally, this line of thought fails to address the political and ideological dimensions of the key concepts of "modernization" and "democracy."

Chapter Five

Dependency:
A Third World Approach

Another group of theorists, focusing on the questions of colonialism, imperialism, and unequal terms of trade between the developed capitalist countries and those of the periphery, has sought to account for social change in a manner quite distinct from social-evolutionary and modernization theorists. Known generally as members of the school of (structural) dependency theory, writers such as Andre Gunder Frank (1967, 1969, 1972), Theotonio Dos Santos (1973), Fernando Henrique Cardoso and Enzo Faletto (1970), Celso Furtado (1970), and Ronald H. Chilcote and Joel Edelstein (1974), among many others, have analysed underdevelopment and poverty in terms of the structure of dependence imposed on the economies of peripheral countries. That structure of dependence, they charge, is responsible for the fact that the periphery produces what it does not consume, and consumes what it does not produce.

The importance placed on the term "structure" in this approach puts dependency thinkers within the tradition of *realism*. Whether referring to the structure of colonial or neocolonial subordination, the structure of world trade and imperialism, the structure of the state, or the social class structures that predominate in advanced and peripheral countries, dependency thinkers subscribe to the realist position that social structure, though not directly observable, is nevertheless real. This sense of realism views scientific theories as making claims about the nature and existence of materially or physically unobservable phenomena. This is where we can distinguish between positivist and realist ontology (Bryant 1985).

Whereas positivists assume the existence of a reality or a real world that is independent of our theoretical conceptions of it, realists argue that reality can never be apprehended without theory. The facts, so to speak, are never theory-neutral. Thus, that which is real does not necessarily have to possess a material or physical existence, for it is possible to identify theoretically social structures and processes that have a major impact on the way we conduct our lives. As John Wilson points out, positivists use a "perceptual" criterion in ascribing reality to an object if it is perceived. If it is not readily observable, it is excluded from the scientific enterprise. But: "Using a 'causal' criterion, by which an object is real if it brings about a change in material things, nonpositivist or theoretical realists are willing to include in the scientific domain entities which cannot be observed and perhaps will never be observed" (Wilson 1983:167).

To the extent, therefore, that empiricism is exclusively identified with positivism and concerned with *generating data* from direct observations and sense impressions, realists are not empiricists. But if empiricism is taken to mean that one seeks to *test theory with data*, irrespective of how those data were obtained, then realists can indeed be seen as empiricists, for the path to scientific knowledge is not unilinear. Science is considerably more than mere experimentation. Along with experimental abstraction and statistical interpretation we also have to consider theoretical abstraction and theoretical interpretation in arriving at conclusions about the nature of reality (McGinnis 1965:3-11; Plange 1984:104).

The realist approach to knowledge, then, is empiricist. But it differs from positivism in that realists operate at the level of social structures and attempt to uncover the deeper "reality" in which those structures are embedded. That deeper reality, although the product of social relations, is neither reducible to those relations nor inferable from them.

Free Will and Determinism

The strong insistence of dependency theorists on the role of social structures in shaping individual or group behaviour can lead to the conclusion that human beings are wholly passive creatures devoid of all will or initiative--so subject to the invisible force called social structure that we appear to be capable only of reacting to its dictates. But nothing could be further from the truth.

Free will and determinism are not all-or-nothing phenomena. They are not absolutes and either-or propositions, because human behaviour is clearly guided by elements of both. Surely we conform to group pressure, laws, norms, and expectations, but as curious, thinking beings who can act volitionally, at times we also resist group pressure, break laws, violate norms, and defy expectations. Social life is not so tightly programmed that every facet of our behaviour can be prescribed. In fact, we are the ones who consciously make laws, collectively produce culture, and determine what is appropriate and inappropriate behaviour for a given situation. The margin for social manoeuvrability is usually quite wide, and the various norms or social conventions are often loosely defined.

As social beings we have what has been described as a "need for belonging." We desire acceptance by friends and family, seek social approval, and in general conform to the expectations of the group(s) we belong to or want to belong to. In this sense social structure clearly influences us. But we also *actively* drop out of groups, join others that we seek to change from the inside, or even establish our own groups with accompanying laws, norms, or customs.

To recognize the importance of social structure for moulding behaviour, then, does not imply a denial of free will. As human beings we are, and always have been, limited to achieving those things that our environmental, physical, and intellectual capacities permit. We are not only limited by such factors as climate and geography, but also by bodily strength, height, age, and existing levels of skill, knowledge, and scientific development. So a certain degree of "unfreedom" has always been with us. Freedom is relative. To produce our basic needs--for example, food, clothing, and shelter--we have had to adapt to physical and biological limitations and integrate those limitations with our intellects in order to survive.

This conception of survival means a more or less constant struggle against the forces of nature, against traditionally established patterns of social organization, even against other human beings. If we did not actively produce our own means of existence and subsistence no one would have done so for us. We would have died out and the species would have disappeared from the face of the earth. In other words, we have never been free not to produce; not to become actively involved with each other; not to create.

In this sense realists argue against the determinism of positivists by showing that we are not just prisoners of social structures. For it is one of the main tasks of social science to expose--to lay bare the hidden constraints and invisible mechanisms that govern a large part of our behaviour--with the understanding that we could actively intervene to modify such structures. Realists, therefore, have a clear *prescriptive* message to convey: wherever social structures are found to limit or distort human fulfilment, they can and must be changed. This issue is of special importance in considering the questions of Marxism and revolution in the periphery.

Dependency Theory
As a group, dependency theorists reject the central ideas of social evolutionism, structural functionalism, and modernization thinking. Societal de-

Dependency 107

velopment, they argue, cannot be adequately understood purely in terms of fixed universal stages or psychological processes. Rather, those within the dependency school view the *overall structure* of the world capitalist system as one that makes development possible for some countries but renders it highly unlikely for others. As the very label attached to this approach suggests, those countries that are "dependent" on others, for whatever reasons, are economically, politically, and socially disadvantaged.

Although there are many varieties of emphasis within the dependency camp, the theorists all agree on one key point. Underdevelopment, they say, is not the original state or stage in which all countries once found themselves. Here the firm distinction between *underdeveloped* and *undeveloped* societies once again comes in. Whereas at one time all countries were undeveloped, not all of them become underdeveloped. The dependency theorists understand development as the active socioeconomic and political process of promoting dependence, which in turn leads to the establishment of structures and institutions that pre-empt development. Hence some countries, such as Britain and the United States, moved from undevelopment to development, while others, such as Trinidad and Haiti, moved from undevelopment to underdevelopment.

The dependency model views the capitalist world system with its internationally structured network of trade relations as the key "cause" of underdevelopment. That system, the "dependentistas" contend, comprises a chain of countries, each of them differentially situated along a continuum from most developed to least developed. The most developed countries belong to the "core" of the system, the "metropole" or the "centre." The least developed are "satellites" that were forcibly brought into the "orbit" of world capitalism, and they belong to the "periphery" or the "hinterland" of that system. Finally, those countries occupying an intermediate position are variously called semicore or semiperipheral (Chirot 1977).

The exploitive relationship between core and periphery is not restricted to dealings among countries, but can also characterize the state of affairs within a given country. In the context of Latin America, for example, Eduardo Galeano talks about a division of labour between and within nations whereby "some specialize in winning and others in losing" (1973:11). Each country, he says, and each region of a given country, can be seen as an "endless chain of dependency that has been endlessly extended. The chain has many more than two links. In Latin America it also includes the oppression of small countries by their larger neighbours and, within each country's frontiers, the

108   Sociology and the Periphery

exploitation by big cities and ports of their internal sources of food and labour" (p.12). This phenomenon has also been referred to as "internal colonialism" by writers such as Pablo González Casanova (1965) and Harold Wolpe (1975).

According to dependency theorists, the *structures* of colonialist and imperialist domination in the periphery represent the point of departure for understanding the present picture of international economic and social inequality. Those structures, both historical and contemporary, include such things as slavery and the historical pattern of race relations, the monocrop plantation economy with its emphasis on the wholesale export of raw or semifinished products, foreign multinational corporations and branch-plant industries that drain the wealth and resources of the peripheral countries back to the metropoles, and political arrangements that favour the (class) interests of those who are in control of such corporations.

Tables 5.1 and 5.2 provide descriptive data on the extent of U.S., Canadian, and European multinational corporations operating in the Caribbean region. The tables are by no means exhaustive, but they do indicate a pattern that can be identified throughout the rest of the Third World.

According to the dependency theorists, the subordination of countries in Asia, Africa, Latin America, and the Caribbean by those of Western Europe and North America has resulted from the virtual stranglehold that these and similar corporations have established over the economies of various peripheral countries. As a consequence, they say, such economic relations of dependence work to the detriment of economic development in the periphery and actually promote underdevelopment. Jean-Paul Sartre explains:

> Underdevelopment is a complex relationship between a backward country and the great powers that have maintained it in this backward condition. Underdevelopment is a violent tension between two nations--the amount of tension is measured in the backwardness of the one in relation to the other (1961:81).

The "relationship" Sartre refers to is one of dependence, which Dos Santos defines as "a situation in which the economy of certain countries is conditioned by the development and expansion of another economy to which the former is subjected." The implied relation of interdependence between two or more economies at the level of the world market leads to

Table 5.1
Selected U.S. corporations in the Caribbean
(6 or more subsidiaries) (Excluding Puerto Rico)

Corporation	Number of Subsidiaries	Main Business
Alcoa	8	mining
Beatrice Foods	7	food
Bristol-Myers	7	home products
Castle & Cooke	6	agriculture
Chase Manhattan	11	banking
Citicorp	18	banking
Coca Cola	13	bottling
Colgate-Palmolive	7	home products
Continental Telephone	6	communications
Esmark	21	manufacturing
Exxon	16	oil
Gulf & Western	26	manufacturing/agriculture
Holiday Inn	13	travel/tourism
ITT	14	communications
RJ Reynolds	13	agriculture
Reynolds Metals	8	mining
Texaco	11	oil
Trans World	7	travel
United Brands	9	agriculture
WR Grace	15	chemicals
Warner Lambert	8	pharmaceuticals
Wometco	9	bottling

Source: Tom Barry et al. *The Other Side of Paradise: Foreign Control in the Caribbean.* New York: Grove Press Inc., 1984.

dependence when the more powerful economies "can expand and can be self-sustaining, while other economies (the dependent ones) can do this only as a reflection of that expansion" (Dos Santos 1973:109).

This is the context in which dependency theorists say that, beginning with the voyages of so-called "discovery" and the capture of colonial territory and continuing to the present time, the economic and political structures of the colonial and ex-colonial territories have been distorted to meet the needs of metropolitan capitalism.

Whether as mining colonies from which gold, silver, and other precious metals and minerals are extracted, or as plantation colonies that produce commodities such as sugar, coffee, cotton, tobacco, cocoa, and bananas for the world capitalist market, the countries of the periphery are not permitted to develop in an autonomous fashion. They are viewed primarily as producers of raw materials destined for export in foreign-owned ships to the metropolitan centres of manufacturing and industry. Once exported, the raw materials are converted into finished products by foreign workers in foreign factories and re-exported to the Third World at greatly inflated prices. In the process, jobs are created for workers in the core countries, where most manufacturing and industrial operations are located, and where capital is accumulated. As a consequence, also, a thriving internal market develops within the centres of advanced capitalism. Wages are increased, and the spread of commercial activity results in higher demand for various other goods and services, greater economic differentiation, "modernity," and higher societal complexity.

Within the mining and plantation colonies the picture is quite different. There one finds rather backward techniques of land cultivation, low levels of technological and scientific development, a heavy concentration on raw or unfinished agricultural and mineral exports, very few centres of industrial production, and highly labour-intensive methods of work (Allahar 1982:32-33). Major decisions regarding what to produce, how much to produce, and what prices to charge are often made outside of the countries in question, thus depriving those countries of any say in determining the structure of their main economic and income-generating sectors. In the economic literature this is referred to as the "declining terms of trade" faced by the periphery, which sees a more or less constant increase in the prices paid for imported producer (and other) goods and a concomitant decline in the prices of staple exports.

Table 5.2
Selected Canadian and European Corporations in the Caribbean
(3 or more subsidiaries) (excluding Puerto Rico)

Home	Corporation	Number of Subsidiaries	Main Business
Canada	Alcan	9	mining
	Bata	3	shoes
	Canadian Pacific	6	travel/food
	Scott's Hospitality	8	travel
	Seagram	5	liquor
	Canadian Imperial Bank	10	banking
	Royal Bank of Canada	35	banking
	Bank of Nova Scotia	40	banking
France	L'Air Liquide	3	gas/chemical
	Club Méditerranée	8	travel
	Banque Nationale Paris	5	banking
	PLM	5	travel
Netherlands	Algemene	5	banking
	Amro	5	banking
	Heineken	5	liquor
Switzerland	Nestlé	13	food
United Kingdom	BAT Industries		communications
	Barclays		
	Berger, Jenson & Nicholson		
	BICC		
	Booker McConnell		
	Cable & Wireless		
	Commonwealth Development		
UK/Netherlands	Unilever	4	food
	Royal Dutch Shell	18	oil

Source: Tom Barry, Beth Wood, and Deb Preusch, *The Other Side of Paradise: Foreign Control in the Caribbean* (New York: Grove Press, 1984).

The economies of the peripheral countries are thus distorted or biased towards activities that favour development in the centres of advanced capitalism. Although the mining and plantation sectors, also known as enclaves, may employ better technology, pay higher wages, and afford their workers a generally higher standard of living than the rest of the society in question, the vast bulk of the population in the country continues to live in poverty, with low levels of skill, education, health care, and housing. The dependency theorists see this economic "rape" of the country's wealth as directly related to its continued dependence and underdevelopment. Table 5.3 contains data from the Commonwealth Caribbean that illustrate the import/export dimensions of the dependency relationship.

Thus, unlike the dualist/diffusionist approach, which views development and underdevelopment as separate or unrelated phenomena, or at times views the less developed sector as a fetter on the modern one, dependency thinkers stress the *relational* character of these phenomena. The underdeveloped sectors or countries are not expected to catch up with the advanced ones when the appropriate institutions and technology are diffused to them. It is clear that the *structures* of dependence and underdevelopment that link these sectors together are themselves responsible for the failure of one sector and the success of the other (Wallerstein 1974). Dependency thinkers reverse the dualist position and see the modern sectors as the main obstacles to development in the periphery. Walter Rodney's classic study, *How Europe Underdeveloped Africa* (1972), is a clear case in point of such dependency thinking in terms of political economy among states. Rodney's central thesis is that Europe became developed through the very same process by which Africa became underdeveloped, and that Africa's underdevelopment was a direct consequence of Europe's process of wealth accumulation.

By tailoring their economics to meeting the needs of the advanced ones, peripheral countries become dependent on the advanced ones for supplies of capital, credit, technology, expertise, and the very market demand that makes possible continued production. Hence local needs and local markets tend to be neglected, for the better part of all economic activity is directed towards external markets and consumers.

Such a situation is perpetuated because political leaders in the dependent countries are generally reduced to being mere pawns of international capitalism. Given their structurally subordinate position within the system of international capitalism, these leaders come to recognize that their class

Table 5.3

Commonwealth Caribbean: Direction of trade, 1984 (percentages)

Countries	Domestic exports						Imports					
	U.S.	Canada	EC	CARICOM	Other	Total	U.S.	Canada	EC	CARICOM	Other	Total
Antigua	0.4	0.0	2.8	59.8	37.4	100.0	49.8	4.4	18.6	9.6	17.6	100.0
Bahamas[1]	31.1	7.3	18.8	0.0	42.8	100.0	78.2	2.9	8.3	0.0	10.6	100.0
Barbados[2]	27.6	1.6	8.1	22.3	40.4	100.0	47.8	5.6	12.0	11.7	22.9	100.0
Belize[2]	49.7	2.1	21.2	7.5	19.5	100.0	45.8	2.8	22.2	2.3	26.9	100.0
Dominica	1.6	0.0	51.4	45.0	2.0	100.0	26.6	7.7	29.6	21.0	15.1	100.0
Grenada	5.6	3.0	53.0	35.7	2.7	100.0	24.6	4.4	24.3	24.7	22.0	100.0
Guyana[3]	18.0	4.2	42.0	13.8	22.0	100.0	18.0	3.2	14.3	41.1	23.4	100.0
Jamaica	48.2	14.4	14.7	7.2	15.5	100.0	45.6	5.4	9.6	3.2	36.2	100.0
Montserrat[3]	25.7	0.0	7.5	65.0	1.8	100.0	38.5	3.6	20.0	21.4	16.5	100.0
St Kitts-Nevis	45.6	1.0	27.8	22.0	3.6	100.0	39.6	4.4	16.4	19.5	20.1	100.0
St Lucia	17.4	0.0	53.1	26.5	3.0	100.0	36.7	4.2	20.7	16.8	21.6	100.0
St Vincent	10.7	0.7	24.2	64.2	0.2	100.0	37.0	3.1	24.4	19.3	16.2	100.0
Trinidad & Tobago	57.7	0.6	15.2	9.2	17.3	100.0	37.9	6.9	19.3	7.3	28.6	100.0

[1] Export and import figures refer only to non-oil trade.
[2] The figures for exports include re-exports.
[3] Domestic exports relate to 1983.

Sources: Official Trade Reports, OECS, Statistical Pocket Digest, 1985; IMF, Direction of Trade Statistics, Yearbook, 1986.

interests are bound up with the interests of foreign capital. As Gunder Frank argues, they "accept dependence consciously and willingly" and as "junior partners of foreign capital" they impose policies that increase dependence on the imperialist metropolis (1972:3-15).

Marxism and Dependency

Although Marxist thinkers agree with the general spirit and thrust of dependency thinking, they find it too descriptive and generally lacking in *class analysis*. For example, to account for the political aspects of underdevelopment, Irving Zeitlin argues that the "full and unhampered" industrial development of the colonies was not in the interests of the imperialist forces; hence it "became the cardinal principle of every imperialist's policy to prevent and retard" such development (Zeitlin 1972:96). Realizing that industrialization would eventually lead to the development of national consciousness, a working-class movement, and opposition to both the imperialist presence and domination by local capitalists--and ultimately to calls for independence--none of which was in the interests of the imperialists, the rich nations cultivated allies among the locally dominant landlord class. In addition: "The imperialist/landlord alliance contributed further to the economic stagnation of the colonies because both groups had a powerful interest in preventing industrialization and the profound changes that inevitably would follow" (Zeitlin 1972:97).

From the Marxian perspective the development of capitalism is closely bound up with how specific social classes have historically come into contact with each other, sometimes working together, sometimes working against each other. However, as an economic system, capitalism developed unevenly throughout the world. That is to say, a country such as Jamaica is no less capitalist than the United States, although it may be less economically developed. Like the United States, Jamaica boasts a free-enterprise economic system and a liberal-democratic political system; nevertheless, the two countries are at polar extremes of the development continuum. This is a crucial point to be kept in mind as a counter to the conservative ideological thrust of modernization thinking, which generally holds that there are three basic types of countries in the modern world: the capitalist, the socialist, and the underdeveloped or poor. A Marxist-informed dependency approach is keen to point out that the underdeveloped countries of today are overwhelmingly capitalist in their economic structures, and large numbers of them also embrace liberal-democratic systems of political rule.

The Marxists, then, account for underdevelopment in class terms. The dependent countries represent both sources of cheap labour and raw materials and viable markets for finished goods. Thus, specific commercial, manufacturing, and industrial classes within the advanced countries are keenly interested in gaining access to those raw materials and markets. During the early colonial period those classes secured such access by outright plunder and conquest. In this way the politically and economically powerful classes in the mother countries benefited largely at the expense of the indigenous inhabitants of the colonies.

In contemporary times, rich nations, led by the United States, have used a variety of new political and economic means to realize the further subordination of the periphery. Examples at the political level are the sham of what Edward Herman and Noam Chomsky call "demonstration elections" and the creation of client states with puppet governments whose financial and military strings are pulled in Washington or London. The wealthy nations also encourage and support military juntas and, in the case of the United States, resort to periodic invasions as effective ways of keeping political control of key peripheral states. Ronald Chilcote and Joel Edelstein (1974:16-17) report, for example, that since the middle of the nineteenth century the United States has led or sponsored almost two hundred military invasions of Latin America.

We know, of course, that such activities did not cease in 1974. The direct invasions of Grenada and Panamá and Washington's proxy wars in Nicaragua, El Salvador, and Guatemala represent the continuation of a fundamental process set in motion before the turn of the twentieth century. Furthermore, a U.S. Supreme Court ruling in June 1992 underlines the length to which the U.S. government is prepared to go to defend its interests. *The New York Times* (June 16, 1992) reported: "The Supreme Court ruled today that the U.S. can kidnap a criminal suspect from a foreign country, over that country's objection and without following the procedures set out in an extradition treaty, to put the suspect on trial in a Federal court." This ruling brings to mind the case of Panamá's Manuel Noriega, whom the U.S. government kidnapped in December 1989 after its invasion of the small Central American country. Before being declared "a criminal suspect," Noriega was an ally of the U.S. leadership and a paid informant of the Central Intelligence Agency. In the unipolar "New World Order" of U.S. pre-eminence, such actions may well become more common. Ted Carpenter, who is no radical, writes of the United States' "morally inconsistent strategy"

116   Sociology and the Periphery

of support for right-wing dictators and its opposition to "democratic governments with a left wing slant" and charges: "It is reprehensible for a government that preaches the virtues of non-interference in the internal affairs of other nations to have amassed such a record of interference" (1991:123-25).

At the same time, the United States has played an active role in undermining democracy globally. For not only does the U.S. government assume that it is possible to violate the principles of democracy in the defence of democracy, as testified by the many invasions, or by the entire Iran-Contra scandal of the 1980s, but it also works to install and maintain dictators in the South, leaving an indelible image in the minds of the masses of people in those countries. While the Northern propaganda machine leads the bulk of the Northern population to believe that the U.S. government is in the business of promoting peace and good government at home and abroad, those who endure dictatorial governments are under no such illusions. Indeed, those people are quick to associate the United States with their own repression, and this explains (a) why anti-American sentiment is so rampant in such countries, and (b) why the people who live in poor countries appear to have so little interest in American-style democracy.

As far as military support for Caribbean and Central American regimes alone is concerned, the information in Table 5.4, supplied by the United States' Department of Defense (DOD), is instructive.

These data must be placed within the context of the political climate during the 1980s. For example, under the Sandinista government Nicaragua received no "assistance," while Grenada in its socialist phase met a similar fate. Politics also explains why Trinidad-Tobago, which was generally supportive of the Bishop government in Grenada and opposed the 1983 invasion, was snubbed for three years running, and why Dominica, which "officially invited" the United States to do something about the state of affairs in Grenada, went from U.S.$4,000 in military aid in 1982 to U.S.$1,042,000 in 1983. In the case of Jamaica, the table shows evidence of the change in 1981 from the left-leaning Manley government to the conservative Seaga administration.

The Marxist analysis of dependency and imperialism seems especially relevant in light of the social, economic, and military turmoil in such Central American and Caribbean countries as Honduras, El Salvador, Panamá, Nicaragua, Grenada, and Suriname within the last decade or so, and given the stunning increase in U.S. military aid under recent U.S. administrations.

Table 5.4

U.S. Military Assistance to the Caribbean Basin, 1980-89<1> (in U.S. $ thousands)

	1980	1981	1982	1983	1984	1985	1986	1987	1988	1989
Caribbean										
Antigua-Barbuda	0	0	0	1,067	353	1,483	686	1,142	380	244
Barbados	30	30	56	55	70	192	344	642	89	961
Belize	0	0	20	48	204	919	612	410	325	288
Dominica	0	8	4	1,042	382	1,322	484	525	159	233
Dominican Republic	239	348	3,883	1,096	6,949	4,385	6,997	5,762	3,042	1,959
Grenada	0	0	0	0	2,335	3,450	464	557	625	80
Haiti	128	110	212	339	770	396	1,464	2,221	63	101
Jamaica	0	95	73	3,472	2,936	5,978	9,288	2,712	1,712	12,677
St. Kitts-Nevis	0	0	0	0	32	2,704	451	412	204	168
St. Lucia	0	2	8	1,065	410	225	429	348	136	236
St. Vincent	0	0	1	31	44	85	2,992	318	173	342
Trinidad-Tobago	0	15	0	5	0	39	50	78	70	11
Subtotal	397	608	4,257	8,220	14,116	21,178	24,261	15,027	6,979	17,300
Central America										
Costa Rica	0	31	46	4,084	2,430	14,825	6,787	1,123	1,650	563
El Salvador	2,535	35,412	66,248	69,032	121,598	139,754	130,551	109,779	109,221	87,002
Guatemala	10	4	0	71	2,669	984	3,911	4,239	10,067	15,354
Honduras	2,653	4,711	10,478	24,977	33,631	81,394	98,745	104,916	39,078	26,116
Panama	517	710	807	644	1,258	17,635	3,256	1,965	0	0
Nicaragua	0	0	0	0	0	0	0	0	0	0
Subtotal	5,715	40,868	77,579	98,808	161,586	254,592	243,250	222,022	160,016	129,035
Total CBI	6,112	41,476	81,836	107,028	175,702	275,770	267,511	237,049	166,995	146,335

[1] Includes foreign military sales agreements, foreign military construction sales agreements, Military Assistance Program, and International Military Education and Training Program.

Source: U.S. Department of Defense, *Foreign Military Construction Sales and Military Assistance Facts as of September 30, 1989* (Washington, D.C.: DOD, 1989).

By far, however, multinational corporations (MNCs) have provided one of the most common ways of cementing the link between dependence and underdevelopment in the periphery. Acting through their respective MNCs, the various fractions of the international commercial, manufacturing, industrial, and financial bourgeoisie come to wield a great deal of power in the countries of the periphery. Taken together these class fractions are seen to represent *imperialist interests*, which "work out deals" with local governments and powerful fractions of dominant classes in the dependent countries and establish operations within restricted sectors of those countries.

Such operations are usually focused on mining and agricultural activities and use cheap, locally available labour, which greatly facilitates the extraction of wealth and the generation of huge profits. Along with the exploitation of cheap labour, the MNCs also manage to secure attractive concessions from local governments, including tax incentives, relaxed customs duties on imported technology, and certain monopolistic privileges. Whatever infrastructural changes the corporations promote are limited generally to transportation and communications networks that serve their own needs-- for instance, linking the mines or plantations with seaports, thus yielding a very lopsided picture of local industrial development. Very often the MNC insists, as a precondition for investing in a given peripheral country, that the local government assume the responsibility and cost for certain infrastructural developments.

Economically the dependence of the peripheral countries is maintained and deepened through the very presence of the multinational corporations and their role in reshaping the local class and economic structures. Although peripheral countries today are no longer unindustrialized, their industrial growth has followed a distorted or uneven pattern (Warren 1980:125-85). The exploits of MNCs have damaged the host countries of the periphery in two essential ways. The first concerns questions of imported technology, recruitment of foreign experts, and the securing of investment and other capital to finance their operations; the second relates to the restructuring of class and economic relations locally.

Technology transfers, the high cost of spare parts, service contracts, control of patents, and royalty payments--or the remittances of profits abroad--all represent a constant drain on scarce foreign exchange resources. When viewed together all these factors contribute to a loss of local or internal autonomy. In addition to this, the reliance on imported technology

Dependency 119

has important consequences for class relations. Apart from rendering existing indigenous enterprises obsolete and inefficient, the new capital-intensive technology, by its very nature, also fails to absorb labour surpluses, and often increases them.

Thus, although the poor countries have achieved a degree of industrialization and a tiny fraction of local business interests has managed to prosper, the general economic situation in those countries is not bright. The entire process of multinational-led "development" has been accompanied by economic denationalization, increasing social inequalities, and greater marginalization of the very poorest segments of the society (Sunkel and Paz 1970). As Alejandro Portes comments: "While the working sector associated with the multinationals may evolve into a veritable labour aristocracy, the masses remain in a subsistence situation where unemployment, scarcity of bare essentials and lack of access to expanding social and economic benefits are the norm" (1976:76).

But what are the actual and potential consequences of such a state of affairs for the marginalized masses? The answer to this question relates to the nature of the link between the economic and political aspects of imperialism as well as to the phenomenon of revolution.

When Marxists speak of U.S. imperialism, for example, they are referring not merely to the economic exploits of U.S.-based MNCs abroad, but also to the full support those economic interests get from U.S. foreign policy. For when *private* U.S. foreign investments are threatened by local uprisings in a dependent country (for example, Cuba 1959-62, Chile 1970-73, Grenada 1979-83, and Panamá 1989-90), the U.S. government, *not* the MNCs, dispatches the armed forces or increases the amount of military aid (via advisors or training programs) to that country in an effort to safeguard the private investment and supposedly protect Americans living there. This type of domination, Marxists say, can create the conditions for revolutionary change in the peripheral countries.

Objectively, imperialist exploitation, linked as it is with the indigenous dominant classes (landowners, or petty industrialists, for example) and their local militia, creates increased misery and poverty for the bulk of the population, very few of whom are employed in the foreign-controlled sectors. The constant draining away of national wealth, the monopolization of the best lands by foreign corporations, the recruitment of trained experts from abroad, and the underdevelopment locally of health or educational facilities: these conditions all accentuate social and economic disparities between the large mass of workers and peasants and the tiny core of privileged classes that benefit from the imperialist connection.

Subjectively, this leads to a growing sense of nationalism as local parties, opposition interests, and lobby groups see the possibility for change and start mobilizing for more responsible government, better wages and working conditions, greater self-determination, or land reform. Depending on the extent of such mobilization and the degree of political education and consciousness that develops, government repression increases (with the able assistance of outside states), which deepens social discontent. Developments in Haiti and the Philippines in the 1980s point clearly to the consequences of increased political consciousness on the part of workers, peasants, unemployed, and poor people. This is not to say that workers and peasants have "won the battle for democracy" in those countries, but tangible gains were made merely by securing the physical removal of the dictators Duvalier and Marcos. Apart from renewing the possibilities for dialogue (albeit with other dictators in the case of Haiti), the people themselves have arrived at a keener awareness of their collective ability to bring about change.

According to the Marxists, then, when the objective condition of misery combines with the subjective condition of consciousness at the correct moment and under favourable conditions, the result is a revolutionary situation. This must not be taken to mean, however, that revolution is a mechanical affair. Other factors such as brutal repression through state terrorism, anti-communist ideological attacks on dissenters, and what Marxists call "false consciousness" can always militate against the effective combination of these two sets of conditions.

This is the case with certain religious, nationalist, or racial ideologies. As a mechanism of social control, ideology can prove highly effective in distracting people from a clear understanding of their problems, and from envisaging possible solutions. Take, for example, the religious teachings that seek to make a virtue of poverty ("the meek shall inherit the earth" or "the poor will be rewarded tenfold") and counsel conservatism ("turn the other cheek"). When these ideas are internalized by significant numbers of people, when they are accepted and used to guide their conduct in the world, the subjective awareness that can lead to revolutionary action is effectively stifled. The same holds for the ideologies of racism and sexism, which serve to divide workers and distract them from realizing the commonality of their condition. Similarly, the ideology of nationalism can unite and mobilize the majority of people of a given nation against an external "enemy," while blinding them to the internal class divisions that characterize their own country and are at the root of their problems. Revolutionary consciousness, therefore, is not to be understood as a simple, mechanical phenomenon (Allahar 1986).

Dependency and Regionalism in Canada

When applied to countries that are unequivocally part of the Third World, the dependency approach, complemented by a focus on social class, is persuasive. But what happens if that perspective is applied to a country such as Canada, which most commentators agree is anything but peripheral? Such a question points to two salient and related issues in the analysis of dependence: (a) the uneven nature of capitalist development; and (b) the theme of regionalism.

In her book *Silent Surrender*, Kari Levitt (1970) describes Canada as the world's richest underdeveloped country. Citing numerous examples of U.S. MNCs operating within Canada, Levitt argues that the Canadian economy has become a branch-plant economy, playing host to a wide variety of U.S. business interests. These branch-plant subsidiaries of parent firms located in the United States serve to drain Canada's wealth out of the country and south of the border. They have served to create a lopsided picture of industrial development in this country--development that is not locally directed. As Harry Hiller argues, multinational enterprises are not necessarily concerned with the local problems or priorities of a given country. They are not compelled to reinvest profits locally, and if pressured by local governments to do so they often threaten to move their operations elsewhere: "It is the very nature of corporations to make decisions according to the norms of capitalism and their desire for profit; national sentiments are rarely able to change these norms" (Hiller 1976:93). It was precisely this type of situation that led Levitt to remark cryptically: "Some sixty years ago Sir Wilfrid Laurier declared that the twentieth century belongs to Canada. By the middle of the century it had become clear that Canada belongs to the United States" (1970:58).

In another study, Jorge Niosi (1985:33-60) agrees that the Canadian economy has been subject to external control and dependence on foreign influences; but he does not go as far as Levitt to claim that Canada is underdeveloped. He speaks of Canada's "dependent industrialization" and outlines in clear detail the processes by which U.S. corporations have "invaded" the Canadian economy and established controlling interests in areas such as telecommunications, utilities, transportation, mining and smelting, oil and gas, lumber, and electronics. Even though, for a short period of time in the 1970s and early 1980s, various Canadian governments (federal and provincial) sought to "buy back" control in several of these areas, the Canadian economy continued to exhibit traits of dependence on foreign technology, foreign markets, foreign capital, and foreign expertise: "Canada, after a century of pursuing a liberal policy towards foreign direct investment and the transfer of technology, now finds itself (although this has begun to change) with half of its technology under outside control--one of the highest percentages of foreign control in the world" (Niosi 1985:30).

How do the dependency theorists account for this situation? In recent years a massive literature has grown around the themes of dependency, regionalism, colonialism, and internal colonialism in Canada. Using the basic dependency model of "centre" and "periphery" (Galtung 1971), "metropolis" and "satellite" (Gunder Frank 1973) and "metropolis" and "hinterland" (Davis 1971), Canadian scholars have attempted to explain the pattern of dependent development in this country. Focusing on the questions of regionalism and uneven development *within Canada*, writers such as Wallace Clement (1980, 1983), Ralph Matthews (1982), and Henry Veltmeyer (1978) have looked to the disciplines of economics, geography, history, and sociology for answers.

Their basic argument is that historically Canada's dependence on foreign powers stemmed from its status as a colony of Britain. Being politically, culturally, and economically dominated by the mother country (Hiller 1976:84), Canadians and Canadian society came to exhibit a pronounced European orientation as distinct from Americans and American society (Lipset 1985). In economic terms, the Canadian economy was geared to the production and export of raw materials processed and manufactured in Britain, thus creating jobs in that country and boosting its industrial development. As well, the host country (Canada) served as a ready market outlet for the manufactured goods produced in the metropole (Clement 1983:55-56). Over the years, as the United States replaced Britain as Canada's foremost trading partner, Canada's external dependence increased greatly and the internal disparities between regions were exacerbated.

The dependency notion of a chain of metropoles and satellites helps explain these processes. As Clement asserts, "Regional economies are tied to national economies and national ones to international ones" (1980:276). This is the idea of the chain. For Canada is neither developed nor

Dependency 123

underdeveloped. Some parts or regions are more developed than others. The least developed are linked to the more developed, and the more developed, in turn, are tied to even more developed international centres: "Canada is not unequivocally an industrial country. Part is industrialized--but the rest [is] a resource hinterland. Most of Canada's industrial capacity is located below a line starting at Windsor, encompassing Toronto and moving to Montreal. This is industrial Canada" (Clement, 1980:276).

When we speak of the underdeveloped regions of Canada, we automatically think of the Atlantic provinces (Nova Scotia, New Brunswick, Prince Edward Island, and Newfoundland). Making up the so-called hinterland of Ontario and Quebec, the Atlantic provinces are not centres of banking, industry, and commerce. As resource-based economies they are sources of wealth; but that wealth is traditionally accumulated and reinvested outside, bringing jobs to outsiders (Ontarians and Quebeckers, for example) and providing those outsiders with a generally higher standard of living than the Maritimers. As Ralph Matthews puts it: "The traditional wealth of southern Ontario is certainly not attributable to any strong resource base there, as there are few resources within several hundred miles of the area. Conversely the Atlantic provinces have always had abundant iron ore, coal, gold, forests, fish and hydroelectric power, but have remained poor" (1982:105).

The economies of the Atlantic provinces are underdeveloped not because they lack resources, but because they are dependent on outsiders for technology, expertise, capital, and markets. Because such "outsiders" usually present themselves in the form of MNCs, and because they do not necessarily have local interests at heart, the peripheral areas and single-industry towns become seriously disadvantaged. Whatever economic or infrastructural development does occur is highly resource-specific and does not lead to integrated development for the region as a whole. Hence social development is neglected; schools, hospitals, and housing are substandard; and the general life chances of the population are not as promising as those of Canadians who live, for example, in the "golden triangle" (Toronto-Montreal-Ottawa).

To explain further the dynamics of underdevelopment and dependency in Canada, theorists such as Clement, Niosi, Veltmeyer, and Joseph Smucker have argued for the value of a class analysis. Specifically, they direct our attention to the structure of the Canadian capitalist class. That class, concentrated largely in the "golden triangle" area, exerts a growing dominance in matters of finance, transportation, and utilities nationally; and internationally it is able to compete effectively with the most powerful capitalist enterprises for profits and markets. At the same time, the Canadian capitalist class has long played a subordinate role as junior partner of U.S. corporate capital in areas such as mining and manufacturing. As Clement says, by the 1960s, when the bulk of the Canadian economy had fallen into foreign hands: "Development was welcomed by many Canadian capitalists [for] they participated in foreign control in a variety of ways.... Canadian capitalists, particularly the powerful ones, have aligned themselves with U.S. corporations and invested heavily in them" (1983:58-59).

Within the underdeveloped regions of the country, the economic structures in place do not provide much opportunity for the advancement of the local populations. The jobs usually available tend to be of an unskilled or semiskilled variety, and the general content of school curriculla reflects the demands of that job market. Housing conditions, health and welfare provisions, and general lifestyles often lag behind those in the more developed regions of Ontario and Quebec. But even within Ontario and Quebec there are large pockets of poverty in the so-called single-industry towns and rural areas that are part of the development-underdevelopment chain. Rex Lucas paints a clear picture of dependence and uneven development in single-industry towns in his classic study *Minetown, Milltown, Railtown* (1971).

Dependency theory, then, can be applied to an understanding of change and development in certain regions of Canada. But Canada cannot be defined as an underdeveloped society, as Levitt implies. Jorge Niosi (1985) supplies a far more accurate view, arguing that Canada today is a major imperialist country whose MNCs have extensive control of banking, mining, insurance, transportation, and communications in peripheral countries. Various fractions of the Canadian capitalist class are allied internationally with other capitalist classes, and together these groups are responsible for much of the underdevelopment that characterizes large parts of both Canada and the Third World. Table 5.5 provides some indication of the extent of Canadian multinational presence in the Caribbean.

Of course, compared to the United States, Canada's profile as an imperialist power is not strong or prominent. In the Caribbean particularly, where Canada has long had a significant commercial and trade presence, recent years have seen a steady decline. This has been due in large part to the increasingly diversified production structure of its southern neighbour, and has been such that Canada supplied (exported) a mere 5 per cent of

Table 5.5
Major Canadian Multinationals in the Caribbean

Banks	Royal Bank of Canada
	Bank of Nova Scotia
	Canadian Imperial Bank of Commerce
Tourism	Scott's Hospitality (Holiday Inn)
	Canadian Pacific
	Air Canada
Manufacturers	Bata Shoe Corporation
Insurance	Sun Life Assurance
	Imperial Life Assurance
	Dominion Life Assurance
	Manufacturers Life Insurance
Agriculture	Maple Leaf Mills
	Quaker Oats of Canada
	Global Food Processors
	Seagram
Minerals	Alcan Aluminum
	Falconbridge Nickel

Source: Barry, Wood, and Preusch 1984: 221.

imports to the Caribbean in 1984, compared to 25 per cent in the late 1920s. Canada now receives a meagre 12 per cent of its total imports from the four largest economies of the region: Jamaica, Guyana, Barbados, and Trinidad-Tobago.

In 1986, in an attempt to counter this trend, the Canadian government introduced its own version of U.S. president Reagan's CBI (Caribbean Basin Initiatives). CARIBCAN is intended to bolster the disappearing market by increasing the range of goods eligible for duty-free entry into Canada (Deere et al. 1990:162-64). But like the CBI, CARIBCAN is not really designed with the best interests of the Caribbean economies in mind, for as Ramesh Ramsaran observes, "Certain key items of interest to the Caribbean such as

126   Sociology and the Periphery

textiles, clothing, footwear, luggage and leather goods, lubricating oils and methanol, are excluded from the scheme" (1989:130). Clearly, then, although Canada's economic presence in the Caribbean is small compared to that of the United States, the logic of imperialism dictates that its economic role will take precedence over any humanitarian concerns. To the extent that foreign aid benefits the donor country more than the recipient (Acosta-Belén and Bose 1990:300), the fact that bilateral aid from Canada to the Caribbean has increased (Worrell et al. 1991:248) suggests that the economic news is not all negative for Canada.

In a country as vast and diverse as Canada, with its twenty-seven million inhabitants, it makes little sense to use the entire country as a unit of analysis when investigating the phenomena of development and underdevelopment, especially given the uneven nature of capitalist development. In smaller countries, for example, Barbados or Trinidad, where the dependent capitalist classes play more of a *comprador* role as junior partners of foreign capital, and where export-oriented plantation agriculture or mining is the norm, regional disparities can be small and one sector can often account for the bulk of the productive activity of the entire country. Alternatively, in a large, resource-rich country such as Canada, the agricultural, mining, manufacturing, industrial, energy, and financial sectors are more easily separated; and distinct fractions of the bourgeois class have varying degrees of strength and autonomy vis-à-vis foreign capital.

Thus, depending on the specific regions and resources in question, the particular fraction of the capitalist class that is involved, and the historical terms and conditions under which they were incorporated into the world capitalist system, there can be wide variations in the rates and patterns of development. Hence, though capitalist, Canada contains regions and pockets of poverty and misery comparable to many countries in the periphery. Capitalism, therefore, does not imply even development and widespread social equality. Nor does it imply an even process of economic underdevelopment, because within the system as a whole the various countries all reflect differing degrees and patterns of economic and industrial growth. The uneven development along racial lines in the United States is a prime example of this, as described in the insert on the following page.

Filling the Gaps

During the 1960s, dependency theorists and other social analysts on the Latin American continent became embroiled in a debate over the political solutions to dependence and underdevelopment. Unlike the social evolu-

ONE COUNTRY, TWO NATIONS

Almost every country has one or more ethnic groups whose level of human development falls far below the national average.

Minorities and indigenous peoples often find it difficult to participate fully in societies that consistently operate in favour of the dominant groups. Sometimes this discrimination is embedded in the legal framework, denying minority groups equal access to education, to employment opportunities or to political representation. But exclusion is generally less a matter of official policy than everyday practice. One of the clearest and best-documented cases is that of blacks in the United States.

Their disadvantage starts at birth. The infant mortality rate for whites is 8 per 1,000 live births, but for blacks it is 19. And black children are much more likely than white children to grow up in single-parent homes. In 1990, 19 per cent of white children were growing up in single-parent households, compared with 54 per cent of black children. Children in black families are also more likely to grow up in poverty. The real GDP for whites in 1990 was around $22,000, but for blacks it was around $17,000.

As Andrew Hacker, the author of *Two Nations* (1992) writes: "Nearly two-thirds of black babies are now born out of wedlock, and over half of black families are headed by women. The majority of black youngsters live only with their mother; and in over half of these households, she has never been married. At last count, over half of all single black women have already had children, and among women in their mid to late thirties, less than half have intact marriages. These figures are from three to five times greater than for white households.... Black Americans are Americans yet they subsist as aliens in the only land they know. Other groups may remain outside the mainstream—some religious sects, for example—but they do so voluntarily. In contrast, blacks must endure a segregation that is far from freely chosen. So America may be seen as two separate nations."

Indeed, if the United States were divided into two "countries," according to the human development index the one with the white population would rank number one in the world, while that with the black population would be only number thirty-one.

Source: United Nations *Human Development Report 1993* (New York: Oxford University Press, 1993), p.26.

tionary and modernization approaches, which were conservative in their recommendations, dependency thinkers adopted a radical position. Beginning with the early dependency school of ECLA (Economic Commission for

Latin America), such writers as Osvaldo Sunkel and Raúl Prebisch couched their arguments in nationalistic terms. Although they were not opposed to capitalism per se, they did criticize the role played by foreign capital in stifling the free development of indigenous capitalism. To remedy the problems associated with dependence they called for a process of import-substitution industrialization that would serve to strengthen the development of local capitalist classes and temper the unfettered exploits of foreign multinational corporations.

Later dependency thinkers such as Andre Gunder Frank and Theotonio Dos Santos were even more radical in their prescriptions. Arguing that underdevelopment in the peripheral countries results from incorporation into the world capitalist system, these writers advocated a complete revolutionary break with that system. In its stead they proposed an economic and political reorganization along socialist lines, giving workers a greater say in the management of their enterprises and also answering to the pressing need for progressive land reform.

Casting their arguments at a very general level that embraced a wide variety of economic and political emphases, dependency theorists soon ran into major criticisms from Marxist academicians. Colin Leys, for example, speaks positively of dependency analysis to the extent that it has succeeded in "sensitizing" us to some of the broad features of peripheral capitalism and has rescued us from the "intellectual deserts" of prevailing developmentalist and modernization thinking. But Leys also outlines a number of serious shortcomings in this perspective: (a) dependency theorists leave obscure the precise meanings of dependence and development; (b) they never analytically discuss the term "exploitation" as a central concept; (c) they largely ignore class relations and the role of the state; (d) they deal with the phenomenon of imperialism in too descriptive a manner; and (e) they never clearly specify the main unit of analysis (social class, nation, region, MNC) (Leys 1977:94-96).

Based on these and other similar criticisms, a number of Marxist and neo-Marxist scholars turned their attention to a closer analysis of the *structures* of colonialism and imperialism, with a view to determining the historical and contemporary character of the mode of production in peripheral economies. Given their general interest in the phenomenon of social change, these thinkers felt that such an approach would enable them to uncover the class and political forces at play and forecast the likelihood of revolutionary social transformation in the periphery.

In the Latin American debate, then, the first task was to determine the specific nature of socioeconomic stagnation in colonial and neocolonial contexts. Was Latin America feudal or capitalist? What form did the exploitation of labour assume (Laclau 1971)? Should revolutionary mobilization be aimed at the overthrow of a basically feudal oligarchy of large landowners and the establishment of a "modern" system? Or were the countries of Latin America already in a bourgeois phase, thereby calling for a socialist revolution (Munck 1984:8-11).

Colonialism and Imperialism

In recent times a great many writers have pointed out that several of Marx's expectations regarding the "progressive" role of capitalism in the less economically developed countries simply have not been fulfilled. In his widely cited article "The Future Results of British Rule in India" (1853), Marx was optimistic that the British introduction of the railway system to that country would have positive spillover effects in numerous sectors and would lead to a process of unbridled (capitalist) development:

> You cannot maintain a net of railways over an immense country without introducing all those industrial processes necessary to meet the ... wants of locomotion, and out of which there must grow the application of machinery to the branches of industry not immediately associated with railways. The railway system will therefore become, in India, truly the forerunner of modern industry ... and will dissolve the decisive impediments to Indian progress. (Marx 1972b:84-85)

Even in 1867, when preparing the preface to the first edition of *Capital*, Marx continued to hold to the view that the penetration of capital into the poor countries served the purpose of creating a world after capital's own image. Betraying positivistic sentiments, he wrote that "the natural laws of capitalist production" worked with "iron necessity towards inevitable results." He concluded: "The country that is more developed industrially, only shows to the less developed, the image of its own future" (*Capital*, Vol. 1:8-9). Lenin, writing some fifty years later in 1916, shared this belief when he stated, "The export of capital affects and greatly accelerates the development of those countries to which it is exported" (1966:76).

Why, then, did these expectations not materialize? Were Marx and Lenin being too mechanical in their application of the laws of capitalist development? Or did they simply misunderstand the historical mission of colonialism and imperialism in the less developed countries?

Irving Zeitlin provides a partial answer to these questions. Zeitlin argues that *if left to itself* (as both Marx and Lenin assumed would happen) the spread of capitalism to the periphery would indeed have resulted in some measure of balanced industrial growth. However, capitalist development was not "left to itself." On the political level, the imperialist interests realized that the free and autonomous development of the colonies could ultimately lead to political independence and economic nationalism and pose serious threats to their own continued high profits (Zeitlin 1972:96-97).

The capitalist powers thus took special precautions to limit and retard any development that would have strengthened the bases of potentially antagonistic local classes: the industrial bourgeoisie and a strong, unionized industrial proletariat, both of which stood to gain from the more balanced and even development of capitalism locally. Instead, the pursued strategy included cultivating, as allies, those specific classes that benefited either directly or indirectly from the export-oriented nature of the dependent economies: the agro-commercial bourgeoisie, which Chilcote and Edelstein (1974) and Ramon de Armas (1977) saw as anti-nationalist because it pursued free-trade policies and put in place certain structures that exacerbated the problems of dependence and distorted development. Very often, too, the imperialist interests would help this class, financially and militarily, gain and maintain political power.

Other writers, such as Hamza Alavi, Jairus Banaji, and J.M. Barbalet, focus on what they call the *colonial mode of production* and try to show how the patterns of capitalist development in the periphery differ significantly from those in the core countries. This is not to imply that all the colonies of the various European powers today reflect identical or similar levels of development or underdevelopment. Former colonies, such as Canada and Barbados, which were both under the colonial tutelage of Britain, have followed greatly dissimilar paths. How can this be explained?

Edgar Thompson, George Beckford, Lloyd Best, and William Demas, among many others, offer answers to this general question. Beckford begins by making a distinction between colonies of *settlement*, on the one hand, and colonies of *conquest* and *exploitation*, on the other. Colonies of settlement such as Canada, Australia, and New Zealand were those in which the colonizer was interested in homesteading and farming or establishing a small business. The family farm, Thompson says, "is a 'human unit of land', that is, it is a piece of land which the farmer and his family have domesticated and made a member of the family as a working partner" (1959:27). In these colonies, after the colonizers had effectively subdued the indigenous populations, they seized the land with the aim of settling and developing it and living there on a more or less permanent basis.

It was not their intention to exhaust the natural resources as quickly as possible, to take without giving, and then return home; for in many cases they left the mother country as convicts and assorted outcasts to escape repression and make a life for themselves in a new environment. Along with their families, they "carried with them patterns of social organization and definite ideas about the kind of society they wished to create" (Beckford 1972:35). Very often, too, these writers say, the colonies of settlement were geographically strategic: they gave certain classes in the metropolitan centres easy access to key trade routes.

The colonies of conquest and exploitation, by contrast, witnessed a different set of circumstances. The colonies of conquest usually included the mainland territories of Latin America, places in which the colonizers were chiefly interested in mining for precious metals. When the colonizers encountered large and well-organized indigenous populations they took control through a variety of military and administrative structures tailored to the extraction of mineral wealth (gold and silver) under conditions of minimal social disruption. They did not develop permanent institutions of settlement and were not normally accompanied by their families.

In a somewhat similar manner the colonies of exploitation were not earmarked for development. Including for the most part the plantation societies of the New World (for example, the Caribbean), exploitation colonies existed largely to service the European demand for agricultural products. Thus, in addition to military and administrative organization, the colonizing power had to develop "an institutional framework for the bringing together of land, labour, capital, management and technology" (Beckford 1972:31). That framework was provided by the plantation system, which subjected slaves, indentured servants, and "free" wage labourers to very stringent controls.

As in the colony of conquest, this situation was not one in which the colonizers tended to migrate with their families. Nor did they have intentions of settling there permanently and building schools, hospitals, roads, and other infrastructural bases not specifically related to the production and export of agricultural commodities. These types of developments were more likely to take place in the colonies of settlement, where the colonizer-become-settler had less antagonistic social and cultural relations and more enduring familial ties with those left behind in the mother country. This contrasted starkly with the situation of enslaved indigenous Indians, import-ed Africans, and indentured Indian and Chinese workers in the colonies of conquest and exploitation.

Along with these considerations, analysts have also advanced a number of other hypotheses to explain the differing patterns of development exhibited by colonial and ex-colonial countries. Population size and natural-resource endowment also appear to be crucial factors (Demas 1975; Best 1974). If a dependent country is to diversify its industrial structure and re-duce its reliance on imported technology, goods, and services, a large population and resource base are definite assets. A small country "suffers from the basic constraints of a narrow range of natural resources and an inadequate market size stemming from a small population" (Demas 1975:62). Also, because in small countries imports and exports tend to account for a greater part of total production, there is less likelihood of autonomous local diversification and the types of social classes associated with such economic diversification.

This problem can become especially acute when small dependent countries are exporting a strategic raw material (such as petroleum or bauxite) that is in high demand on the world market. The inadequacy of effective demand locally (owing to the small consumer market) and the need to generate foreign exchange dictate that these countries must look to outside buyers. But on the outside market they usually lack bargaining power and the ability to set prices for their product. They therefore suffer from declining terms of trade in their dealings with the larger, more developed countries. the prices of their exports are usually lower than the prices they have to pay for imported necessities. Given such a situation, then, large-scale manufacture is not very viable. As Lloyd Best puts it, "The small economy, unlike the large, needs to specialize in fewer lines of production, to rely on exports and to depend on imported supplies" (1974:30). This cements the link between imperialism and underdevelopment in the peri-phery. As Table 5.6 and Table 5.7 show, the foreign debt of Third World countries has been steadily increasing over the years. According to the theorists of this school this trend is directly related to the presence of foreign MNCs in those countries.

In the case of Latin America, according to a report in *The New York Times*, the region as a whole is burdened with a debt of "more than $435 billion in loans, and the debt is still climbing. It is expected to reach $442.7 billion next year" (August 1, 1992:1, 40).

The Colonial Mode of Production

Using the impact of imperialism on social and economic structure as a point of departure, a number of writers have sought to explain the situation in the peripheral countries by using the concept "mode of production" (Foster-Carter 1978). This concept, which embraces both the economic substructure of forces and relations of production and the ideological superstructure of politics, religion, science, art, and morality, serves as a useful analytical tool. Not only does it enable researchers to grasp the totality of a given situation, but it also simultaneously affords insight into the complex interplay of the various parts of the social system and the forces that make for change.

These theorists argue that various modes of production, understood almost as ideal types, exhibit distinct features. Each possesses its own inner logic and structure. For example, there are clearly discernible differences in a feudal and a capitalist mode of production: between the class of peasants and the class of proletarians; between extra-economic coercion and purely economic coercion; between levels of scientific and technological know-how as applied to the respective production processes; or between simple reproduction associated with the manor and expanded reproduction characteristic of the factory.

But ideal types are not empirical realities; ideal-typical modes of production do not exist in pure or unadulterated form. For wage relations, markets, and the production of exchange values, though not predominant or widespread, were nonetheless known to exist even in the heyday of feudalism. In certain capitalist countries, similarly, semifeudal, patron-client types of relations, non-market labour coercion, and systems of debt peonage also persist up to the present.

With these points in mind several writers have theorized about a colonial mode of production (Banaji 1972, 1973; Alavi 1975; Barbalet 1976). Their argument is that, while serving the wider interests of metropolitan capitalism, the economies of the colonies and former colonies have not quite followed the pattern of capitalist development in the metropole. In other words, though derived from a capitalist mode, the colonial mode of

134   Sociology and the Periphery

Table 5.6

Third World External Debt, Selected Regions, 1982, 1988-91

Figures are in U.S.$billion, current prices.

Region	1982	1988	1989	1990	1991
Africa	122.4	203.7	208.5	225.1	235.6
Latin America and the Caribbean	331.2	409.3	408.0	414.1	414.5
Third World Debt	839.2	1,234.8	1,237.0	1,302.6	1,353.8
Total Third World Debt-Service Payments	135.9	165.8	153.0	167.6	190.1

Source: International Monetary Fund, World Economic Outlook, October 1990.

Table 5.7

Third World Long-Term Debt, Financial Flows, Official Development Assistance, and Arms Imports, 1985-89

Figures are in U.S.$billion.

Year	Total debt	Debt-service[a]	Principal	Interest	Net transfer[b]	ODA	Arms imports
1985	781.3	107.3	53.1	54.2	-19.7	29.4	32.5
1987	1,001.3	122.5	68.9	53.6	-34.2	41.6	43.8
1989	988.5	129.8	70.3	59.5	-42.9	46.7	39.3

[a] Debt-service is expressed in total and as principal and interest.
[b] Net transfer is the remainder of new loans minus debt-service.

Sources: World Bank, Annual Report 1990 (Washington, D.C., 1990); U.S. Arms Control and Disarmament Agency, World Military Expenditures and Arms Transfers 1989 (Washington, D.C.: U.S. Government Printing Office, 1990); Organization for Economic Co-operation and Development, Development Co-operation (Paris, 1990); author's estimates.

production is unique in many respects. We have already seen that to preserve their positions of privilege and dominance at the level of world economy, the imperialist classes deemed it necessary to limit or retard the spread of industrial growth in the periphery. Thus the emerging international division of labour witnessed a process by which various national economies were fused together through a hierarchy of forms of dependence and domination. The results of capitalist penetration into the colonies, however, were not uniform. In some cases, for example, in the colonies of settlement, this penetration had the effect of dissolving precapitalist modes of production and creating the conditions for capitalist development. In specific parts of the colonies of conquest and exploitation the penetration could be seen as preserving precapitalist relations in accordance with the dictates of capitalist interests:

> In these colonies, unlike the others, capitalism did not eradicate tribal modes of production and fill the vacant spaces with industries and markets. The populations it encountered consisted largely of peasants and far from uprooting their existing forms of production through their expropriation and conversion into wage labourers, so as to lay the foundations for an internal expansion of its own mode of production, capitalism imparted a certain solidarity to those forms and even extended them to new territories not previously inhabited. (Banaji 1973:394-95)

By definition a capitalist mode of production implies the development of the society in which it is operative along capitalist lines; it would seem to include the widespread occurrence of commodity production, the predominance of wage relations, and the reinvestment of surplus converted into constant capital, leading to an increase in the organic composition of that capital. This mode of production also presupposes the existence of a powerful indigenous capitalist class and a proletariat imbued with a national consciousness, both working for the positive and autonomous development of the society instead of trying to promote economic dependence and deformed or lopsided development.

The mode of production that emerged in the colonies of conquest and exploitation, however, is quite distinct and only resembles the capitalist mode at certain levels. Some writers say that in the plantation colonies, for example, the dominant mode of production is only "formally capitalist" because its main beneficiaries participate in a world market in which the leading productive sectors are already capitalist: "This enables the landowners in the plantation economy to participate in the general movement of the capitalist system without, however, their mode of production being capitalist" (Laclau 1971:27).

Accordingly, then, the central characteristics of the colonial mode of production include: (a) a heavy concentration on *export* activities with emphasis given to raw and semiprocessed agricultural (as opposed to industrial) products; (b) high expenditures on both *imported* necessities and luxury goods that are consumed by the numerically small but economically and politically dominant local bourgeoisie; (c) the retarded development of full capitalist relations of production in agriculture; (d) comparatively low productivity of peasant and semiproletarian labour; and (e) widespread backwardness in overall scientific and technological development.

These factors serve to distinguish the colonial mode of production from its capitalist counterpart insofar as the surplus required for revolutionizing the conditions of production locally is drained away to the metropolitan centres, where it is invested and enables expanded industrial production and accumulation. Whatever capital investments are made in the colonial agrarian economies are restricted largely to infrastructural projects related to the import/export interests and are not tailored to bring about the industrial development of these colonies. Thus, the colonial mode of production, like the capitalist mode of production, is indeed a system of expanded reproduction, though of a deformed nature because the imperialist bourgeoisie appropriates a substantial part of the surplus produced in the colonies and enters that surplus into expanded reproduction at the imperialist centres. As Hamza Alavi says, such "expanded reproduction benefits the imperialist bourgeoisie rather than the colony from which the surplus is extracted" (1975:183).

Today, therefore, many of the peripheral countries are characterized by monocrop economies as a direct carry-over of colonial commercial practices established when those countries were viewed mainly as markets to which metropolitan goods could be exported and as sources of abundant food supplies and cheap raw materials. Hence these are the types of economic activity that were encouraged and supported when the peripheral countries became subordinated to the demands of the world market. The resulting "internal disarticulation" of their economies is an important feature of their continuing underdevelopment (Amin 1974). Alavi describes the

Dependency 137

Table 5.8
UN Human Development Index (HDI) Ranking
and National Income for Selected Countries

Country	World Rank (HDI)	Total GNP (US billions 1989)	GNP Per Capita Annual Growth Rate		Annual Rate of Inflation	
			1965-80	1980-89	1980-90	1991
Japan	1	3,141	5.1	3.5	1.5	1.9
Canada	2	543	3.3	2.4	4.4	2.7
Sweden	5	202	2.0	1.8	7.4	7.0
USA	6	5,446	1.8	2.2	3.7	3.6
UK	10	924	2.0	2.5	5.8	6.9
Israel	19	51	3.7	1.5	101.4	—
Hong Kong	24	66.7	6.2	5.5	7.2	—
Trinidad & Tobago	31	4.5	3.1	-6.0	6.3	16.5
Venezuela	50	50.6	2.3	-2.0	19.3	21.2
Mexico	53	214.5	3.6	0.9	70.4	19.2
Brazil	70	402.8	6.3	0.6	284.4	428.5
Jamaica	69	3.6	-0.1	-0.4	18.3	60.7
Dominican Rep.	97	5.8	3.8	-0.4	21.8	53.5
El Salvador	110	5.8	1.5	-0.6	17.2	11.9
Kenya	127	9.8	3.1	0.3	9.2	8.9
India	134	294.8	1.5	3.2	7.9	12.8
Haiti	137	2.4	0.9	-2.3	7.2	-1.4
Rwanda	149	2.2	1.6	-2.2	3.8	14.6
Ethopia	151	6.0	0.4	-1.2	2.1	7.7
Somalia	166	0.9	-0.1	-1.8	49.7	—
Aggregates: Industrial, Developing Countries and the World						
Industrial	—	16,820	2.9	2.5	9.4	—
Developing	—	2,950	2.9	2.5	27.9	39.9
World	—	19,770	2.4	2.3	21.6	—

Source: United Nations Development Programme (UNDP), *Human Development Report 1993* (New York: Oxford University Press, 1993), pp.188-89.

entire process: "Segments of the colonial economies do not trade with each other; they are articulated only via their links with the metropolitan economies and they are subordinated thereby to the latter. The concept of internal disarticulation of the colonial economy is crucial for the understanding of the colonial mode of production" (1975:184).

What happens in this type of socioeconomic exchange is that metropolitan capital disarticulates the internal economy of the colony and reintegrates its segments externally into the metropolitan economy, thus perpetuating the fragmentation of the colony and its structural dependence on the imperial centre. The consequences of this can be seen in Table 5.8, which addresses national income levels in both the metropole and the periphery.

From Realism to Revolution

For the dependency and Marxist writers, the realist approach is foremost. At the same time, in analysing such structured processes as dependence, colonial relations, the impact of imperialism on class structure, and modes of production, these writers all share the view that the object of scientific inquiry need not have a material or physical existence in order to be studied. This is so because the concepts of social relations or social structure are no more open to direct sensory observation than is Freud's notion of the "unconscious." To the realist, nevertheless, those relations and structures, like our unconscious, have a definite influence on us and our societies, and hence must be treated as if they were real.

This is not to imply that we are all total prisoners of social structures and institutions. After all, we are the ones who created them in the first place, and it is up to us as conscious human actors to change or continue to live with them, as we see fit. Thus, what the realist is interested in specifying is the wide range of social behaviour that falls between the polar extremes of ultradeterminism and unconditional voluntarism. These realist approaches to social conditions can in turn be linked to the concerns of dependency and Marxist writers. Where the structures of dependence, underdevelopment, or imperialist exploitation--and the social relations they engender--are deemed harmful to specific human groupings and societies, they can be changed. At the macro level of whole societies, this movement involves the formidable question of revolution.

Chapter Six

Peasants and Revolution

Marx's theory of revolution was the result of careful investigation into the nature and functioning of the capitalist system as it grew out of feudal England to the level attained in the Western Europe of his time. His forecast that revolution would occur in the most advanced capitalist countries seemed to him quite consistent with the available empirical evidence. For Marx, sustained participation in revolutionary activity required the prior development of class consciousness among the insurrectionaries. In other words, the transition from a "class in itself" to a "class for itself" speaks to the development of that consciousness through the process of forming political parties and having a clear articulation of common interests (Giddens 1973).

The capitalists themselves create the conditions for the emergence of such consciousness within the working class as a natural outcome of the oppressive conditions under which the workers are forced to live and work. The pressures faced by capitalists to revolutionize the forces of production and raise the productivity of workers, Marx argued, would lead to greater consciousness among those workers, and as the excesses of the system became more blatant the capitalists would come to realize, too late, that they had "created their own gravediggers." As the mass of misery grows, so too do oppression, degradation, and exploitation: "But with this too grows the revolt of the working class, a class always increasing in numbers, and disciplined, united, organized by the very mechanism of the process of capitalist production itself" (Marx, *Capital*:715). These objective conditions of misery, poverty, and inequality in turn combine with the subjective component of consciousness to produce class-based political and revolutionary action.

This, in very crude form, is the essence of Marx's view of the revolutionary transformation of capitalist society. That view, as we know, has not met with historical confirmation. Where, then, is the theory deficient? It seems to me that the answer to this question lies in the fact that neither Marx nor Engels had a clearly worked-out theory of imperialism. As Michael Barratt Brown (1972:14) notes, the term "imperialism" never appears anywhere in their voluminous writings. They make references to the process in their early works, but do not trace out or systematically develop the actual implications: "The need of a constantly expanding market for its products chases the bourgeoisie over the whole surface of the globe. It must nestle everywhere, settle everywhere, establish connections everywhere" (Marx and Engels 1955:13).

The development of imperialism, which saw a geographical shift (over-seas expansion) in the locus of capitalist investment, production, and surplus extraction, tied the countries of the periphery more firmly into the international network of trade and commerce. As a consequence, various classes in those countries came to assume the brunt of capitalist (imperialist) oppression. This is in contrast, for example, to the workers in the imperialist centres who, though themselves exploited, derive certain comparative benefits from the exploitation of workers and peasants in less advanced countries. Workers in the imperialist centres enjoy a generally higher material standard of living (Shanin 1970; Caldwell 1970), along with far greater access to higher quality educational, medical, and social facilities.

In this context it is interesting to see what Engels, in a letter to Kautsky (in Avineri 1968:447-48), had to say about the proletariat in England in 1882:

> You ask me what the English workers think about colonial policy. Well, exactly the same as they think about politics in general: the same as the bourgeois think. There is no workers' party here, you see, there are only Conservatives and Liberal-Radicals, and the workers gaily share the feast of England's monopoly of the world market and the colonies.

The workers and peasants in the less developed Third World societies are thus subject to the most coercive aspects of the process of capitalist accumulation. They are less well educated (in a formal sense), employ more basic technology and techniques of production (Zhukov 1970:35-39), and are generally paid lower wages than their metropolitan counterparts (Gunder Frank 1973:18; Stepanov 1970:126-69; Jalée 1969). They are also faced with higher costs of living (Zhukov 1970) and have considerably fewer, if any at all, state welfare programs they can rely on. Unions are either non-existent, very weak, or else government controlled, all of which makes for the extremely high level of labour disorganization. In the agrarian sectors of these countries, workers and peasants suffer from seasonal unemployment and insecure land-tenure arrangements (Stavenhagen 1970; Feder 1971; Chirot 1977), along with the other factors already mentioned.

At this point two interesting questions suggest themselves: (1) If the vicissitudes of capitalist production and exploitation create the objective conditions for, and facilitate the emergence of, revolutionary consciousness and action among workers, will not those who suffer most from these conditions be most revolutionary? And (2) where, then, are we to look for the revolutionary class(es) of our time?

Marxism and Revolutionary Classes

The Marxist literature has expressed two diametrically opposing views on these questions. The orthodox Marxist position states that the most advanced technology and the centres of power and knowledge lie in the industrial societies and therefore make them more materially suited for pursuing the path of socialist economic development. Further, the social character of the industrial working class, its unity on the shop floor, its level of skills, and its discipline, size, alienation, and lack of property ownership accentuate its structurally antagonistic position vis-à-vis the capitalist class, rendering it the *only* consistently revolutionary class (Wolf 1971b; Hobsbawm 1973; Duggett 1975).

> Of all the classes that stand face to face with the bourgeoisie today, *the proletariat alone* is a really revolutionary class. The other classes decay and finally disappear in the face of modern industry; the proletariat is its special and essential product.
>
> The lower middle class ... the artisan, the *peasant*, all fight against the bourgeoisie, to save from extinction their existence as fractions of the middle class. They are therefore not revolutionary but *conservative*. Nay more, they are *reactionary*.
> (Marx and Engels 1955:20; emphasis added)

The second major school of thought represented in the literature opposes this orthodox view and seems to be more favoured by empirical evidence. Using the theory of imperialism as their point of departure, these writers argue that the peripheral countries have now emerged as the areas in which revolutionary movements are most likely to be sparked off and to persist. As a matter of fact, the major social revolutions of the twentieth century

(Mexico, Russia, China, Cuba, Algeria, Angola, Nicaragua, and Vietnam, among others), have all occurred in the less industrially advanced countries of the world, contrary to orthodox expectations.

What, then, is the significance of this? It seems to me that the process of imperialism, in exporting some of the more *immediate* contradictions of capitalist development in the advanced countries, has also served to export conditions that exacerbate the development of revolutionary consciousness and action. Hence, as opposed to the orthodox view, I would argue that the revolutionary class in society today is not the industrial proletariat of the advanced societies, but rather must be sought in these less economically developed countries, among the proletariat in the industrializing sector, the peasants in the rural areas, or some combination of both: rural proletarians (Mintz 1974). "The masses in the exploited dependencies constitute a force in the global capitalist system which is revolutionary in the same sense Marx considered the proletariat of the early period of modern industrialization to be revolutionary" (Sweezy, 1968:33).

This second argument seems more consistent with the trends in revolutionary movements in the twentieth century. Related to this category of "the masses in the exploited dependencies" are four fundamental questions: (1) Do these masses constitute a homogeneous group or class? (2) If so, according to what criteria? (3) If not, on what basis can we distinguish between them? (4) From these distinctions, what subgroups or classes are likely to act in the most consistently revolutionary manner?

Given actual conditions obtaining in these territories, the answer to the first question must be a categorical "no." Hence the second one does not apply. With respect to the third, James Petras (1975) and Robin Cohen (1976) note that imperialism has clearly conditioned the class structure of those societies it has touched. In some cases it has tended to undermine the existence of certain classes (small peasantry), preserve the continuity of others (absentee landlords), and even create new ones (*comprador* bourgeoisie and rural proletariat). Thus one general trend that accompanies the penetration of capitalist relations of production into the largely agrarian economies of these peripheral countries is "depeasantization and proletarianization" (Talib and Majid 1976). But what happens to the urban proletariat in these countries? How are they affected?

This is a very contentious area in the debate, for the non-orthodox Marxists charge that the conditions that made the proletariat revolutionary in the early phases of capitalist development certainly cannot be accurately applied to the proletarians in the industrially advanced countries today who benefit (indirectly) from the spoils of imperialism. But this does not mean that Marx's expectations were totally unrealistic, for given the conditions at the time he was writing, his position was not unreasonable. The forces of the Industrial Revolution were just being unleashed, with machinery progressively abolishing certain crafts and skills. The results were widespread unemployment along with high levels of poverty and increased child labour. Wages generally fell to subsistence levels or even below, while hours of work were lengthened and machines set an increasingly intense work tempo:

> The nature of work in the modern factory requires the organisation and disciplining of the workers, thereby preparing them for organised and disciplined action in other fields. The extreme exploitation to which they are subjected deprives them of any interest in the existing social order, forces them to live in conditions in which morality is meaningless and family life impossible ... these workers form a proletariat which is both capable of, and has every interest in, revolutionary action to overthrow the existing social order. (Marx and Engels, quoted in Caldwell 1970:51)

In *The Holy Family* Marx and Engels (1975:36-37) focused specifically on the objective conditions of poverty, misery, and dehumanization that faced the proletariat, concluding that on the basis of those conditions, structurally, the proletariat would be "compelled by unavoidable and absolutely compulsory need to revolt" against its degradation. At the time they were writing "the abstraction of all humanity was practically complete in the proletariat," and its conditions of existence represented "the focal point of all inhuman conditions in contemporary society."

Now, however, those conditions and the contradictions they engender are far more pronounced among the various producing classes in the peripheral countries. Writing about the case of pre-revolutionary China, for example, Malcolm Caldwell sought to apply Marx's description of the conditions facing the working class of early capitalism to the situation of the peasantry in that country:

"The abstraction of all humanity, even the appearance of humanity" was "practically complete"; their [peasants'] living conditions represented "the focal point of all inhuman conditions in contemporary society". In the war-lord and Kuomintang recruitment systems--a veritable trade in human souls and human flesh--the ultimate in dehumanization may be observed, while widespread starvation, the selling of female children into prostitution, etc., complete a pattern uncannily true to that portrayed in *The Holy Family*. (Caldwell 1970:59)

This means that the classical picture of proletarian revolution has to be modified, for three main reasons: (1) due to the process of imperialism and the rise of multinational corporations, the centre of capitalist exploitation and oppression has shifted away from the advanced countries to the periphery; (2) in the periphery the classical revolutionary proletariat is too small in sheer numbers, too vulnerable and disorganized, to perform its historic task; and (3) the very class consciousness of this tiny proletariat is lacking. With respect to this final point, some writers (Furtado 1962; Caldwell 1970; Shanin 1970) have argued that the small urban proletariat in the towns and enclave sectors of the dependent societies are quite privileged in comparison with their rural counterparts. In fact, it is said, those urban people are the pillars upon which the system of neocolonial exploitation is erected, and hence they constitute a conservative and reactionary force. According to Fanon (1963:108-9):

In the colonial territories the proletariat is the nucleus of the colonized population which has been most pampered by the colonial regime. The embryonic proletariat of the towns is in a comparatively privileged position.... [It] has everything to lose; in reality it represents that fraction of the colonized nation which is necessary and irreplaceable if the colonial machine is to run smoothly: it includes tram conductors, taxi drivers, miners, dockers, interpreters, nurses, and so on.

The Peasantry as a Class

If the proletariat of both the advanced and dependent countries, along with the indigenous bourgeoisie of the dependent countries, have limited potential as a consistently revolutionary force (Furtado 1962; Carroll 1970), we are left with that broad mass of rural producers referred to as peasants, who make up "the majority of mankind" (Shanin 1966).

The peasantry as a whole, however, forms a "class" that defies definition (Shanin 1966:239, 254), for the simple reason that it does not constitute a homogeneous group. Attempts to treat the peasantry as such have frequently resulted in great confusion and distortion of their political, economic, and revolutionary roles throughout history. For example, Marx, whose writings reflect extreme ambivalence about the peasantry (Duggett 1975), wavers between outright condemnation and poetic praise for them. Writing about the French peasants in the middle of the nineteenth century in *The Class Struggles in France 1848-1850*, he says they are:

> clumsily cunning, knavishly naive, doltishly sublime, a calculated superstition, a pathetic burlesque, a cleverly stupid anachronism, a world historic piece of buffoonery and an undecipherable hieroglyphic for the understanding of the civilised ... the unmistakable physiognomy of the class that represents barbarism within civilization. (Marx, 1972a:71)

But elsewhere (*The Eighteenth Brumaire of Louis Bonaparte*) Marx argues that these same peasants, when they come to realize that neither private property nor Napoleon represents their own interests, will become revolutionary and anti-capitalist:

> When he is disappointed in the Napoleonic Restoration, the French peasant will part with his belief in his small holding, the entire state edifice erected on this small holding will fall to the ground and the proletarian revolution will obtain that chorus without which its solo song becomes the swan song in all peasant countries. (Marx 1963:148)

This view of the peasantry is clearly contradictory and has led to inconsistencies in analysis and to ambivalence about its political role throughout history and today. For Marx, the peasants would not constitute a class simply by virtue of the fact that they share the same relation to the means of production, or because they possess a consciousness of common interest. "Classness" extends beyond this and presupposes a common political organization directed against other classes and actively engaging in class struggle (Marx 1963:124; Duggett, 1975:171).

Two opposing views of the peasantry emerge from this definition of class. Firstly, those who conceive of peasants as rural "folk" living in traditional, stable, isolated communities (Redfield 1956; Fischer-Galati 1963;) see peasants not as forming a class or set of classes, but rather as an undifferentiated mass of country people who in general possess very "low classness" (Shanin 1971a; Hobsbawm 1973b) in comparison to industrial workers. Secondly, the peasantry is seen as being made up of several different classes defined according to specific relations of production; the amount of land owned; the nature of capital invested; or the kind of labour utilized (Alavi 1973:291-95). In this view, different strata of peasants possess differential amounts of social, economic, and political power, and although their class interests may not always be overtly translated into "class struggle," they nonetheless see themselves as being different from other classes they come into contact with, and they have a clear idea of their own situation (Alavi 1973; Deal 1975; Hutton and Cohen 1975; Redclift 1975; Cohen 1976).

How, then, can one explain these apparently contradictory views? And which one is correct? In fact both positions represent conceptions of the peasantry at different historical moments, in different contexts and from different points of view. For example, when they examine non-European peasants of a later time period, people such as Raymond Firth (1946 and 1950) and Robert Redfield (1956) use categories that are more applicable to the European peasantry in the early period of capitalist development. Further, a functionalist framework of analysis quite characteristic of anthropologists writing in the 1940s and 1950s limits their scope of investigation (Foster 1967:2-8). Hence we get a picture of the peasantry as comprising "communities of producers on a small scale, with simple equipment and market organisation, often relying on what they produce for their subsistence" (Firth 1946:22). In another study Firth leaves us with the impression that small-scale producers, such as fishermen and rural craftsmen, belong to "the same social class as agriculturalists," and that as occupational

148   Sociology and the Periphery

groups they may be separable only in theory: "Since many a peasant farmer is also a fisherman or craftsman by turns, as his seasonal cycle or his cash-needs influence him" (Firth 1950:503).

This view contrasts with later commentators such as James Petras (1975), B.D. Talib and A. Majid (1976), and Robin Cohen (1976), who use the processes of "depeasantization" and "proletarianization" as their points of departure. These writers argue that the penetration of capitalist relations of production into agriculture had two major related consequences for peasant social organization: first, it destroyed the basis of existence of the small subsistence peasant economy (depeasantization), partly to facilitate the rational application of capitalist techniques of production to agriculture (large tracts of land were required to ensure economies of scale); and second, it created a class of rural proletarians (Alavi 1973; Mintz 1974), drawn from the ranks of the ex-small peasants whose plots were reduced to such an extent that the land no longer provided a subsistence living. These people then had to attach themselves to the large plantations, estates, and *latifundia* as wage workers (proletarianization) in order to stay alive. In most cases, reliance upon wages came to play a far more important role in their physical survival than did the produce from their subsistence plots.

Given this, it is misleading to view the peasantry today as an undifferentiated, homogeneous mass of country dwellers, all engaged in subsistence activities. Hence it is necessary to investigate further the other peasant "classes" in the periphery to see how they interact with these other two classes--small-scale producers and rural proletarians--and how they can be related to our general concern of "class and revolution."

Peasant Social Organization: Past and Present

The type of social organization governing peasant communities or villages reveals a great deal about class structure and various pressures towards revolutionary change. Eric Wolf (1971a:264) argues that peasants in villages or communities not extensively penetrated by market relations would find it difficult to go "from passive recognition of wrongs, to political participation as a means for setting them right"--referring to situations in which a relatively low degree of social differentiation exists, and where peasant families generally work alone and on their own land. For Joel Migdal (1974:27) such a village is more likely to have members whose cash needs are small and rare, and who as a consequence (a) engage in little or no external wage labour and (b) use primarily local peasant markets or local traders to sell any surplus and buy any goods.

Peasants in such cases tend to be technologically primitive (Shanin 1971a), at the mercy of nature, and excluded from the world that lies "beyond the bamboo hedge" of their villages. Any disputes that arise are generated and resolved locally, usually to the mutual satisfaction of the contending "families." Any kind of mobilization on the basis of class tends to be extremely rare, since "primordial ties or loyalties" (Alavi 1973) cut across class boundaries and make for more social stability than in other cases where kinship does not play as prominent a role in social organization.

Today, however, relatively isolated peasant villages of this type are scarce, because most such villages now have varying degrees of contact with wider communities in which market relations are more developed and formalized. As a consequence, class divisions tend to be much clearer or more distinct, since a variety of new relations of production are created in accordance with a given village's degree of incorporation into local, regional, or national markets. However, it must not be supposed that participation in these markets was open to just anyone. Local lords realized that unrestricted involvement by peasants in such relations would tend, after a while, to afford a certain amount of economic independence and personal freedom to the peasants, and thus undermine the lords' own basis of power in the village. In enterprises like the Latin American *hacienda* or *latifundio*, the *hacendados* or *latifundistas* (lords) were traditionally the only people who forged external links, and they took special precautions to ensure that the poor peasants beneath their control did not seek alternative arrangements outside the community with other lords or members of other classes such as merchants and traders.

The poor peasants (for example, sharecroppers) did not own any land and hence did not undertake cultivation on their own account. This was the source of their dependent status, for they were placed in a situation in which they had to offer their labour services to a lord who controlled the land and who could make demands upon them that they were generally too powerless to reject. Here Peter Blau's (1964) notion of "social exchange" is instructive, for it shows how these lords could maintain an "inward orientation" (Migdal 1974) among the subordinate peasants and prohibit them from seeking alternate means of satisfying their needs. The vast monopoly over scarce resources enjoyed by the lord enabled him to maintain his position of superiority over the poor peasants who: (a) needed to have access to these resources; (b) could not obtain them elsewhere (lords usually stuck together in dealing with peasants); and (c) could not force the lord to yield them. The

150   Sociology and the Periphery

result was a patron-client arrangement between lord and peasant embodying certain reciprocal obligations, as in the case of the Latin American *hacienda* where peasants were bound to give their lords loyalty and respect, serve in the lord's armies, provide domestic service, and above all render a certain number of work days each week. "In return peasants received a hut, a small piece of marginal land on which to grow subsistence needs, and advances for capital (such as seeds and tools). Also the lord gave special favours such as fiestas, medical aid etc." (Migdal 1974:36-37).

Similar cases have been documented for India (Lemarchand and Legg 1972; Powell 1970) and Vietnam (Sansom 1970), where similar patron-client relationships were found to be quite common.

Power Relations within the Community

Realizing that their position of superiority within the community depended on the continued "inward orientation" of the peasants, the most powerful lords and nobles took special precautions to ensure that the peasants remained dependent on them and did not establish external ties. Within any given community there was a variety of hierarchical statuses of lords and peasants measured on a scale of economic independence: the quality and amount of land possessed; degree of market involvement; amount of capital owned (tools and animals); and the size of the army. Depending on the size and population of the community the most powerful lords and nobles appointed lesser lords and nobles, who in turn appointed others all the way down to the poorest peasants. In this way both control and the maintenance of inward orientation among the broad mass of peasants were effectively realized.

In cases where the lords' local power was insufficient to ensure compliance, state bureaucrats and government agents (even in freeholding villages) were called upon to maintain order. The bureaucrats and agents usually made informal agreements to assist the lords in this way, in return for various types of rewards. Hence the entire structure of social inequality within the community was integrated, and each peasant "felt the cumulative effect of all the layers on top of him, because in the system of reciprocity, each layer could often call on the layer above to help maintain the status quo through the application of sanctions" (Migdal 1974:41). The key to the power of the lords could thus be found economically in their varying degrees of monopolistic control of essential rural resources, and politically in the fact that they could summon external, governmental forces to protect them from any perceived internal threats.

The peasant family households thus became the only social institution permitted to flourish. But even here the lord made sure that there was no significant interpeasant co-operation that might lead to the consolidation of interests and the formation of a peasant power bloc. This was accomplished by the promotion of vertical, dyadic relationships (Foster 1967) between the lord and individual peasant households, in which the peasants were bound to the lord, who was the sole supplier of all peasant needs. The more the lord could fulfil these needs, the less demand and opportunity there were for the development of community institutions and organizations. The result was the perpetuation of a one-to-one dependence on the lord and greater community fragmentation owing to the active discouragement of horizontal social relations among peasant households.

In a situation such as this, revolutionary mobilization among the peasants is rare, if not totally impossible, because class formation and the birth of revolutionary consciousness are stifled by the isolation of both social (political) and economic production at the level of separate households. Any protest tends to take the form of spontaneous individual acts of aggression directed at fellow family members, or of "social banditry" (Hobsbawm 1959; Quijano 1967;) against other families. The pervasive control exercised by the lords, the effective isolation of the various productive units, and the community's almost total insulation from the wider society militate against the possibility of organized rebellion, let alone revolution.

Such examples of relatively enclosed and self-sufficient *hacienda*-type enterprises do not exhaust the variety of possible lord-peasant relationships. In fact, at least three other patterns can be identified. Firstly, there can be a situation in which there is only a single lord whose power does not extend to all the peasants in a given area. There we find a class of "independent or middle peasants" who own land and who do not have to rely upon a lord for employment and the granting of other services. These independent smallholders are generally self-sufficient and have no real need to hire labour or hire themselves out as labourers on a constant basis, or as part of a regular practice (Rudra 1976). The lord's formal control over the activities of this class is thus not as total as in the case of the landless sharecroppers, but this does not mean that their external involvement in markets goes unchecked. As Benno Galjart observes with respect to the *fazeda* owner in Brazil, the small independent owners in the neighbourhood had to be careful to stay in the lord's favour, "since they depended on him for occasional

152   Sociology and the Periphery

employment, a loan, an introduction to a bank, a favour. A conflict with him could cost them their land" (Galjart 1964:6).

A second pattern of lord-peasant interaction is that which obtains when several lords control all the peasants in a given community, but no one lord has complete monopoly over vital resources. In one sense this type of situation makes for a certain degree of stability because the lords must co-operate to preserve their position of dominance, and it is only through this co-operation that total inward orientation among the subordinate peasants can be maintained. Although the degree of control here is not as absolute as in the *hacienda*-type system, some check on peasants' activities can still be enforced.

Finally, a third pattern of relations exists in those communities where a group of independent peasants lies outside the combined scope of authority exercised by the local lords, even though they all live within the same community. In this case the peasants, though still not totally free, have a greater measure of relative autonomy (theoretically) than their counterparts in the *hacienda* or the two other systems of social organization. This means that pressures to maintain their inward orientation cannot be as great, and hence they can constitute a greater force of potential resistance to the established powers in the community, in comparison to landless sharecroppers and other objectively powerless rural classes.

These "independent middle" peasants are not necessarily better off economically than those classified as "poor" peasants (such as sharecroppers, or migrant wage workers) although as Hamza Alavi (1973) points out, this is the impression conveyed traditionally by academic sociology. To clarify this situation, Alavi prefers to talk about differentiation among the peasants, as opposed to stratification, which implies a hierarchical structuring of peasants on the basis of pure economic factors. Hence he uses such designations as "capitalist farmers," "independent smallholders," "sharecroppers," and "farm labourers," instead of the imprecise terms of "rich," "middle," and "poor" peasants. Although I agree with him, I have continued to use the more traditional terms, with qualifications when necessary, simply because they have been so widely employed in the literature.

The importance of this point becomes evident in situations in which one finds particular sharecroppers (poor peasants) cultivating more land and having greater incomes than independent (middle) peasants. What makes the middle peasants more potentially revolutionary, then, is a combination of two factors: (a) though classified as middle peasants, they are really quite poor in comparison to the landlords and capitalist farmers, and they experience all the harsh realities of life that beset poor peasants in any country; and (b) the greater level of personal freedom enjoyed by members of their class (owing to their relative economic independence) allows for more latitude of movement, in comparison to sharecroppers who are much more constrained by the powers of the landlords, or the rural proletarians who are placed in a similar situation given their relationship to their employers (the capitalist farmers). For this reason, any discussion of peasant classes must be premised on the notion of relations of production, and not simply on economic criteria like wealth and income. The Marxist concept of class, Alavi reminds us, has to be understood structurally and within the context of the prevailing relations of production. "Where several modes of production coexist, classes cannot be arranged in a single linear hierarchical order because they must be structurally differentiated" (Alavi 1965:293).

Peasant Revolts and Rebellions

Given this discussion, then, on what basis does mobilization among these independent smallholders occur? And towards what ends?

The first of these questions relates to the peasant struggles for more freedom, more market involvement, and more sharing in some of the material goods brought from the city and consumed by the lords. Peasants are quite aware of their oppression and deprivation, but what is more important, they realize the possibility of doing something to alter their conditions of existence (Davidson 1974).

The second question focuses more on the actual limitations of such a struggle, and its political form. This class of independent smallholders, it has been argued (Shanin 1966; Hobsbawm 1973; Duggett 1975;), is quite capable of organizing and carrying out a *revolt* or *rebellion*, when the particular peasant community is located in a peripheral area, far removed from centres of state influence and pervasive policing (Wolf 1969:270-71). Their very peripherality and isolation, however, render them incapable of escalating the struggle to a *revolutionary* stage, because this process involves the capture of state power and the total social, economic, and political reorganization of the society. The breadth of changes required in this type of social reconstruction presupposes a broader consciousness of certain issues that the institutional structure of the peasant community does not foster. In this context Douglas Deal argues that any definition of revolution must set it apart from rebellion, which is thought to be a much more limited and ephemeral phenomenon. While both are seen to represent forms of collective violence, "Revolution is said to entail the aim of transforming society itself, whereas rebellion seeks redress of specific injustices within the framework of the existing social order" (Deal 1975:414).

The independent peasants living in peripheral areas, then, are seen to possess more strategic freedom than other peasants, and hence are potentially more rebellious. This hypothesis has been borne out in the villages of Morelos in Mexico; in the communes of the central agricultural regions of Russia; in Northern China, Vietnam, and among the "fellahin" of Algeria (Wolf 1969). Even the squatters of Cuba's Oriente province displayed such rebellious characteristics, which led Ché Guevara (1961) to conclude that the final triumph of the revolution would have been impossible after the early setbacks had it not been for these peripheral peasants (squatters) and the assistance they rendered to the guerrillas. As a matter of fact, rural guerrilla forces find indispensable allies in these peripheral areas and their inhabitants (Debray 1967). For Teodor Shanin (1971a:260), over the years guerrilla warfare has proved to be the most likely form of successful peasant resistance.

The effectiveness of such guerrilla campaigns is greatly enhanced by two additional factors: (a) if the area contains defensible mountainous terrain that can offer protection to the guerrillas, as in the cases of Morelos (Mexico), Kabylia (Algeria), and Oriente (Cuba); and (b) where there is an ethnic linguistic difference between the peripheral and the surrounding populations. Again, the same examples support this point: the villagers of Morelos spoke Nahuatl, while those from Kabylia were Berber-speaking. Although in Oriente the Spanish spoken was similar to that heard elsewhere in Cuba, the significant Afro-Cuban element there, mixed with a hint of French from Haitian immigrants and refugees, gave Eastern Cuba a unique ethnic and cultural identity. Ethnic distinctions enhance the solidarity of the rebels, while possession of a special linguistic code provides for an autonomous system of communication (Wolf 1969:271; Quijano 1967:304-5).

Such peasant movements, though not necessarily revolutionary at the outset, have been known to lead to revolutionary conclusions, as the peasants, tempered in their own struggles, come to acquire a broader consciousness and forge links with movements of other oppressed people, both rural and urban (Mintz 1974).

Peasant Communities in the Age of Imperialism

If the structural-institutional limits placed upon the peasants' acquisition of the type of consciousness necessary for transforming rebellions or revolts into revolutions are inherent in relatively self-sufficient and enclosed villages and communities, where powerful lords and nobles force the peasants to be inwardly oriented, what, then, are the forces or processes that liberate these areas from tradition, destroy the lords' basis of power, and create a peasantry that is revolutionary in the true sense of the word?

There are very few peasant communities in the world today that have not been influenced in some form or fashion by the global expansion of capitalism. Accompanied by the forces of the scientific and technological revolutions, the process of imperialism has served to alter the basis of existence of even the most remote rural villages, upsetting traditional patron-client relationships and creating entirely new lifestyles. Peoples who for centuries had lived in isolation from one another have now been brought together in a competitive market economy, over which they have very little control, and about which they have even less understanding.

In the push for profit maximization and the accumulation of wealth, imperialist relations and structures have been established in the urban centres of Third World countries, which imperialists use as a base for their operations--for the transfer of wealth from the peripheries. Subsequently, local states and governments have been subordinated and made to serve the interests of international capitalism (Jacoby 1970)--interests consisting primarily of cheap labour, cheap raw materials, and markets or outlets for goods produced in the metropolitan centres.

The imperialist presence has also wrought fundamental changes in the rural areas of the peripheral countries, leaving peasant populations almost totally dependent on the factors of cash, markets, and wage labour. In the urban centres imperialism has developed more effective administrative techniques and more complex and coherent bureaucracies, thus facilitating the penetration of rural areas on a much broader scale than previously (Migdal 1974:92). What, then, was the nature of these changes? How did they influence the social organization of the peasants and serve to create a revolutionary consciousness among them?

Eric Wolf (1969), Clifford Geertz (1966), and Harold Frederiksen (1961), among others, have pointed to the rapid increase in population growth as a major factor in disrupting traditional inwardly oriented peasant communities. In countries such as Mexico, China, Russia, Vietnam, Algeria, and Cuba, the demographic changes in peasant populations since the turn of the century have been phenomenal. Those changes can be explained by three main factors: (a) the spread of knowledge about preventive medicine; (b) lower infant mortality rates; and (c) higher birth rates. The changes are in turn linked to the revolutions in technology and biological sciences that occurred in the more industrialized countries during the same period and were later diffused to the less industrialized areas.

In peasant communities rapid population expansion meant increased pressure on land, which was disproportionately held by various peasant, landlord, and capitalist-farmer classes. Those individual households, families, or groups who could not meet expanding domestic needs, due either to insufficient land or inadequate technology for exploiting that land efficiently, were forced to find alternative means for satisfying their needs. This invariably meant becoming involved in external cash and market relations: proletarianization. Mahmood Mamdani (1976), Konrad Kingshill (1960), and Geertz (1966) have documented case studies of these changes for India, Northern Thailand, and Indonesia respectively.

Developing concomitantly with this process was the rapid undermining or destruction of the patron-client bonds that traditionally held peasant communities together (Pearse 1972). The more powerful lords now saw the opportunity for obtaining "new sources of prestige" (Migdal 1974:103) by participating in the wider status systems of towns and developing urban centres. The increasing external involvement on the part of the lords meant that they could no longer devote as much time and attention to their village duties and obligations to their peasants, who had come to expect economic, political, social, and even medical services of them. B. Hutchinson (1966) clearly documents and analyses this situation for Brazil, arguing that the lords' absence created a source of tension, because while they attempted to maintain the lord-tenant bond they were also unwilling to furnish the customary patronage benefits to the peasants.

Hence the relatively secure, communal, and protected existence of the peasantry was upset, and they were thrown into a market situation demanding individualism, competition, and high personal risk. In the case of China, Shu-ching Lee (1951) shows how this situation was even further aggravated when the lords, in order to be able to afford the luxuries and comforts of the cities, increased their demands on the peasants, in terms of higher rent, interest, and taxes, and even used the wives and daughters of the peasants as domestics in their new homes in town.

The overall impact of this process weakened the degree of control that the lord exercised over his peasants, if only because his physical presence was no longer felt in the same way. In addition, there was now greater penetration of state institutions into the rural sector, a development that provided peasants with new and alternative sources for satisfying their needs. In the case of Southeast Asia, for example, James Scott (1970) noted that schools, regional banks, agricultural services, and public employment opportunities substituted for traditional services furnished by the lord. Susan Bourque (1971) identified similar patterns in her description of the Peruvian situation, in which the expansion of modern, large-scale agricultural enterprises to the sierra accentuated the inefficiency of the *latifundia*. Indeed, as the *gamonal* or landlord fell under increased financial pressure he tended to pass the burden onto the peasants, thereby incurring both their tacit support for the system and their political opposition. In addition: "The growth of commercial centres in the sierra was expanding the impact of coastal society and the opportunities of the campesino. All of these factors combined to weaken the control of the traditional authority structure, the closed system of the 'gamonal'" (Bourque 1971:34-35). Samuel Huntington (1968) and Gunnar Myrdal (1968) have noted similar trends in the agrarian sectors of various other peripheral countries.

A third factor associated with the imperialist presence in the underdeveloped countries and serving to upset traditional peasant arrangements was the generalized commercialization of agriculture with its deepening reliance on cash transactions, which reflected an increased demand for farm products on the part of the centres. Faced with increasing taxes to pay, the subsistence peasants (both dependent and independent) with fixed levels of land and technology were forced to engage in cash cropping, hence opening themselves up to the vicissitudes of the market. When the prices of their products fell, or when they were faced with a particularly bad harvest, these peasants would experience severe household economic crises, which were further aggravated by the absence of a lord or patron they could rely on in such times. With the increasing application of technology to agricultural production, employment opportunities declined, and many of these peasants (sharecroppers, independent smallholders, and farm labourers) found themselves displaced and unemployed.

Their way of life was thus seriously threatened, because it was becoming extremely difficult for them to "balance their accounts." Their subsistence plots of land were no longer adequate enough to support their families, which were expanding numerically, let alone yield a surplus that would help meet the increasing tax burdens. These peasants were also traditionally viewed as bad credit risks, so that, in the absence of widespread employment opportunities, they were often forced into the voracious grips of rural usurers, who were swift to forfeit their lands upon default of repayment. In the case of China, Barrington Moore Jr. (1966:219) notes that as the peasants fell increasingly into debt, they tended to borrow more heavily and at higher interest rates, which spelled an end to any independence they may have held: "When they could not repay, they had to transfer title to the land to a landlord, remaining on the soil to work it indefinitely." Gunnar Myrdal (1968) and P.C. Joshi (1974) have analysed many cases of such practices in India and Pakistan, and there was usually a common result: either these impoverished and landless peasants found jobs in the growing capitalist rural enterprises or corporations, or they became part of the rural or urban reserve armies of the unemployed--proletarianization.

Peasants and Revolution

The penetration of peasant villages by market forces resulted in a heightened degree of exploitation and an increase in rural proletarian consciousness among former peasants (Mintz 1953, 1974). Apart from the oppression they suffered, peasants were also subject to manipulation by rapacious middlemen who took advantage of their dire need for cash by paying ridiculously low prices for their products. John McAlister and Paul Mus (1970) clearly depict this process in the context of Vietnam; Fei Hsiao-Tung (1939) does the same for China; and Shephard Forman and Joyce Riegelhaupt do likewise (1970) for Brazil.

All this meant that the huge capitalist operations moving into the countryside could now be supplied with a ready-made workforce, because the displaced peasants were both physically and psychologically prepared for such employment. Writing about plantation economies in the Caribbean, specifically Puerto Rico, Sidney Mintz notes that the increasing industrial character of work in these agrarian capitalist enterprises led to the formation of a rural proletariat that was "landless, propertyless, wage earning, store buying (the stores being a chain owned by the corporation with few competitors), [and] corporately employed" (1953:139). In time, Mintz notes elsewhere (1974:300), these rural proletarians "come to behave sociologically in ways associated with such characteristics as wage labour, dependence on imported goods, lack of productive property (especially land), and so on."

The situation, then, is reminiscent of that described by Marx and Engels (1955, 1975) with respect to the revolutionary potential of the industrial proletariat of their time. However, there is an important contextual difference in that we are dealing with a class of rural producers that is sensitive to the hardships of both peasant and proletarian existence. One would thus expect that if the conditions of abject poverty, objective exploitation, and alienation were to make the industrial proletariat revolutionary, these rural proletarians would be doubly so.

Unlike the peripheral peasants who are capable only of revolt or rebellion (Wolf 1969; Hobsbawm 1973), this class is more integrated into a wider societal context, possesses a clearer understanding of state and market functions, and is often better educated and more urbanized. It is hence more potentially likely to pursue revolutionary paths and carry other peasant fractions along. Writing about Latin America generally, Aníbal Quijano (1967:309) observes that revolutionary "movements developed in rural areas closer to the urban zones, and in those places where agriculture had been modernised and the countryside urbanised.... It is safe to say that in the long run these movements were very influential in paving the way for subsequent peasant movements." This analysis supports the position of Wolf (1969), who argues that as long as peasants remain isolated and enclosed within their own villages and communities, the likelihood of them organizing or even participating in revolutionary activity is remote. However, the imperialist penetration of these peripheral areas breaks the traditional bonds keeping peasants in subordination and ignorance, thus enabling them to develop a wider social consciousness and to come to a fuller understanding of the true nature of their oppression. With this in mind James Petras examines the revolutions in Russia, China, and Cuba, and concludes that social revolution was not the special product of the underdeveloped areas of the periphery, but rather was "more likely initiated in those areas most penetrated by the metropolis, where capitalist social relations predominate and where productivity approximates that of the metropolis" (1975:306).

What, then, is the catalyst that unites the harsh, objective conditions of existence with this "new" type of consciousness and produces sustained *revolutionary* action? The answer to this must be sought in the type of leadership present in a given situation, that is, in the links between the more advanced elements of the rural proletariat and other urban-based forces of support.

The Question of Leadership

In any discussion of revolutionary movements the question of leadership is always paramount, because leadership moulds the ideology, aims, and directions of such processes. Stated differently, this crucial factor determines whether or not a movement remains consistently revolutionary or becomes revisionist or reactionary. It is thus important to have leaders who are not only informed but also sincere and dedicated--leaders who are not elitist, but are willing to be educated. The tendency towards elitism has plagued many so-called revolutionary movements in which the leaders put themselves above and separate from those who are led, and where interaction between the two groups is minimal, tokenistic, and involves a one-way flow of information.

Many people who have (mis)read Lenin's *What Is To Be Done?* (1969) have levelled the charge of elitism against his program of revolutionary organization and his notion of the vanguard party. A careful reading of Lenin's position serves to dismiss this charge, for, as Duncan Hallas points out, a key feature of elitist thinking involves the assumption that the "observable differences in abilities, consciousness and experience are rooted in unalterable genetic or social conditions, and that the mass of the people are incapable of self-government now or in the future" (Hallas undated:15). This clearly does not reflect Lenin's position or intentions.

Revolution, indeed, is a complex process in which the participants do not all make the same types of contributions. It is necessary to create a division of labour to accomplish the varied tasks to be performed, and not all members of the movements are equally prepared for every undertaking. The "uneven development" characteristic of capitalist society permeates social structure, social institutions, and social consciousness, and produces extreme inequalities in such areas as schooling and intellectual development. As a consequence, those persons who are "more developed" in these respects, given the revolutions in the fields of transportation and communications networks, and the spread of literacy, have a greater awareness of regional, national, and world trends in social, economic, and political developments. These people are, it can be argued, best equipped to provide revolutionary leadership to peasant or other types of movements. Of course not all intellectuals are revolutionary, and not all revolutionaries are intellectuals (Hobsbawm 1973a). But for that group of intellectuals who are revolutionary, the question becomes: What makes them revolutionary and critical of the society that nurtures them?

Antonio Gramsci (1971) and his discussion of intellectuals--traditional and organic--provide one answer to this question. Gramsci sees organic intellectuals as structurally created by the ruling class in any capitalistic society for the purpose of giving that class a certain homogeneity and consciousness of its functions: "The capitalist entrepreneur creates alongside himself the industrial technician, the specialist in political economy, the organizers of a new culture, of a new legal system etc." (p.6). These organic intellectuals do not form a class in themselves, but rather have the social function of providing ideological justification for the hegemonic class and its system of production and control. In this sense, they too are "technically proletarianised, inasmuch as the bulk of them are no longer 'free professions' or private entrepreneurs, but salaried employees" (Hobsbawm 1973a:258).

Traditional intellectuals--people like priests, medical practitioners, teachers, writers, and creative artists--are said to have no structural or organic relationship to the dominant classes and have traditionally been seen as free of control, of obligation to support the status quo, and even of censorship. Gramsci sees their pursuits as transcending narrow class interests, because their work is meant to benefit all humanity. Such intellectuals often believe that they are members of an autonomous group who can act independently of ruling or dominant class pressures, because historically their social status and function as intellectuals have remained unchanged despite great social and political upheavals. This type of "relative" independence, coupled with their broader consciousness, has enabled such intellectuals traditionally to recognize and speak out against excesses and contradictions within the system. As a result the state perceives them as a potential source of disruption, and in many instances denies them academic and intellectual freedom of expression (Shanin 1970:30-31). In liberal societies especially, this denial tends to make them even more critical. This is the very group that Marx and Engels (1955:20) describe in *The Communist Manifesto*:

> In times when the class struggle nears the decisive hour ... a small section of the ruling class cuts itself adrift, and joins the revolutionary class, the class that holds the future in its hands....
> A portion of the bourgeoisie goes over to the proletariat, and in particular, a portion of the bourgeois ideologists, who have raised themselves to the level of comprehending theoretically the historical movement as a whole.

In underdeveloped societies, members of this segment or group of traditional intellectuals, usually educated in Western universities, return home and become a potential source of tension and conflict. They potentially constitute an independent social entity, possessed of a high degree of knowledge of the outside world, but at the same time they are marginalized and frustrated by the limitations placed on them in their own countries. They become associated with various local protest movements and, having the ability and consciousness, serve to direct and guide such "causes." Shedding their status of traditional intellectuals, individuals from this group are well placed to become organic intellectuals of the oppressed classes in their society. Indeed, they are the ones who can and do provide the necessary leadership and organizational skills required for escalating protests and revolts to the level of revolutionary movements, in both industrial and agrarian settings. The case of Cuba provides a classic example of this.

The Cuban Experience

The period from 1868 to 1959 in Cuba was marked by intense class struggle and revolutionary mobilization of both peasants and workers. During the Ten Years War (1868-78), the War of Independence (1895-98), the crisis of the state in the 1930s, and the "Castro revolution" (1956-59), various class interests coalesced, disintegrated, and recombined in different forms, yielding an extremely complex picture of Cuba's recent economic and political history.

The massive influx of foreign (U.S.) capital into Cuba at the turn of the century (Thomas 1971; Huberman and Sweezy 1960, 1969; Boorstein 1968) had a tremendous impact upon the class structure of the entire country. This impact ranged from peasants to the national bourgeois elements. The peasantry was being increasingly proletarianized as U.S. investments sought profitable outlets in the lucrative sugar industry (O'Connor 1970; Aguilar 1972), which tied the country to a monocrop economy. By the 1950s this investment had subjected Cuba's overall prosperity to the very unstable character of sugar prices on the world market. The national bourgeoisie was rendered impotent, because it did not have the wherewithal to compete with the foreign investors, and its members found themselves relegated to the status of "junior partner" in most ventures: "The Cuban bourgeoisie in fact, lacked almost any homogeneity or history.... It was profoundly and fatally integrated into the U.S. imperial economy" (Blackburn 1963:62-64). Along with these two extremes, other intermediate classes

Peasants and Revolution   163

were also experiencing the consequences of the imperial penetration of their economy and coming increasingly to realize the source of their oppression:

> Support for many basic reforms was forthcoming from segments of nearly all of the island's major classes. The peasants and rural workers had been made aware by their hunger and enforced idleness of the abundance of unused lands; the teacher and doctor by illiteracy and disease, of the backwardness of the educational system and health services; the small businessman, by his sluggish profits, of state corruption, and irrational labour; many urban industrial workers were made conscious by their lack of training and underemployment, of the under-utilization of both their own and the island's productive potential. (O'Connor 1972:68)

Agitation among the rural workers dating back to the 1920s (Thomson 1935) was heightened when the student movements threw in their lots with various rebel groups and set the scene for the arrival of the Castro forces, which provided the necessary revolutionary leadership and served to galvanize the masses (Wolf 1969a). This leadership came not from among the ranks of the peasants and rural proletarians, but rather from middle-class (traditional) intellectuals who challenged the status quo and sought to capture state power and transform the entire social order. Of this group, some were students (Raúl Castro, Faure Chomón), some lawyers (Fidel Castro, Osvaldo Dorticos), some doctors (Ché Guevara, Faustino Pérez, Réné Vallejo), and some teachers (Frank País). As Guevara wrote, "None of the first group who came in the 'Granma', who established ourselves in the Sierra Maestra, and learned to respect the peasant and worker while living with them, had worker's or peasant's backgrounds" (quoted in Wolf 1969a:269).

This leadership, however, was not received with eager and open arms, for in the early days of the movement peasant recruitment to the revolutionary army was slow and, as Guevara (1968) noted, this was not without reason. Many times in the past these very peasants had been betrayed and cheated by so-called urban revolutionaries who had supposedly come to deliver them from their miseries. Hence it was not until the guerrillas gave up their "city ways," became "peasantized," and proved their sincerity that they won the confidence of the poor peasants:

164   Sociology and the Periphery

In order for the peasants to become rebels, the rebels became peasants. They took part in the field chores. It wasn't enough to know the needs, the poverty of the rural people. It was necessary to suffer from these hardships and at the same time to combat them. The farmer would be that much better disposed to listen to them, the more he recognized them as his own kind. (Sartre 1961:50-51)

In the meantime, those workers and rural proletarians in the vicinity of Oriente province were joining the revolutionary army much more readily and receiving training in the tactics of guerrilla warfare, while teaching the guerrillas how to survive in the jungle.

After a few months the guerrillas began to "blend" in with the local peasants and started to develop modest operations for improving the conditions of existence of the peasants. They rendered medical services and financial assistance, helped with the provision of food, and, most importantly, began the process of political education. Before long the guerrilla leadership and organization penetrated the remotest rural areas, encompassing various isolated peasant struggles and giving them revolutionary direction. This served both to increase the ranks of the rebel army and to heighten the commitment to revolutionary change on the part of the members: "At the beginning the 'campesinos' merely hid the rebels; before many months had passed the 'campesinos', *as a class*, were backing the rebels. They changed from passive onlookers to active participants" (Huberman and Sweezy 1960:57; emphasis added).

Political consciousness grew at each different stage of the struggle as the revolutionary leaders took every possible opportunity to explain the consequences of their actions to the people and broaden peasant awareness of wider societal goals. This is the crucial element in revolutionary struggle--an element missing, and impossible to attain, in the context of isolated rural uprisings, which are geared more to redressing individual acts of transgression or in rare cases to reforming certain aspects of social structure. In the Cuban countryside such superficial responses to deeper social problems quickly began to disappear as peasant political consciousness and organization increased, and as the class struggle became more crystallized. For the first time the rural poor were able to arrive at a wider understanding of the causes of their poverty. For the first time they felt themselves in a position to make dramatic changes; and they did.

Revolution in the Periphery

The development of imperialism and its effects mean the arguments in favour of a revolutionary proletariat in the advanced industrialized countries have to be revised. The centre of capitalist exploitation and oppression shifted to the Third World in general, making those countries more potential sources of social tension because the masses there are relatively worse off than those in the advanced centres. These peripheral masses, however, do not constitute a homogenous group, and their respective patterns of social organization greatly influence any identification and analysis of potential conflict areas.

In these largely agrarian-based economies, peasants predominate and the inwardly oriented structure and institutions of their communities limit their general level of social class consciousness. Hence poor peasants in this type of environment are more likely to engage in protest movements that take the forms of social banditry, rebellions, or revolts, but these incidences rarely escalate into full-blown revolutionary movements.

As the development of capitalism in agriculture proceeds, this inward orientation is undermined and increasing proletarianization results. With the break-up of traditional social arrangements the factors of cash, markets, and wage labour begin to play a prominent role in rural social organization. This leads to the peasants' acquisition of a broader consciousness as they come to interact with a wider community and to experience more direct contact with state officials and government agents. The destruction and replacement of their old secure existence by the formal and impersonal relations characteristic of market society produce greater disorientation. They begin to search for renewed security by means of a change in the prevailing system of oppression; and they become in a position to understand that system more fully than when they were confined by the "bamboo hedges of their villages."

Given these changed circumstances, unrest can be triggered by a wide variety of factors, ranging from traditional peasant demands for land reform through rural proletarian concerns with stable year-round employment to even more typical proletarian issues such as higher wages. Whatever the specific demands, these peasants, ex-peasants, and rural proletarians must be able to bargain from a position of strength, and, as we know, their main strength lies in their numbers. To make their demands more effective, they realize that their "numbers" must be organized, educated, and prepared for struggle. This is when the questions of leadership and direction enter the picture.

The traditional intellectuals in the Third World societies are the ones best suited to performing these tasks, given their greater social and political consciousness and their traditional freedom to criticize the status quo. Coupled with these two factors is the consideration of the marginal position occupied by such people in their own societies. In most cases they have travelled and lived abroad and received formal "higher education" in foreign universities, which affords them a comparative context. Returning home armed with their metropolitan experiences, high ideals, and hopes of reforming their own societies, they soon run into a wall of tradition and institutional conservatism, and they discover that entrance to the main decision-making positions is generally governed more by seniority and political patronage than by merit. This type of situation often produces a great sense of frustration and alienation among the ranks of these middle-class intellectuals, both in their wider societal dealings and even in relations with close family and kin.

For those who return home and secure comfortable positions as organic intellectuals within government departments and large corporations, the picture is different. For whatever reasons, they experience no serious ideological conflicts and manage to re-adapt to the society relatively smoothly. Sharing interests consistent with the prevailing status quo in their own countries, such people often rise to positions of prominence and serve to reproduce the system politically and ideologically. The others, however, have the potential to become more radicalized. They are the ones who tend to establish alliances with other marginalized individuals and groups who speak out against the system. When such links are forged with groups in areas where rebellious sentiments already prevail, for example in the rural sector, revolutionary mobilization is most likely to occur.

Social revolution, then, is not a one-class affair, but rather varies historically according to the specific context and incorporates different classes or fractions of different classes. Variations in the nature of oppression, exploitation, state intervention, class formation, and consciousness produce widely varied trends in revolutionary activity. But the changes wrought by imperialism on the agrarian sectors of the peripheral countries seem to point to those areas and their inhabitants as the loci and portents of revolutionary insurrection.

Chapter Seven

Race, Gender, and Development

This book started with Saint Simon and Comte, so it is only fitting that it should end with reference to them. As the founding fathers of sociology, they gave to the discipline much that was useful; but they were also the social and intellectual products of their own times, reflecting the thought and attitudes of that time. This was true especially when it came to the twin questions of racism and sexism, questions that receive so much attention in contemporary society and scholarship.

For example, in trying to account for some of the chaos that ensued from the French Revolution, Saint Simon blamed the "revolutionaries who applied the principles of equality to negroes. If they had consulted the physiologists they would have learned that the negro, because of his basic physical structure, is not susceptible, even with the same education, of rising to the intellectual level of Europeans" (quoted from Saint Simon's *Lettres d'un habitant de Genève à ses contemporains*, in Manuel 1956:408). Irving Zeitlin writes that for Comte, "The female sex is in a state of perpetual infancy." In Comte's own words: "Sociology will prove that the equality of the sexes, of which so much is said, is incompatible with all social existence" (quoted in Zeitlin 1987:68).

As we prepare to greet the twenty-first century, it appears that these views, expressed in the early eighteenth century, have not entirely lost their currency. In certain political and intellectual circles today, the debate over the social and "natural" aspects of race and gender inequality rages on at the macro level of whole countries. The long history of the racially driven apartheid system in South Africa and the lingering residue of bitterness and uncertainty mixed with the jubilation as that country undergoes political transformation provide one example. Closer to home, the charge by some critics that the Canadian constitution does not guarantee equal rights for women is another case in point. This final chapter addresses the historical and contemporary dimensions of race and gender in relation to the periphery.

BLACKS IN SOUTH AFRICA: STILL A PEOPLE APART

South Africa has officially abolished apartheid, yet the country's black people continue to live in a world apart.

Assets: The richest 5 per cent of the population, mostly white, owns 88 per cent of all private property.

Poverty: Half the population, mostly black, lives below the poverty line.

Children: Many poor black children are being stunted by malnutrition: 40 per cent of rural children and 15 per cent of urban children.

Literacy: One-third of the black population over fifteen years of age (some three million people) is illiterate.

Education: Three-quarters of black teachers are either unqualified, or underqualified, for their job. The education system thus perpetuates a vicious circle of deprivation and discrimination.

For South African blacks, the achievement of full political rights will be a vital step towards greater participation. But unravelling apartheid completely will be a complex and difficult task in the years ahead.

Source: United Nations *Human Development Report 1993* (New York: Oxford University Press, 1993), p.27.

Racism

Whether or not "black" people and "white" people actually exist is not as important as the fact that human beings *behave* as if they do. Peoples' colours are seen to be associated with their races; they are thus identified, and they identify themselves, as lying somewhere along a colour continuum that runs from blue-black to pinkish-white. The number of races that can be identified today is correspondingly very large. Indeed it is so large that the term "race" has itself become quite meaningless. Robert Miles says it best when he asserts that "race" is "an idea that should be explicitly and consistently confined to the dustbin of analytically useless terms" (1989:72).

Meaningless or not, the concepts of colour and race continue to act as key social markers providing individuals and groups with packaged meanings of themselves and others. The attribution of meanings linked to phenotypical and genetic characteristics is the basis on which categorizations are made with their attendant expectations as to what various individuals and

170   Sociology and the Periphery

groups are like, what they are capable of, and even what their sense of morality entails. When such categorizations are informed by negative meanings, and when those meanings serve to relegate people to subordinate positions in a system of hierarchical social rankings, racism is the result. For along with its ideological message, racism is the practice of including and excluding individuals and groups from participating fully in the social economy and of denying them access to certain services and resources on the basis of some imputed racial similarities or differences.

Phenotypical differences--that is, differences in physical appearance-- have existed throughout history and have been used positively and negatively depending on the circumstances. In a general sense, those who are phenotypically different also tend to be seen as having different religious, political, and social beliefs and practices, which makes it all the more possible to set them apart as outsiders or "others," as belonging to distinct nations, tribes, or races. Further, the combination of military strength with the ideologies of nationalism, tribalism, or racism creates the possibilities for widespread conflict and domination. While human beings have always operated with the ideas of the "in-group" and the "out-group," the actual mechanics of inclusion and exclusion have run the gamut from total assimilation to outright decimation. Always, however, the members of an in-group, those in the powerful positions, have used ideological justifications or rationalizations for their actions. In the case of racism the members of an in-group often refer to their so-called *natural* superiority as a group.

Like other concepts, the ideas developed around the question of race can assume a life of their own, divorced from their original context. They have therefore come to be applied in different ways throughout history, serving diverse ends here and there. Thus, whether or not the ancient Egyptians were racist towards the Ethiopians, or whether the colour symbolisms of the Old Testament were meant literally, these considerations still served greatly to inform the later practices of slavery and colonialism and to justify the historic actions of slave owners and colonizers, both to themselves and to others.

In this sense, racism became a relation of production; for it was an indispensable aspect of the process of primitive accumulation of colonial capital, which was vital to the consolidation and development of capitalism at the global level. As part of the process, African enslavement was seen as "the appropriate position for a population at a different stage of human development, for a different (and inferior) kind of human being" (Miles 1989:111). But the roots of that rationalization antedated African slavery by several millennia, and throughout the post-slavery period those same roots have continued to support, albeit in altered form, the processes of labour recruitment and exploitation.

Where, then, does this all begin? When did black people come to be worth less than others? Why? Who is black? And how *black* is black? It may not be possible to answer all these questions, but I hope that posing them will afford some insight into the phenomenon of racism; and that by extension we will gain an understanding of the politics of race.

Contrary to much popular belief, racism did not cause black people to be oppressed and enslaved. "Slavery was not born of racism," Eric Williams states. "Rather, racism was the consequence of slavery" (1966:7). In addition, slavery was not to be identified solely with the African and the African's subjugation by the white European. Long before Europeans went to Africa, (white) slavery was commonplace in ancient Greece and Rome, and Asians had invaded, conquered, and enslaved other Asians. Often with the help of black African rulers, "Arabs had exploited and enslaved black Africans" (Shils 1968:2). Together with the indigenous inhabitants of the Caribbean region, poor whites from Europe were among the first to experience the privations of human freedom in the New World. Slavery, therefore, was neither unique nor peculiar to Africans.

The institution of slavery was more of an economic than a racial phenomenon per se: "It had to do not with the color of the laborer, but with the cheapness of the labor" (Williams 1966:19). Where in history, then, does the concern with blackness or negritude arise? If slavery is not to be wholly or exclusively associated with blacks, whence arose the socio-religious ideas that blacks were evil and sinful, and that enslavement was their just punishment? (Moreno Fraginals 1976:53; Lewis 1983:139). Partial answers to this question can be sought in many places, including the history of art and literature as well as in the rise of Christianity as a religion embraced by white Europeans as a counter to Islam.

History of the Idea of Race
If we are to accept the views of Frank M. Snowden Jr., the writings that cover the period from the Pharaohs to the Caesars are to be noted for their accurate and benign portrayal of blacks in the ancient world. To be sure, the literature did remark on differences between blacks (Ethiopians) and others (primarily the Egyptians), but according to Snowden the writers made no attempt to link phenotypical characteristics with social standing. This may have been due

to the fact that "from earliest times Egyptians had been acquainted with blacks, and had fought alongside black mercenaries at least as early as 2000 B.C." (Snowden 1983:5). Throughout most of this period blacks were seen as formidable, keen soldiers who defended their interests, national and personal, and who protected their own territory as expertly and skilfully as any others. Whether as ally or as enemy, they were roundly respected.

Can the views of Snowden be uncritically accepted? After all, he is the same person who defends as non-racist those classical authors who showed a decisive preference for northern or "white" beauties over their southern or "dark" counterparts. As part of that defence he offers an intellectually feeble comment: "It is questionable whether individuals should be called racist because they accept the aesthetic canons prevailing in their country" (Snowden 1983:63). He also chides modern scholars for seeing "color prejudice where none existed" in the paintings, sculptures, and engravings of the period (p.64). Among those he singles out are: C.T. Seltman (1920:14), who challenges the unquestioned portrayal of the Negro as ugly in works of art; Arthur Lane (1971:55), who rejects the depiction of the Negro as grotesque; and D. von Bothmer (1963:161), who opposes the image of black people in classical art as purely comical caricatures.

For Snowden, any focus on ugliness and comic distortion is largely the product of projection on the part of modern commentators--a product of the mind of the beholder. On this score he continues to support an assertion he made in an earlier work that extended into the Greco-Roman period: "There is nothing in the evidence to suggest that the ancient Greek or Roman established color as an obstacle to integration into society" (Snowden 1970:217-18). But because he did not find any evidence, this does not mean that none existed. Indeed, it may well be the case that, for whatever reasons, Snowden is the one engaged in projection. But this still does not exempt him from the responsibility of dealing with Aristotle's well-known justification of slavery on the basis of the innate differences and capacities of individuals. To argue that the justification was cultural and not racial (Snowden 1970:170) hardly clarifies the issue. In fact it only begs the question and leaves unresolved the problem of the relationship between "race" and "culture" and the actual definition of the vexing concept of race.

John Block Friedman (1981) presents a somewhat different view. He surveys the period from antiquity through the Middle Ages with a view to identifying both the existence of "race" prejudice and its origins. For Friedman the search is centred on medieval art and thought, and it concerns what were called the "monstrous races." Beginning with the writings of Homer as early as the ninth century B.C. and moving through the work of Virgil in the last century B.C., as well as the travel reports of men such as Alexander the Great, Pliny the Elder, Ctesias, and Megasthenes, Friedman finds a virtual obsession with the strange or *monstrous* races that were supposed to live on the margins of the Greco-Roman world. For like other tightly knit cultures, the Hellenes were xenophobic, fearful, and suspicious of outsiders, whom they tended to view as inferior and untrustworthy barbarians.

The Ethiopians were the first to be so viewed. Derived from the Greek word *Aethiops*, meaning "burnt-faced," the Ethiopians of earliest times were seen not only to be different, but also to be inferior, savage, and lacking in morals. Indeed, this image was so powerful that even the famous Father Bartolomé de las Casas, who was sent to the West Indies to protect the native "Indians" from extermination at the hands of the Spanish *conquistadores*, could have held the view that among the African slaves were some "as black as Ethiopians, so malformed in their faces and bodies that they appeared to those who looked at them to be the image of another and lower hemisphere" (quoted in Wagner 1967:247). It is not difficult, then, to understand why Friedman can argue that "color polarities were easily interchanged with moral polarities" and in time being black came to signify inferiority and immorality just as being white implied salvation (1981:26, 64–65). Friedman documents how the homiletic writers of the period associated blackness with sin, vice, and the Devil. Blackness was the punishment meted out to them by God. In the Dutch Calvinist version of Christianity, which would provide the religious justification for apartheid in South Africa, the association was unmistakable: "Since Calvinism came to see the slave as a sinner, slavery was thought to be an appropriate social condition for this inferior race. The Dutch Calvinist clergy came eventually to describe a slave as dirty, black, lazy and polluted" (Turner 1986:81).

This was the message of church men such as Paulinus of Nola and Fulgentius of Ruspe. Fulgentius saw the Ethiopian as "one not yet whitened by the grace of Christ shining upon him." Then there was Theodulus's definition of the word *Ethyopum*: "Ethiopians, that is sinners. Indeed sinners can be rightly compared to Ethiopians who are black men presenting a terrifying appearance to those beholding them" (quoted in Friedman 1981:65). Even Snowden (1970:217), in his apology for the racism that was rife in classical antiquity, notes the generally accepted view at the time that held that later "Christ came into the world to make blacks white."

During this early period, given the general state of ignorance and confusion that abounded in the areas of geography, biology, and science, the popular imagination was filled with ideas of monstrous peoples who lived on the periphery of the then-known world. Together with Amazons, Cyclopes, Androgini, Cynocephali, Blemmyae, and others, black people came to be viewed as just one among scores of hairy, tall or short, ugly, speechless, and savage peoples, actual and imagined, who composed the monstrous races of antiquity. Because their pigmentation, hair texture, and facial features differed radically from the European norm, they were seen as deviating from the natural order of things or as going against nature, and throughout the Middle Ages they were generally regarded with the fear, suspicion, and intolerance born of ignorance. Black people became anomalies, prodigies, and portents from God. As Robert Miles indicates, it was a time when "natural events considered to be indicators of God's intentions towards human beings were defined as *portenta* or *monstra*" (1989:16).

Although these terms were used synonymously at times, *portenta* retained its meaning of "warning" and *monstra* its meaning of "demonstration" or "revelation." But over time the term *monstra* came to be used by Greek travellers in reference not only to the "anomalous" Indian and African races, but also to all peoples and cultures appearing in any way different from the Western norm. The term became linked or equated with the idea of "monster." Throughout the ages its different uses and meanings were consistent: they all seemed to carry negative connotations that were usually meant to indicate a warning from God that all was not well. In this context the influential writer Isidore of Seville, who made the first leap from individual monstrous births (for example, Siamese twins or children born with physical deformities) to entire monstrous races, is a case in point. Arguing that such anomalous births signified a message from God, he asserted: "Just as among individual races there are certain members who are monsters, so also among mankind as a whole, certain races are monsters" (quoted in Friedman 1981:116).

Given the rampant xenophobia that attended the encounters between different peoples at the time, it was not long before those in the majority in the world of European "civilization" came to develop rationalizations, scientific and theological, for what they saw and experienced in the relations with "others." As we know, the "scientific" explanation for "blackness" was the environmental theory that had certain peoples living too close to the sun and as a consequence developing their unique burnt colour, their "unusual" hair, and a whole host of supposedly abnormal physical and facial features. In all of this, however, the important point is that the skin pigmentation and deviant (in the statistical sense) physical appearances of black peoples set them apart from the norm in Greco-Roman society and automatically cast them in a negative light. Coupled with their physical appearances and their unfamiliar social conventions and cultural practices--especially their preference for wearing little or no clothing--black people became thought of as not only savage but also cannibalistic, immoral, and, like animals, sexually uninhibited (Jordan 1968:4; Sanders 1978:211-25; White 1972:21-22; Stevenson 1992:27-45).

The Ideological Context

On the ideological level it is possible to understand such representations of blacks in two ways. The first concerns the dominant image of blacks in the minds of the European travellers, who, according to Philip Curtin, were imbued with a very deep sense of curiosity about the exotic lives of non-Europeans. Continuing into the modern period of European colonization of the New World, much of this curiosity was sexually voyeuristic, concentrating on "a libidinous fascination for descriptions of other people who break with impunity the taboos of one's own society" (Curtin 1964:24).

In the case of the Africans, this attitude accounts for the numerous references to their nakedness, the size of their genitalia, their frequency of sexual intercourse, and even their supposed mating with apes (Jordan 1968:151-59; Fryer 1984:138-40, 159). As a result a great deal of the travellers' reports concerning the peoples they encountered emphasized the social and cultural practices that were most different and outrageous in comparison to their own societies and cultures, while tending to ignore the similarities that would have suggested a common human link between Europeans and Africans: "The reporting often stressed precisely those aspects of African life that were most repellent to the West and tended to submerge the indications of a common humanity" (Curtin 1964:23).

The second ideological context in which the European mentality was formed relates to the politico-religious opposition between Islam and Christianity. For Europeans, knowledge of the wider world beyond Europe was almost entirely restricted to the Islamic world as represented by the Middle East, North Africa, and India. For centuries prior to the colonization of the New World, Europeans, particularly the Iberians, had come into contact and conflict with the Moslems (Moors), who had occupied parts of the Iberian peninsula for some seven hundred years. The vast majority of the Moslems were seen to be Arabs, and the strength of Islamic belief among the darker-skinned Arabs, coupled with the occupation of the Iberian peninsula, made Europeans both fearful and resentful of the Arab peoples. Given as well the significant economic might of the mercantile and commercial interests of the Islamic countries, their counterparts in Christian Europe saw fit to employ whatever means they could find, ideological and military, to combat these people.

Because it is customary for the enemy to be portrayed in as negative a light as possible, Muhammad, the prophet of Islam, and indeed the entire religion were depicted by the Christian Europeans "as barbaric, degenerate and tyrannical," given to violence, polygamy, sodomy, and general sexual promiscuity (Miles 1989:18). As a consequence, the leading European economic interests used the pretext of defending Christianity to launch the so-called Crusades or Holy Wars against the Islamic infidels (Saracens), and during the eleventh and twelfth centuries those wars were "justified theologically in the name of the Christian God" (Miles 1989:19). Hence, what was at root an economic conflict became cast as a battle between rival religions and "races." N. Daniel states: "In a period when Europe was in a mood of aggression and expansion, its surplus energy created an attitude to its Arab and Arabic-speaking neighbours which was based, not on what the Arabs were like, but on what, for theological reasons, they ought to be like" (1975:248).

Race, Colour, and Christianity

Unlike the supporters of scientific and environmental explanations of human physical differences, Christians were committed to the notion of monogenesis and a common human origin. This belief is related to the question of "creationism," according to which all human beings are created by God and descended from Adam and Eve: we are all God's children. The creationist doctrine, nevertheless, encountered a special difficulty when it came to accounting for the infinite variety of the human species. In other words, if all humans have common ancestors, whence arose the physical, phenotypical, pigmentational, and other differences that characterize the species?

Uncomfortable with standard scientific explanations, many of which challenged and controverted biblical claims, Christians had to look elsewhere for answers to the questions relating to the different races and colours of human beings. Like the Greeks and Romans before them, a great deal of myth and fantasy attended their responses. Thus, for example, we have the stories of Cain and Abel, the sons of Adam and Eve, and of Noah and his son Ham. Both Cain and Ham were guilty of misdeeds and disobedience, and their punishment from God included exile from the kingdom of God. Consequently Cain, we are told, was often seen in early Christian commentary as the parent of the monstrous races; and it was common to believe that the monstrous races inherited Cain's curse and all the torments associated with exile from the kingdom of God.

What is important here is not the exact nature of the term "curse" as reported in the Bible; but rather the *interpretations* of it by Old Testament scholars and Christians alike. One of the popular explanations concerns the question of equating punishment, evil, and sin with negritude. Thus we are told that God placed a mark (or horns, as some interpretations have it) on Cain and his progeny so that they would be easily recognized as troublemakers, wrongdoers, and receivers of God's wrath. For many that mark or curse was a black skin (Bastide 1968:36). Saint Simon, for example, states: "Know that Europeans are the sons of Abel. Know that Asia and Africa are inhabited by the descendants of Cain. See how bloodthirsty Africans are. Note the indolence of Asiatics" (quoted in Manuel 1956:408).

In the case of Ham the association between blackness, evil, and punishment is more explicit. *Genesis* 9:21 tells the story of a drunken Noah (one of his jobs was to tend a vineyard) who fell asleep naked and was seen in that state by Ham. Instead of covering up his father as any dutiful and loyal son would have done, Ham--who had been chastised by his father for sexual incontinence on the Ark--called his brothers to witness the sight and proceeded to mock Noah. Japheth and Shem, however, refused to countenance their brother's behaviour and, without looking, covered their father's naked body. Once awakened, Noah realized what had happened and again chastised Ham and called down God's curse on him.

According to several popular biblical interpretations (Utley 1941:243) the curse, which was to extend to all Ham's descendants, was that they be forever (a) black and (b) servants (and eventually slaves) of his brothers' children. Thus Friedman quotes an eleventh-century traveller who presents us with a vivid portrait of Ham's son Canaan "as having black skin, red eyes, a deformed body, and horns on his forehead" (1981:101).

The key point--and one that must be strongly emphasized--relates to W.I. and Dorothy Thomas's oft-repeated statement to the effect that "if men define the situations as real they are real in their consequences" (Thomas and Thomas 1928:572).

In other words, the crucial issue is not so much the actual punishment meted out by God to Cain and Ham, but rather the fact that later Christians came to understand that punishment in a specific way and *acted on the basis of that understanding*. This is similar to Max Weber's discussion of the Calvinist belief in predestination, which, even if it were not true, was nevertheless accepted as true by the believers and came to have a direct impact on the conduct of their daily lives. In the same way that some non-Calvinists also came to share the belief in the doctrine of predestination, so too non-Christians came in time to associate the idea of blackness with wrongdoing and the more sinister aspects of human existence and life in general.

In numerous later interpretations of *Genesis*, Ham's link with evil and sin was routine and unquestioned, and it also became frequently used as a moral justification for the enslavement of black people (Friedman 1981:101-2). This reading of the literature, then, is at odds with the interpretation of Frank Snowden Jr. (1970 and 1983), who, while acknowledging the existence of black demons, and the association of black with death and ill omens, nevertheless insists on the existence of a generally favourable view of black people in antiquity. He is also adamant about the fact that "the early Christians did not alter the classical color symbolism or the teachings of the church to fit a preconceived notion of blacks as inferior.... In the early church blacks found equality in both theory and practice" (Snowden 1983:107-8). Nowhere, however, does Snowden deal with the existing interpretations related to Cain and Ham or with the entire question of "monstrousness" as treated by J.B. Friedman.

Race, Christianity, and Colonialism

The writer Roger Bastide provides a more recent insight into the symbolic dimension of race and colour in the context of Christianity. Bastide seems to favour the view that Christianity as a doctrine or body of thought is replete with examples of racial stratification and colour prejudice. "Christianity," he states, "has been accompanied by a symbolism of color. This symbolism has formed and cultivated a sensitivity to color that extends even to people who claim to be detached from religion" (Bastide 1968:35).

Bastide is therefore in essential accord with Weber and the argument holding that an ideology, once having taken root in a concrete context, can develop a life of its own and spread to encompass different individuals and groups in different situations far removed from the ideology's original context. He states: "It is not surprising, then, that a symbolism of color associations could survive the disappearance of its mystical Christian roots" (p.48). The color symbolism of the Old Testament has thus permeated the consciousness even of non-Christians down through the years and has come to be applied very generally in social contexts that have nothing to do with God and religion.

This is the sense in which we can understand the close relationship between slavery and racism in the Americas. In their desire to justify the enslavement of African blacks in the New World, Catholic monarchs, the church, and all manner of Christian (Catholic and Protestant) slave-owning planters relied heavily on the claim that blacks were evil, cursed by God, and fully deserving of punishment (enslavement) for their reported sins and misdeeds in biblical times. In this vein the historian Manuel Moreno Fraginals, commenting on the situation in Cuba between the years 1760 and 1860, observes that the local church there had built up an elaborate body of "doctrine justifying slavery. It was based on the belief that the chief reason for bringing the black savage from Africa was to redeem him by work and teach him the road to Christian salvation" (Moreno Fraginals 1976:53). In other words, if the African were ever to become civilized, slavery was a necessary penance.

The church, therefore, which participated in and sanctioned the institution of slavery, was warmly embraced by certain fractions of the slave-owning plantocracy; and given the practical necessity of maintaining social order and control within their enterprises, the slave-owners in turn found a ready-made ally in the church. Both groups invoked the medieval, Christian notion that man will earn his bread only by the sweat of his brow, and they applied this belief generously to the slaves. In this way the consciences of both planter and priest could be soothed by regarding the entire socioeconomic complex of sugar and slavery almost as a redemptive undertaking, while the slave trade itself could be recast as an unselfish, missionary activity. Bryan Turner points out a curious contradiction here: "Christians saw that they had a mission towards the slaves to convert their souls but this left the institution of slavery unquestioned" (1986:81).

The vital importance of the two related economic activities of slavery and slave trading is to be found in the flow of tremendous amounts of wealth in the form of mineral and plantation products from the colonies back to the mother countries. This facilitated the consolidation of "ownership," further colonization, and settlement of individual countries at a time when European competition for the building of rival colonial empires was most intense. It also afforded an independent source of royal income through taxation as slave traders were required to pay taxes (often in gold) on each individual slave landed in the colonies (Allahar 1990:18).

Thus, although Christianity did not *cause* racism against blacks, it did provide a unique ideological justification for black enslavement. Through its unmistakable colour symbolisms, Christian teachings (both Catholic and Protestant) aided greatly in the establishment of the secular institution of African slavery and gave a spiritual impetus to anyone benefiting from the odious trade in human flesh. According to those symbolisms, white expresses the idea of purity and innocence as associated with the Virgin Mary, while "black" represents the devil and his agents. The ideological implications are evident; and their consequences for black people did not disappear when slavery ended. For the symbolisms of colour and race have remained with Christianity to the present, manifesting themselves in both the sacred and secular domains.

The figure of Christ himself, for instance, is supposed to transcend all colours and races. But in the contemporary Western imagination, in paintings and sculptures, Christ has been conventionally portrayed as a person with white or European features. His Jewish origins are now difficult to detect phenotypically, because of "the deliberate whitening or bleaching effort that changed Christ from a Semitic to an Aryan person" (Bastide 1968:37). As novelist Harold Ladoo puts it, Jesus may have been King of the Jews, but "he was a Jew in the English fashion: blonde hair, blue eyes, red beard and a pink face" (1974:39).

Owing to the firmly established colour symbolisms, this metamorphosis of Christ from Semite to Aryan had become quite necessary. As the incarnation of God on earth Jesus had to be distanced, as far as possible, "from everything that could suggest darkness or blackness, even indirectly" (Bastide 1968:37). Ironically, it seems that the old Judeo-Christian belief that God made man in his own image and likeness was reversed: man (white man) had now remade God in *his* own image and likeness. Once performed, this act of spiritual hygiene ramified throughout Western society and served to promote a virulent form of discrimination based on race and legitimized by religious doctrine.

Gender and Colonialism: The Woman of Colour

Discussions of colonialism and racism have most often focused their attention on men: white masters and black male slaves. But the colonial enterprise embraced a great deal more than an intramale dialectic, for from its very inception miscegenation or race mixing (which necessitates the involvement of women) was as much a part of the process as were slavery, violence, and plunder.

At the outset the primary ethnic elements were clearly distinct from each other: Iberians, Native Indians, and Africans. It was not long, however, before sexual pairings among these three groups served to produce entirely new ethnoracial categories of people. The general pattern involved the white male, from his position of dominance, taking the initiative vis-à-vis the Indian and African women; and the results of their liaisons were *mestizo* (white-Indian) and *mulatto* (white-African) offspring. A third combination known as the *zambo* in Spanish America (or *cafuso* in Brazil) resulted from the union of Africans and Indians. Further complexities arose as well when, for example, a *zambo* and a *mulatto* would have a child--*calpanmulato*; or a Spaniard and a *mulatto--morisco*; and so on.

As Angel Rosenblat (1954:168-79) indicates, the possibilities were infinite, and the designations of the offspring from such unions were as imaginative as they were funny. Thus we are told that the child of a *calpanmulato* and a *zambo* was known as a *"tente en el aire"* (hold yourself high), implying pride in some degree of blood purity, while the child of a *tente en el aire* and a *mulatto* was known as a *"no te entiendo"* (I don't understand your origins). Similarly, if a *morisco* mated with a *mulatto* the issue was called a *"salto atras"* (a jump backwards) owing to the implied darkening of the skin that resulted from such a pairing.

For our discussion, the most relevant of these interracial relationships is the union of the white male and the Indian or African female within the general context of Christianity and its colour symbolisms. What is of particular interest is how the church, both Catholic and Protestant, regarded the unmistakable and key role that the brown Native-Indian and the black African woman were coming to play in the shaping of the emerging New World society. For in time the white colonists accepted and applied the

Christian view not only to the Indian and the African, but also to all women of colour, who became thought of as evil temptresses leading men astray.

Given that men conceived and executed the colonial undertaking, it is no great surprise that women, especially white women, played such a relatively minor role in the entire enterprise. Certainly in the first century or so of the colonization of the New World, whether as wives, mistresses, or servants, white women were largely absent, and white men freely sought the companionship of those women who were available. Once begun, the practice occasioned numerous myths concerning the unbridled sexual passion, sheer capacity for orgasm, and very morality of these women. Speaking of colonial Brazil, for instance, Simon Collier observes that the "dark-skinned woman seemed to have enjoyed an excellent reputation as a source of erotic satisfactions" (1974:149), while Bastide reports: "The black woman will make love at any time, and with anyone.... Making love to a coloured woman does not mean anything, will have no consequences, for 'the blacks don't marry, they just pair off'" (1961:11-12).

It was not long before greatly embellished stories began to make their way back to Europe, and as early as 1512 Ferdinand, the king of Spain, ordered the authorities at the Casa de Contratación to make provision for sending white Christian females to the colonies to temper the miscegenative practices of the Spanish colonizers (Hoetink 1973:59). It would seem, therefore, that the Spanish crown was concerned with the questions of race and religion, but less so with civil status. For like the Amerindian and African concubines of the colonists, the white, Christian females sent to the Americas were also slaves.

Although it was obeyed, the king's order did not result in a large-scale migration of white women, slave or free, Christian or non-Christian. In fact, for most of the colonial period, especially the first hundred years, European women were vastly outnumbered by their Amerindian and African counterparts; and as a consequence, during the sixteenth century, the *mestizo* and *mulatto* populations grew at an amazing rate. A statement attributed to one of the *conquistadores* of Chile, Francisco de Aguirre (1508-81), who claimed to have fathered over fifty *mestizo* children, sums up the mentality of the day: "The service rendered to God in engendering *mestizos* is greater than the sin incurred in so doing" (quoted in Ojeda 1929:31).

The religious argument was not the only justification used. By the nineteenth century in Cuba, for example, the planter class was caught in an interesting bind. On the one hand they were concerned about the acute

Race, Gender and Development 183

shortage of labour, and on the other they were cognizant of the risks involved in having the black population grow too large. Thus was born the plan of having white men mate with slave women to increase the numbers of workers and simultaneously "whiten" the population: "The idea was not crossing black men with white women, but white men with black women.... The white woman must not obstruct the island's whitening process by having mulatto children; the black woman, on the other hand, would procreate mulattos [instead of black children] and thereby hasten the process" (Moreno Fraginals 1976:134).

Indeed, the Indian woman held a special enchantment for the Iberian man (Freyre 1964:19), and the African woman had an almost mystical allure (Collier 1974:145). As Gilberto Freyre argues, the principal reason why these women appeared so desirable had to do with the Iberians' long contact with the Saracens (Moslems who had invaded and occupied the Iberian Peninsula), which left in them a sense of romantic adventure involving "the idealized figure of the enchanted Moorish woman, a charming type, brown-skinned, dark-eyed, enveloped in sexual mysticism, roseate in hue" (Freyre 1964:19). Significantly, this attraction was not limited to the lay-colonist, for there were many more than a few priests whose sexual fantasies were fuelled by the innocence and powerlessness of these women and who, while eagerly granting absolution to their fellow compatriots for their sexual promiscuity, were quick to forego their own vows of chastity and were also living in the same manner. In his inimitable style, Freyre tells us that "in place of ascetics austerely concerned with their vows of virginity there flourished formidable stallions in clerical garb," themselves fathering *mestizo* and *mulatto* children. He even relates the case of a Jesuit priest who one day asked his congregation for a "Hail Mary for the Bishop's woman who is in labour" (Freyre 1964:391).

In their New World adventure, the Catholic Spaniard and Portuguese, both priest and layman, were able to free themselves of the restrictions imposed by their socio-religious upbringing on the enjoyment of sexual intercourse. According to that upbringing, sex (which is forbidden to the priest) is cast as being somewhat "unclean" and not really to be enjoyed. It is to be engaged in for the express purpose of procreation--to do the Lord's bidding. However, removed from the religious-cultural baggage of their homelands, where sex and marriage were limited largely to one's own colour and where "a too carnal enjoyment of the wife would have taken on the aspect of a kind of incest, degrading to both the white man and the white woman" (Bastide 1968:40), European males regarded the woman of colour as a legitimate outlet for all that they were taught was sexually perverse, but nonetheless totally desirable and satisfying.

This experience became the source of many of the sexual myths and delights surrounding the woman of colour, whose unbridled sexuality was constantly compared to the white woman's supposed restraint. The sheer voluptuousness of the woman of colour was said to be sexually enticing to men. Her slightest gesture, Bastide tells us, "such as the balanced sway of her body as she walks barefoot, is looked upon as a call of the female sex to the male." At the other extreme, "The white woman is desexualized, if not disincarnated or at least dematerialized" (Bastide 1968:40). Thus a popular jingle in Brazil (quoted in Collier 1974:149) holds that:"*Moça morena é quitute; moça branca é canja fria.*" (A dark girl is a delicious tidbit; a white one like cold chicken soup.)

The sexism directed at women of colour was fundamentally political in that it involved white men's abuse of *power* over the women, and the use of "race" to justify such abuse. The priests (who were doubtless not entirely innocent with regard to the white women in their own societies) especially felt a great deal freer to act with impunity against women of colour because those women were really of no consequence and had no social base they could use as a support in calling the priests to task. It was thus possible for priests to become sexually engaged openly with women of colour, who were by definition less socially empowered than their white, European counterparts.

The discrimination against the woman of colour, therefore, was very much like the discrimination against the Amerindian or the African. It was part of a set of Old World beliefs and attitudes used to buttress a set of New World practices. The Europeans saw themselves as having an inherent capacity and desire for democracy and freedom, while they saw the non-Europeans who lived in the periphery, particularly Africans, as a lower order of human being, not really capable of appreciating "true" freedom. Power, in this case both economic and political, was the driving rationale, and the biological conception of race was confused with its social definition.

Biology and race became independent variables explaining the rate of social advancement and economic progress; and the religious ideology of Christianity was the justification or pretext used to explain away any guilt incurred along the way. In the process, as the historical roots of racism disappeared, racism itself did not. Rather, as a key mechanism of maintaining the availability of cheap labour in the era of modern capitalism, new racist ideas have evolved all the way from Classical Antiquity, utilizing the images of medieval thought and the colour symbolisms of Christianity to inform discriminatory practices right into the modern period. For although races are socially imagined and not biologically real categories, human beings continue to act as if they were real; and as long as they do so, race becomes real in its consequences. The same can also be said about gender and the ideology of sexism, which speaks to the supposed *natural* inferiority of women and serves similarly to undervalue their labour.

Women and Development

Given the nature of exploitation in the capitalist economies of the periphery, as well as the historically structured patterns of social inequality found there, it is clear that a full understanding of contemporary economic and political reality must move beyond the dimensions of class and race. Indeed, the critical analysis of underdevelopment is incomplete without the consideration of one other crucial factor--gender.

Women today find themselves among the poorest of the poor and the most powerless of the powerless in the underdeveloped countries of the periphery: "The place of poor women of color at the bottom of the second tier of the global economy, and their exploitation ... as cheap labor that drives the 'free market' economy of the First World illustrates the inseparability of gender, race and class as a unitary system of oppression" (Lorber 1990:293).

Women do not constitute a homogeneous category, and my focus here will be on the most populous groups: the working poor and the unemployed. Within these groups, the most disadvantaged are single mothers. These are the women who bear a large part of the economic burden facing peripheral countries. They are the frontline victims of what is euphemistically called "structural adjustment"--the harsh terms and conditions imposed by the International Monetary Fund (IMF) on the governments of the Third World as a precondition for receiving credit. Such terms and conditions routinely require the devaluation of the currency of the recipient country, the elimination of food, health, and education subsidies, along with the curtailment of social programs that benefit the poor. They also produce higher unemployment levels, increased costs for such basics as transportation and utilities, and lower real wages. The upshot is a decline in the country's overall standard of living, which generally hits women harder than men, and poor, single mothers the hardest of all.

Related to the structural adjustment policies of the IMF and the hardships they bring are the similar demands and consequences of policies held by the World Bank and the U.S. Agency for International Development (AID), two other sources of so-called "development" funds that plunge peripheral economies even deeper into the debt and dependency trap discussed in chapter five. In all of this, poor women emerge as the net losers, because they have less stable employment, lower wages, and more limited access to resources than men and other women who enjoy more privileged class situations. For even in working-class families that have two parents living at home, the economic crunch usually forces the woman (who already has a full-time job within the home) into the labour force, where she is paid minimum wages or lower, endures substandard working conditions, and must often contend with the sexist insults and attitudes of male co-workers (Berger 1990:415; Safa 1990:356-57).

In a comparative study dealing with Jamaica and the Dominican Republic, Carmen Diana Deere and her co-authors focus on the situation of poor women and conclude, "The impact of the present debt crisis and the structural adjustment policies has been devastating for poor women" (1990:52). They identify three principal areas of trouble: (a) the sharp decline in wages and the concomitant increase in female unemployment; (b) the unequal burden that the rising cost of living thrusts upon women; and (c) the absolute government cutbacks to social welfare programs that poor women rely on so heavily.

Using Jamaican data, these authors point out that whereas women on average have slightly higher education than men and outnumber men in professional, clerical, and sales jobs, in 1985 "average weekly earnings for men stood at J\$86.9, compared to J\$68.3 for women" (p.52). They also show the severity of the crisis, given that 45 per cent of households in Kingston in 1985 were headed by women, and female unemployment stood at 36.6 per cent (over twice the rate for men). In general, in the midst of a deteriorating international economic situation, Jamaica, the largest of the English-speaking countries of the Caribbean, ranks among the least prosperous in its Gross Domestic Product (GDP). Table 7.1 indicates changes in minimum food costs and minimum wages in Jamaica for a six-year period.

Deere and her group note a similar pattern of female disadvantage in the Dominican Republic. There, women's wages in 1980 were 50 to 60 per cent lower than men's, and within poor, urban households headed by women the situation was far worse. The weekly cost of a family food basket more than

Table 7.1
Changes in Minimum Food Costs (Family of Five) and
in Minimum Wage, Jamaica, 1979-85

Period	Cost of Basic Set of Meals (J$)	Weekly Minimum Wage (J$)	Cost as Percentage of Minimum Wage
June 1979	24.27	26.4	91.9
September 1983	65.31	30.0	217.7
December 1983	77.00	30.0	256.7
August 1984	101.46	40.0	276.2
July 1985	128.43	52.0	247.0

Source: Omar Davies and Patricia Anderson, "The Impact of the Recession and Adjustment Policies on Poor Urban Women in Jamaica," paper prepared for UNICEF, 1987, table 10.

Table 7.2
Indicators of the Rising Cost of Living, Dominican Republic, 1980-86
(in Dominican pesos)

	Cost of Family Food Basket	Price Index	Purchasing Power of Dominican Pesos
1980	162.00	1.3652	1.00
1981	156.94	1.4681	0.93
1982	167.44	1.5802	0.86
1983	173.48	1.6897	0.80
1984	212.81	2.1027	0.65
1985	291.75	2.8918	0.47
1986	334.24	3.1735	0.43

Source: Miguel Ceara, "Situación Socioeconómica Actual y su Repercusión en la Situación de la Madre y el Niño," paper prepared for UNICEF (Santo Domingo: INTEC, 1987), table 18.

doubled in 1980-86 (Deere et al. 1990:55-56), and since then the condition of poor women has only grown more dismal. The situation is aggravated by the fact that while minimum-wage legislation is loosely enforced by governmental agencies, most women work at jobs that are not even covered by such legislation. Table 7.2 provides information on the rising cost of living in the Dominican Republic for a seven-year period.

Table 7.3
Women and Employment: Selected Third World Countries

Country	Labour Force as % of Total Pop	Women in Labour Force as % of Total Pop	Percentage of Labour Force in					
			Agriculture		Industry		Services	
	1989-91	1990	1965	1989-91	1965	1989-91	1965	1989-91
Trinidad & Tobago	38	27	20	10	35	41	45	49
Brazil	43	35	49	28	20	25	31	47
Cuba	44	32	33	24	25	29	42	47
Panamá	36	27	46	12	16	21	38	67
Jamaica	45	31	37	25	20	12	43	63
Dominican Republic	30	15	59	46	14	15	27	39
Guyana	36	21	—	27	—	26	—	47
El Salvador	41	45	58	10	16	35	26	55
Nicaragua	35	34	56	46	16	16	28	38
Guatemala	34	26	64	48	15	23	21	29
Zimbabwe	41	35	79	64	8	6	13	30
Haiti	41	40	77	50	7	6	16	44
Rwanda	46	48	95	90	2	4	3	6
Developing Countries	44	33	72	61	11	14	17	25
Industrial Countries	49	42	22	7	36	26	42	67
World	45	34	57	48	19	17	24	35

Source: United Nations, Human Development Report 1993 (New York: Oxford University Press, 1993), pp.168-69.

Women's Economic and Political Responses

Throughout the countries of the periphery, poor women have been increasingly active and innovative in responding to their social and economic plights, with four main patterns of response: (a) a higher number of them are seeking jobs outside of the home, particularly in the manufacturing and export-processing industries (Berger 1990); (b) they have increased their level of participation in the informal economic sector (Lorber 1990:293); (c) they are modifying or scaling down their living and consumption patterns at the household level (Deere et al. 1990:61); and (d) like their male counterparts in earlier decades, they are becoming increasingly visible in the statistics on migration out of the periphery (Nash 1990:350).

As a consequence of the first two developments, women in many peripheral countries have significantly transformed the terms on which they participate in the wider economy and polity. As Judith Lorber (1990:293) observes, women in the periphery do not make a distinction between work for the family and paid labour. For them a "job" can mean anything from the exchange of services for money or for payment in kind, through selling home-made goods, doing domestic labour or child care, to part-time or seasonal employment in a sweatshop, factory, or even on a farm. These are some of the *practical* gender interests around which women have begun to organize themselves. The result is that they are now so incorporated into the public domain that it is no longer possible for them to retreat back into the private domestic sphere or for them to be treated as belonging exclusively or even predominantly to that sector.

In the context of Latin American women, Helen Icken Safa argues that they have become key members of the labour force and that their contributions to household finances are now indispensable. In political matters, Latin American women are at the forefront of social movements for human rights and social welfare, as well as making their presence felt in labour unions and organized political parties: "Women are demanding more 'democracy' in the home as well as in the State" (Safa 1990:366). Or, as Teresa Valdés and Marisa Weinstein (1989) note, these women are seeking to forge a new relationship with the state based not on subordination, control, and dependency, but on rights, autonomy, and equality.

On this score Maxine Molyneux calls for a greater analytical understanding of the points at which gender, ethnicity, and class intersect. In other words, she recognizes the historically structured relations of class, race, and gender domination and acknowledges the contradictions between men and women of all classes and races. "Since 'women's interests' are significantly broader than gender interests, and are shaped to a considerable degree by class factors, women's unity and cohesion on gender issues cannot be assumed.... Such unity has to be constructed; it is never given" (Molyneux 1986:285). Precisely because women have multiple identities, then, there is no logical reason why gender or social position based on gender attributes should be assumed uniformly to override class, ethnic, or other identities that may divide women. Thus, the false homogeneity conveyed by a term such as "women's interests," which presumes a political unity among all women, needs to be replaced by a more careful articulation of *gender interests* (female or male).

Gender interests, in turn, are of two types: strategic and practical. In the case of women, strategic gender interests are feminist interests and speak to the theoretical and philosophical conceptualization of such elements as sexual subordination and inequality, abortion rights, and the right to be free from physical violence and sexual assault. The political struggle involved in these issues requires the development of a "feminist" consciousness and usually implies an alternative, non-capitalist vision of society. Practical gender interests are more concrete and issue-specific. Again, for women, given the place they traditionally occupy in the sexual division of labour, these interests may include, along with the ones listed above, mobilization around the need for child care or school-bus service or, in a rural setting, for the more efficient delivery of water and electricity to homes. This theme is also picked up by Marxist-feminists such as Helen Safa and Norma Chinchilla. Safa, for example, is not content with calls for a feminist revolution pure and simple. She recognizes the historically structured relations of class, race, and gender domination and acknowledges the contradictions between men and women of all classes and races. She endorses the useful distinction between women's *practical* domestic demands around such issues as child care and communal kitchens and their strategic claims to equality and participation in the traditionally male institutions of labour unions and political parties. It is within these institutions that women encounter most opposition from men, even those of their own class and race. The solution, then, "is not simply one of women's incorporation into a male-defined world but of transforming this world to do away with the hierarchies of class, gender, race and ethnicity that have so long subordinated much of the Latin American population, men as well as women" (Safa 1990:367).

For Norma Chinchilla (1990), who addresses the question of women's empowerment within a socialist or revolutionary context, there is no doubt that the general condition of women and their future prospects for greater recognition and integration into the wider society are considerably improved under socialism. She cautions, however, that socialism alone is not sufficient. Based on an analysis of women in the Nicaraguan and Cuban revolutions, she calls for (a) the admission on the part of revolutionary leaders that sexism is a serious problem and (b) the continuation of the political education and empowerment of women both within and outside the revolutionary party. Linking the arguments of Safa and Chinchilla, Edna Acosta-Belén and Christine E. Bose (1990:314) state that the organization of women around "practical" gender issues must be transformed into organization around "strategic" gender interests that are "articulated with class, race, ethnicity, and national identity issues and challenge women's subordination."

In this way the traditional and current divisions within working-class liberation movements could be addressed, which would serve to strengthen the forces of all those who suffer class, race, and gender oppression. For in the minds of these writers, if race was the principal mechanism of exploitation in the colonial era, in the contemporary neocolonial period "it is women's unpaid or underpaid labour that is at the core of new development programmes and policies" (Acosta-Belén and Bose 1990:300). Viewed, therefore, as "the last colony" (Mies, Bennholdt-Thomsen, and Werlhof 1988) of capitalist and imperialist exploitation, women, especially the poor and the working poor in the periphery, cannot be left out of any analysis of economic development today, or out of any proposals for meaningful and progressive political change in the future.

Socialism and Feminism: Some Reflections on Cuba
In the same way that theorists can identify a "worker's state" or a "capitalist state" based on the principal *interests* that are legally served and protected, so too feminists have invoked the question of *women's interests* to determine whether or not a given state can be characterized as patriarchal. Such an approach is particularly important when considering socialist states and how women have fared within them. Thus, when comparing the general situation of women before and after a socialist revolution, Maxine Molyneux

concludes that under socialism "women could be considered to be worse off than they were before the revolution" (1986:280). Commenting on all actually existing socialist countries in 1985, and especially Cuba, one feminist writer notes, "The Cuban experience with relation to women is problematic" (Bengelsdorf 1985:41).

Among other things, such writers point to the fact that far from standing still or being lightened, women's workloads actually increase, as they have done in Cuba, to encompass domestic and childrearing responsibilities, full-time wage work, compulsory study, military duty, and political activism. In addition, these writers argue that women in socialist states do not enjoy domestic sexual equality with men, nor do they have parity with men in governmental bodies, let alone economic emancipation. On this basis Molyneux declared her liberal, non-Marxist orientation and stated categorically that "women's interests are not served by socialist revolutions" (1986:281) given the essential patriarchal structure of the new administrations. What she fails to grasp is the essential difference between the sacrifices, albeit greater, that women (and men) make under socialism and the work they do under capitalism. In the case of a socialist state they are working towards the enhancement of their own country, destiny, and dignity, whereas under capitalism the fruits of their labour enrich others, perpetuate their fragmentation and alienation, and deny their personal dignity.

The inability of many North American and European feminists to grasp the practical problems of constructing socialism given the hostile economic and political context of global capitalism is worth noting. Loaded down by their own societal and cultural baggage, North Americans and Europeans are known to travel to non-North American and non-European countries, and in the case of Cuba, a non-capitalist country, and seek to impose bourgeois political concerns and concepts onto those countries. Very often those political concerns are shared only by a very restricted group within their own home societies. Feminism is a case in point. It is no great revelation that the principal beneficiaries of the North American and Western European feminist movements have been white, middle-class women, who are usually attached to powerful, white, middle-class men in their own countries. In the less advanced countries such as Cuba, however, women do not make a distinction between work for the family and paid labour.

It is in this sense that Vilma Espín, the president of the Federation of Cuban Women (FMC), is often heard to say about Cuban women: "We are feminine, not feminist" (Bengelsdorf 1985:36; Casal 1980:200). But "feminine" here is not used, as Elizabeth Sutherland suggests, to mean home-oriented, passive, needing to be guided and protected" (Sutherland 1969:181). Rather, Margaret Randall said it best when she observed that "the Cuban woman today drives a tractor, hoes a field, and carries an AK-47" (Randall 1974:23).

The point, then, is that these women do unpaid labour in the home, paid labour outside the home, contribute voluntary labour in the community, study part-time, and participate in the militia primarily to serve their country, rather than to serve their own narrow, individual interests as women. For the Cuban woman is under no illusions that her own liberation can be separated from her country's. As class phenomena, underdevelopment and imperialism are far greater threats to her than sexism in Cuban men. Thus, after acknowledging that gender contradictions do persist in certain areas, the FMC president quickly adds: "Fidel has always been a dedicated defender of the policy of women's equality.... The Party systematically struggles to advance in this area. So the battle for equality is not just for women, but for the whole society, which must overcome, step-by-step, its own objective and subjective limitations" (Espín 1990:22).

From the perspective of North American and Western European feminists, it is sometimes difficult to see the difference between their feminism, which speaks to their individual liberation, and the women's movement in Cuba, which is first and foremost in the service of socialism. Thus, when Carolee Bengelsdorf (1985:41) observes that one of the problems of socialist theory is that it has failed to take account of women, it may equally be argued that feminist theory, born as it is of the contradictions of capitalist society, has failed to take account of socialism and the conditions under which socialist states are forced to struggle for their survival. The conditions that gave rise to feminist politics in the advanced, industrial, Western societies are peculiar to those societies, and contain their contradictions. This is why the feminist movement there continues to reflect the entrenched classism and racism of the larger society (Hooks 1988; Hill-Collins 1990). The issues identified are those close to the hearts of white, middle-class women, and to the extent that the movement has had some success, the benefits have accrued precisely to those women.

The women's movement in Cuba has a totally different point of departure. It has governmental sanction and works with various state agencies to develop and implement policy. On this basis it has access to state funds and other resources to be used in the promotion of its agenda, and it also has the security of knowing that the government "has swept from the books most laws based on differential treatment of the sexes" (Lewis, Lewis, and Rigdon 1977:xii). As a consequence, the average Cuban woman today is very different from the traditional model of the domesticated, dependent, subservient, apolitical Latin woman. She instead boasts an image of a militant, independent, politicized, and community-minded activist (Lewis, Lewis, and Rigdon 1977:xiii), who is "not about to huddle in a corner begging for compassion" (Espín 1990:46).

In talking about socialism, feminism, and women, the central questions become, as Norma Chinchilla (1979:142) asks, how can women "be mobilized on behalf of or as part of the working class?" How can they "be mobilized on behalf of their own liberation in ways that also advance the movement for socialism?" From the perspectives of liberal and radical or separatist feminists, these are non-questions. Liberal feminists are reform-minded as far as the economic and political system is concerned--they are neither working class nor in favour of socialism; while radical or separatist feminists, who view men and patriarchy as the main problem, are also opposed to working-class politics and socialism given the prominent roles played by men in both. But from the perspective of the socialist woman in a country such as Cuba: "The problem of the liberation of women is a class problem and we can't speak of women's liberation as long as the oppressed classes do not free themselves from the exploitation of the oppressing classes" (Espín in Hahner 1976:168).

Vilma Espín is here echoing the Marxist concerns of writers such as Helen Safa and Norma Chinchilla. For criticizing the liberal and radical feminists, Chinchilla argues that they are unable to comprehend the liberation of women in the context of the liberation of the entire society, "nor do they see that the conditions for liberation can only be created in the process of fighting for socialism" (1979:142). Stated differently, the establishment of socialist society is the prerequisite for the liberation of women. But such liberation is neither automatic nor guaranteed. It is part of a continuous process of struggle and depends on the empirical reality facing each given socialist society. To the extent that the strategic and practical gender interests of women (and men) are not intrinsically inimical to socialism, the liberation of women is properly tied, in the first instance, to the more broad-based struggle for socialism; for in practical terms the socialist movement seeks to unite class, sex, gender, race, and ethnic groupings against the divisive forces of capitalism, imperialism, and patriarchy.

Reflections and Conclusions

Clearly, there has been a great richness and diversity throughout the sociological debates on social change and development in the periphery. Covering various theoretical perspectives from the macrostructural to the microinterpretive, the participants in these debates, whether conceived of as individual writers or as whole schools of thought, reflect a range of conflicting and complementary approaches to understanding society. The fact that sociologists may not always be in total agreement on the sources, causes, and directions of change must not, however, be taken as a sign of weakness. For within any discipline controversy and argumentation over ontological and epistemological differences are bound to arise, and these will always tend to serve as guarantees against intellectual stagnation and dogmatism. Through the clash of ideas, scientific knowledge is strengthened.

But ideas are neither arbitrary nor neutral. When formulated as theories and hypotheses, ideas assume an active role in shaping reality or our perceptions of it. This is the sense in which we speak of the *ideological* content of various theories. Given the fact that theorists often act as economic planners, advisors to governments, and business consultants, it is crucial that we clearly understand the ideological assumptions guiding their recommendations.

Taken as a system of beliefs and ideas that reflects the interests of specific groups and classes, ideologies seek to simplify social reality. In doing so they present distorted and incomplete images of that reality by masking some aspects of it while magnifying others. Depending on the ideology in question and the particular group or class that promotes it, we can expect to find a clear relation between the interests of that group or class and the ideas being advanced.

These general observations hold true for the three main theories of socioeconomic change: social-evolutionary, modernization, and dependency. Evolutionary thinking counsels an ideologically conservative response to the challenge of development. According to this school, just as humans could not intervene to alter the speed and course of their own biological evolution, so too are they powerless to affect the process of societal evolution. In other words, because evolutionary change is above human agency, because attempts to control it are futile, it should just be accepted as a fact of life.

For somewhat different reasons the main thrust of modernization theory can also be seen as ideologically conservative. Though differing from

196   Sociology and the Periphery

evolutionary thinkers insofar as they recognize the efficacy of human action, modernization theorists fail to appreciate the class and political biases of their prescriptions. By arguing that underdevelopment in the periphery is the product of defective psychological, attitudinal, and value structures, and that development will result when modern behavioural traits, scientific practices, and technology are diffused to the periphery, these thinkers actively mask the full picture. They pay little or no attention to history and consequently ignore the roles played by colonialism and imperialism in promoting underdevelopment.

In this way both evolutionary and modernization theorists provide ready-made defences for the classes that benefited most from colonialist and imperialist exploits. The concepts these theorists develop and employ in the construction of their arguments are such that underdevelopment comes to be viewed as "nobody's fault." According to the evolutionists it is a more or less natural state; and for the modernizationists the "blame," to the extent that there is blame, must be assigned to the victims. The very inhabitants of the underdeveloped countries are themselves responsible for their backwardness, and if they wish to escape, they should change their values, attitudes, and psychological make-up. They should become more like those in the advanced countries.

The dependency theorists, also, are no less ideological in their prescriptions. They are, however, more critical of the status quo and more radical than their evolutionary and modernization counterparts. They note that in a number of peripheral countries the problems of dependency and underdevelopment seem to be attenuated when their dependent links with the advanced countries are reduced. During the Great Depression and World War II, for example, when the ties of economic dependency were relaxed or entirely undone, the countries of the periphery registered significant levels of indigenous growth. Finding themselves cut off from such things as foreign consumer goods and imported technology, various producing, manufacturing, and commercial classes in the periphery began to look inwardly and to develop their own resources and local business operations, creating jobs and expanding the domestic markets.

Dependency theorists point to this process, known generally as import-substitution industrialization, as proof that the periphery can become developed independently of the metropolitan countries. In fact they go so far as to argue that balanced industrial development will occur only if countries of the periphery sever their ties of dependency and exploitation with the metropole. Thus, at the ideological level, dependency theorists are united in their opposition to metropolitan capitalism, though it is not clear that they are all opposed to capitalism per se. Some, for example, see the transition to socialism as a solution to the problems of dependency and underdevelopment; but others, particularly the earlier members of this school, advocate a form of local or home-grown capitalism for the countries of the periphery. This followed from their emphasis on the external causes of underdevelopment and their almost total neglect of the internal class dynamics within specific countries.

Among those who favour a move to socialism there is a tendency to adopt a Marxist or neo-Marxist understanding of social change and development. This tendency emphasizes class analysis and employs the "mode of production" approach, and it manages to give a clearer political and ideological focus to dependency thinking. Members of this school of neo-Marxist dependency writers identify with the basic thrust and sentiments of the early dependency thinkers, but go further and openly call for a class revolution against capitalism, both foreign and domestic.

Within the countries of the periphery, the question of social and political revolution is enormously complex. The generally low level of development of the productive forces, the preponderance of peasant and rural-proletarian classes, the greater agricultural as opposed to industrial base of their economies, and the insecurities that result when traditional social arrangements are undermined by multinational corporations penetrating the countryside: these factors all combine to make the agrarian sectors crucial for any consideration of social transformation or revolution. This means that orthodox Marxist expectations concerning the revolutionary role of the industrial proletariat in the advanced countries must be seriously rethought in the case of the periphery. For given the major qualitative and quantitative changes that have taken place over the hundred years or so since Marx's death, it is totally unreasonable to expect that his analyses and insights are still as accurate in the era of late capitalism as they were in the early era.

The foregoing notwithstanding, Marx's *method* and the tradition of neo-Marxist scholarship that it has inspired have proved fruitful for analysing the related problems of dependence, underdevelopment, and revolution in the periphery. The careful use of historical evidence and the dissection of the logic of capitalist accumulation combine to give this perspective a clear advantage over the evolutionary and modernization explanations of change and development. This is not to say that these other approaches have nothing to offer. For, as we know, the positivistic assumptions and empiricist methods of the early evolutionary thinkers figured prominently in the development of Marx's thought and continue to exert an influence on much current Marxist-oriented research. The same can also be said of the interactionist tradition, which provides much of the theoretical foundation for the modernization school. Emphasizing the voluntaristic aspects of social action and the fact that individuals and groups are capable of interpreting social and cultural symbols and assigning meaning to them, this school adopts a firm social-psychological perspective. Although the Marxists do not share the same assumptions or agree with the conclusions of modernization theorists, they nevertheless acknowledge the importance of values, attitudes, and beliefs in either promoting or retarding change and development.

Above all else, this great clash of ideas has served to further our scientific knowledge and understanding of society. And in this respect theory plays a crucial role. The various theories and ideas addressing questions of development and underdevelopment in the periphery must be seen as contributing to a continuing process: building on criticism, modifying assumptions, borrowing concepts, refuting beliefs--and on and on. That process, we trust, is never-ending.

Bibliography

Abercrombie, Nicholas, Stephen Hill, and Bryan S. Turner. 1980. The Dominant
Ideology Thesis. London: George Allen and Unwin.

Acosta-Belén, Edna and Christine E. Bose. 1990. "From Structural Subordination to
Empowerment: Women and Development in Third World Contexts." Gender and
Society, Vol.4, No.3.

Aguilar, Luis. 1972 Cuba, 1933 London: Cornell University Press.

Alavi, Hamza. 1963 "U.S. Aid to Pakistan." Economic and Political Weekly, special
number, July.

———. 1973. "Peasants and Revolution." In Imperialism and Revolution in South Asia,
ed. K. Gough and H. Sharma. New York: Monthly Review Press.

———. 1973. "Peasant Classes and Primordial Loyalties." Journal of Peasant Studies,
Vol.1, No.1.

———. 1975. "India and the Colonial Mode of Production." In The Socialist Register.
London.

Allahar, Anton L. 1986. "Historical Patterns of Change and Development." In The
Social World, ed. Lorne Tepperman and R.J. Richardson. Toronto: McGraw-Hill
Ryerson.

Allahar, Anton. 1986. "Ideology, Social Order and Social Change." In The Social
World, ed. Lorne Tepperman and R.J. Richardson. Toronto: McGraw-Hill Ryerson.

———. 1990. Class, Politics, and Sugar in Colonial Cuba. New York: Edwin Mellen
Press.

———. 1982. "Colonialism and Underdevelopment." Two-Thirds: A Journal of
Underdevelopment Studies, Vol.3, No.2.

Amin, Samir. 1974. Accumulation on a World Scale. New York: Monthly Review
Press.

Aron, Raymond. 1965. Main Currents in Sociological Thought. Vol.1. London: Penguin
Books.

Ashley, David and David Michael Orenstein. 1985. Sociological Theory: Classical
Statements. Toronto: Allyn and Bacon.

Avineri, Shlomo. 1968. The Social and Political Thought of Karl Marx. Cambridge:
Cambridge University Press.

Ballantine, Jeanne H. 1989. The Sociology of Education: A Systematic Analysis. 2nd.
ed. Englewood Cliffs, N.J.: Prentice-Hall.

Banaji, Jairus. 1973. "Backward Capitalism, Primitive Accumulation and Modes of Production." Journal of Contemporary Asia, Vol.3, No.4.

Banaji, Jairus. 1972. "For a Theory of Colonial Modes of Production." Economic and Political Weekly, Vol.7, No.52.

Baran, Paul. 1957. The Political Economy of Growth. New York: Monthly Review Press.

Barbalet, J.M. 1976. "Underdevelopment and the Colonial Economy." Journal of Contemporary Asia, Vol.6, No.2.

Barratt Brown, Michael. 1972. Essays on Imperialism. Nottingham, England: Spokesman Books.

Barry, Tom and Deb Preusch. 1986. The Central America Fact Book. New York: Grove Press.

------. 1988. The Soft War: The Uses and Abuses of U.S. Economic Aid in Central America. New York: Grove Press.

Barry, Tom, Beth Wood, and Deb Preusch. 1983. Dollars and Dictators: A Guide to Central America. New York: Grove Press.

------. 1984. The Other Side of Paradise: Foreign Control in the Caribbean. New York: Grove Press.

Bastide, Roger. 1961. "Dusky Venus, Black Apollo." Race, Vol.3.

------. 1968. "Color, Racism, and Christianity." In Color and Race, ed. J.H. Franklin. Boston: Houghton Mifflin.

Beckford, George L. 1972. Persistent Poverty: Underdevelopment in Plantation Economies of the Third World. New York: Oxford University Press.

------. 1975. Caribbean Economy: Dependence and Backwardness. Mona, Jamaica: Institute of Social and Economic Research.

Bell, Daniel. 1960. The End of Ideology. London: Collier Books.

Bengelsdorf, Carollee. 1985. "On the Problem of Studying Women in Cuba." Race and Class, Vol.XXV11, No.2.

Benjamin, Harold. 1965. Higher Education in the American Republics. New York: McGraw-Hill.

Benton, T. 1977. Philosophical Foundations of the Three Sociologies. London: Routledge and Kegan Paul.

Berger, Iris. 1990. "Gender, Race, and Political Empowerment: South African Canning Workers, 1940-1960." Gender and Society, Vol.4, No.3.

Bergmann, Gustav. 1951. "Ideology." Ethics, Vol.LXI (April).

Best, Lloyd. 1974. "Size and Survival." In Readings in the Political Economy of the Caribbean, ed. Norman Girvan and Owen Jefferson. Tunapuna, Trinidad: New World Group.

Blackburn, Robin. 1963. "Prologue to the Cuban Revolution." New Left Review, No.21.

Blau, Peter. 1964. Exchange and Power in Social Life. New York: John Wiley and Sons.

Blumberg, Abraham S. 1974. "Auguste Comte in Retrospect." Introduction, New Edition of the Positive Philosophy. New York: AMS Press.

Blumer, Herbert. 1967. "Sociology as Symbolic Interaction." In Symbolic Interaction: A Reader in Social Psychology, ed. Jerome G. Manis and Bernard Meltzer. Boston: Allyn and Bacon.

Bodemann, Y. Michal and Anton Allahar. 1980. "The Micro-Organization of Backwardness in Central Sardinia." Journal of Peasant Studies, Vol.7, No.4 (July).

Boeke, J.H. 1942. The Structure of the Netherlands Indian Economy. New York: Institute of Pacific Relations.

Boorstein, Edward. 1968. The Economic Transformation of Cuba. New York: Monthly Review Press.

Bottomore, Tom, ed. 1983. A Dictionary of Marxist Thought. Cambridge, Mass.: Harvard University Press.

Bourque, Susan. 1971. Cholification and the Campesino: A Study of Three Peruvian Peasant Organizations. Dissertation Series. Ithaca, N.Y.: Cornell University Press.

Bryant, Christopher G.A. 1985. Positivism in Social Theory and Research. New York: St. Martin's Press.

Burke, Peter. 1980. Sociology and History. London: George Allen and Unwin.

Caldwell, Malcolm. 1970. "The Role of the Peasantry in the Revolution." Journal of Contemporary Asia, Vol.1, No.1.

Cardoso, Fernando Henrique and Enzo Faletto. 1970. Dependencia y Desarrollo en América Latina. México: Siglo Veintiuno Editores.

Carpenter, Ted Galen. 1991. "The U.S. and Third World Dictatorships: A Case for Benign Detachment." In Third World 91/92. Guilford, Conn.: The Dushkin Publishing Group.

Carroll, Thomas. 1970. "Land Reform as an Explosive Force in Latin America." In Agrarian Problems and Peasant Movements in Latin America, ed. R. Stavenhagen. New York: Doubleday and Co.

Casal, Lourdes. 1980. "Revolution and Conciencia: Women in Cuba." In Women, War, and Revolution, ed. Carol R. Berkin and Clara M. Lovet. New York: Holmes and Meier.

Cashmore, E. Ellis and Bob Mullan. 1983. Approaching Social Theory. London: Heinemann Educational Books.

Chilcote, Ronald H. and Joel Edelstein. 1974. Latin America: The Struggle with Dependency and Beyond. New York: John Wiley and Sons.

Chinchilla, Norma Stoltz. 1979. "Mobilizing Women: Revolution in the Revolution." In Women in Latin America: An Anthology from Latin American Perspectives. Riverside, Cal.: Latin American Perspectives.

--------. 1990. "Revolutionary Popular Feminism in Nicaragua: Articulating Class, Gender, and National Sovereignty." Gender and Society, Vol.4, No.3.

Chirot, Daniel. 1977. Social Change in the Twentieth Century. New York: Harcourt, Brace and Jovanovich.

Chodak, Szymon. 1973. Societal Development. New York: Oxford University Press.

Chodorow, Nancy. 1978. The Reproduction of Mothering. Berkeley: University of California Press.

Chomsky, Noam. 1988. "Propaganda, American Style." Utne Reader, September-October.

Clement, Wallace. 1980. "A Political Economy of Regionalism in Canada." In Structured Inequality in Canada, ed. John Harp and John R. Hofley. Toronto: Prentice-Hall.

--------. 1983. Class, Power and Property. Toronto: Methuen.

Cohen, Robin. 1976. "From Peasants to Workers in Africa." In The Political Economy of Contemporary Africa, ed. Peter Gutkind and Immanuel Wallerstein. London: Sage Publications.

Collier, Simon. 1974. From Cortes to Castro: An Introduction to the History of Latin America 1492-1973. New York: Macmillan.

Collins, Randall and Michael Markowsky. 1984. The Discovery of Society. 3rd ed. New York: Random House.

Comte, Auguste. 1855. The Positive Philosophy. Trans. Harriet Martineau. New York: Calvin Blanchard.

Cooley, Charles Horton. 1962. Social Organization. Glencoe, Ill.: The Free Press.

Côté, James E. and Anton L. Allahar. Forthcoming. Coming of Age in Advanced Industrial Society: The Prolongation of Youth and the Manufacture of Dissent.

Coulson, Margaret and Carol Riddell. 1980. Approaching Sociology. 2nd ed. London: Routledge and Kegan Paul.

Craig, Susan, ed. 1982. Contemporary Caribbean: A Sociological Reader. 2 vols. Maracas, Trinidad: The College Press.

Curtin, Philip D. 1964. The Image of Africa: British Ideas and Action, 1780-1850. Madison: University of Wisconsin Press.

Daniel, N. 1975. The Arabs and Medieval Europe. London: Longman.

Davidson, Basil. 1974. "African Peasants and Revolution." Journal of Peasant Studies, Vol.1, No.3.

Davis, Arthur K. 1971. "Canadian Society and History as Hinterland vs. Metropolis." In Canadian Society: Pluralism, Change and Conflict, ed. R.J. Ossenberg. Toronto: Prentice-Hall.

de Armas, Ramon. 1977. "La Burguesía Latinoamericana: Aspectos de su Evolución." In Feudalismo, Capitalismo, Subdesarrollo, ed. L. Vitale and S. Bagú. Madrid: AKAL Editor.

Deal, Douglas. 1975. "Peasant Revolts and Resistance in the Modern World." Journal of Contemporary Asia, Vol.5, No.4.

Debray, Regis. 1967. Revolution in the Revolution? New York: Grove Press.

Deere, Carmen Diana et al. 1990. In the Shadows of the Sun: Caribbean Development Alternatives and U.S. Policy. Boulder, Col.: Westview Press.

Demas, William. 1975. "Situation and Change." In Beckford 1975.

Deutchman, Iva Ellen. 1991. "The Politics of Empowerment." Women and Politics, Vol.11, No.2.

Dos Santos, Theotonio. 1973. "The Structure of Dependence." In The Political Economy of Development and Underdevelopment, ed. Charles K. Wilber. New York: Random House.

Duggett, Michael. 1975. "Marx on Peasants." Journal of Peasant Studies, Vol.2, No.2.

Durkheim, Emile. 1933. The Division of Labour in Society. New York: The Free Press.

Eisenstadt, S.N. 1966. Modernization, Protest and Change. Englewood Cliffs, N.J.: Prentice-Hall.

———. 1964. "Social Change, Differentiation and Evolution." American Sociological Review, Vol.29, No.3 (June).

Eliot, T.S. 1944. "Burnt Norton." In Four Quartets. London: Farber and Farber.

Espín Guillois, Vilma. 1990. Cuban Women Confront the Future. Australia: Ocean Press.

Evans, Peter B. and John D. Stephens. 1988. "Development and the World Economy." In Handbook of Sociology, ed. Neil J. Smelser. London: Sage Publications.

Fancher, Raymond E. 1979. Pioneers of Psychology. New York: W.W. Norton.

Fanon, Frantz. 1963. The Wretched of the Earth. New York: Grove Press.

Feder, Ernest. 1971. The Rape of the Peasantry. New York: Doubleday.

Fei, Hsiao-Tung. 1939. Peasant Life in China: A Field Study in the Yangtze Valley. London: Routledge and Kegan Paul.

Feyerabend, Paul K. 1981. Realism, Rationalism and Scientific Method. Philosophical Papers, Vol.1. Cambridge: Cambridge University Press.

Firth, Raymond. 1946. Malay Fisherman: Their Peasant Economy. London: Kegan Paul, Trench, Trubner and Co.

Firth, Raymond. 1950. "The Peasantry in South-East Asia." International Affairs, Vol.26.

Fischer-Galati, S. 1963. "The Peasantry as a Revolutionary Force in the Balkans." Journal of Central European Affairs, Vol.XXIII, No.1.

Flax, Jane. 1987. "Postmodernism and Gender Relations in Feminist Theory." Signs: Journal of Women in Culture and Society, Vol.12, No.4.

Forman, Shepard and Joyce Riegelhaupt. 1970. "Market Place and Marketing System: Toward a Theory of Peasant Economic Integration." Comparative Studies in Society and History, No.12.

Foster, G.M. 1967. "What Is a Peasant." In Peasant Society: A Reader, ed. Potter et al. Toronto: Little Brown and Co.

Foster-Carter, Aidan. 1978. "The Modes of Production Controversy." New Left Review, No.107 (January-February).

Franklin, John Hope, ed. Color and Race. Boston: Houghton Mifflin.

Frederiksen, Harold. "Determinants and Consequences of Mortality Trends in Ceylon." Public Health Reports, No.76 (August).

Freyre, Gilberto. 1964. The Masters and the Slaves. Trans. S. Putnam. New York: Knopf.

Friedman, John Block. 1981. The Monstrous Races in Medieval Art and Thought. Cambridge, Mass.: Harvard University Press.

Fromm, Erich. 1966. Marx's Concept of Man. New York: Frederick Ungar.

Frondizi, Silvio. 1967. La Realidad Argentina. 2nd ed. Buenos Aires: Praxis.

Fryer, P. 1984. Staying Power: The History of Black People in Britain. London: Pluto Press

Fuentes, Carlos. 1985. Latin America: At War with the Past. Toronto: CBC Enterprises.

Furtado, Celso. 1970. Economic Development of Latin America: A Survey from Colonial Times to the Cuban Revolution. Cambridge: Cambridge University Press.

———. 1962. "Reflexiones sobre la Pre-revolución Brasileña." El Trimestre Economico, Vol.XXIX, No.115.

Galeano, Eduardo. 1973. Open Veins of Latin America. New York: Monthly Review Press.

———. 1992. "Are the Gods Crazy? Or Is It Me?" The Nation, August 31-September 7.

Galjart, Benno. 1964. "Class and 'Following' in Rural Brazil." America Latina, No.7.

Galtung, Johan. 1971. "Structural Theory of Imperialism." Journal of Peace Research, Vol.2.

Geertz, Clifford. 1966. Agricultural Involution: The Process of Ecological Change in Indonesia. Berkeley: University of California Press.

Gerth, Hans and C.W. Mills. 1958. From Max Weber: Essays in Sociology. New York: Oxford University Press.

Giddens, Anthony. 1973. The Class Structure of the Advanced Societies. London: Hutchinson and Co.

———. 1982a. Sociology: A Brief but Critical Introduction. New York: Harcourt, Brace and Jovanovich.

———. 1982b. Profiles and Critiques in Social Theory. Berkeley: University of California Press.

Gilligan, Carol. 1982. In a Different Voice: Psychological Theory and Women's Development. Cambridge, Mass.: Harvard University Press.

Goldthorpe, John H. 1969. "Herbert Spencer." In The Founding Fathers of Social Science, ed. Timothy Raison. Great Britain: Penguin Books.

González Casanova, Pablo. 1965. "Internal Colonialism and National Development." Studies in Comparative International Development, Vol.1, No.4.

Grabb, Edward G. 1984. Social Inequality: Classical and Contemporary Theorists. Toronto: Holt, Rinehart and Winston of Canada.

Gramsci, Antonio. 1971. Selections from the Prison Notebooks. New York: International Publishers.

Griffin, Keith B. and Ricardo French-Davis. 1964. "El Capital Extranjero y el Desarrollo." Revista Económica, Vols.83-84.

Guevara, Ernesto (Che). 1961. Guerrilla Warfare: A Method. New York: Monthly Review Press.

------. 1968. Reminiscences of the Cuban Revolutionary War. New York: Monthly Review Press.

Gunder Frank, Andre. 1967. Capitalism and Underdevelopment in Latin America. New York: Monthly Review Press.

------. 1969. Latin America: Underdevelopment or Revolution? New York: Monthly Review Press.

------. 1972. Lumpenbourgeoisie, Lumpendevelopment: Dependence, Class, and Politics in Latin America. New York: Monthly Review Press.

------. 1973. Sociology of Development and Underdevelopment of Sociology. London: Pluto Press.

Hagopian, Mark. 1974. The Phenomenon of Revolution. New York: Harper and Row.

Hahner, June, ed. 1976. Women in Latin American History. Los Angeles: UCLA Latin American Center Publications.

Hallas, Duncan. n.d. "Towards a Revolutionary Socialist Party." In Party and Class, ed. Cliff, Hallas et al. London: Pluto Press.

Haralambos, Michael and Robin M. Heald. 1980. Sociology: Themes and Perspectives. Slough, England: University Tutorial Press.

Harding, Sandra. 1986. The Science Question in Feminism. Ithaca, N.Y.: Cornell University Press.

------, ed. 1987. Feminism and Methodology. Bloomington: Indiana University Press.

Hare-Mustin, Rachel T. and Jeanne Marecek. 1988. "The Meaning of Difference: Gender Theory, Postmodernism, and Psychology." American Psychologist, June.

Harrison, Lawrence. 1985. Underdevelopment Is a State of Mind: The Latin American Case. Lanham, M.D.: University Press of America.

Herrick, Paul and Robert Robins. 1976. "Varieties of Latin American Revolutions and Rebellions." Journal of Developing Areas, Vol.10, No.3.

Hill-Collins, Patricia. 1990. Black Feminist Thought: Knowledge, Consciousness, and the Politics of Empowerment. London: Unwin Hyman.

Hiller, Harry. 1976. Canadian Society: A Sociological Analysis. Toronto: Prentice-Hall.

Hindess, Barry. 1977. Philosophy and Methodology in the Social Sciences. Sussex, England: The Harvester Press.

Hobsbawm, E.J. 1959. Primitive Rebels. Manchester, England: University of Manchester Press.

--------. 1973a. "Intellectuals and the Class Struggle." In Revolutionaries. London: Weidenfeld and Nicolson.

--------. 1973b. "Peasants and Politics." Journal of Peasant Studies, Vol.1, No.1.

Hoetink, H. 1973. Slavery and Race Relations in the Americas. New York: Harper and Row.

Hooks, Bell. 1988. Talking Back: Thinking Feminist; Thinking Black. Toronto: Between the Lines.

Hoselitz, Berthold F. 1960. Sociological Aspects of Economic Growth. Glencoe, Ill.: The Free Press.

Huberman, Leo and Paul Sweezy. 1969. Socialism in Cuba. New York: Monthly Review Press.

Huberman, Leo and Paul Sweezy. 1960. Cuba: Anatomy of a Revolution. New York: Monthly Review Press.

Hunter, Alfred A. 1981. Class Tells: On Social Inequality in Canada. Toronto: Butterworths.

Hunter, Guy. 1969. Modernizing Peasant Societies. New York: Oxford University Press.

Huntington, Samuel. 1968. Political Order in Changing Societies. London: Yale University Press.

Hutchinson, B. 1966. "The Patron-Dependent Relationship in Brazil." Sociología Ruralis, No.6.

Hutton, Caroline and Robin Cohen. 1975. "African Peasants and Resistance to Change." In Oxaal, Barnett, and Booth 1975.

Inkeles, Alex. 1966. "The Modernization of Man." In Modernization: The Dynamics of Growth, ed. Myron Weiner. New York: Basic Books.

--------. 1973. "Making Men Modern." In Social Change: Sources, Patterns and Consequences, ed. Amitai Etzioni. New York: Basic Books.

Jacoby, Erich. 1970. "Revolution and Intervention." Journal of Contemporary Asia, Vol.1, No.1.

Jalée, Pierre. 1968. The Pillage of the Third World. New York: Monthly Review Press.

--------. 1969. The Third World in World Economy. New York: Monthly Review Press.

Jordan, Winthrop D. 1968. White Over Black: American Attitudes Toward the Negro, 1550-1812. Chapel Hill: University of North Carolina Press.

Joshi, P.C. 1974. "Land Reform and Agrarian Change in India and Pakistan Since 1947." Journal of Peasant Studies, Vol.1, Nos.2-3.

Keat, Russell N. 1981. The Politics of Social Theory. Oxford: Basil Blackwell.

Keat, Russell N. and John R. Urry. 1975. Social Theory as Science. London: Routledge and Kegan Paul.

Keen, Mike. 1992. "The FBI and American Sociology." Footnotes, American Sociological Association, May.

Kemp, Tom. 1978. Historical Patterns of Industrialization. New York: Longman Group.

Kingshill, Konrad. 1960. Ku Daeng--The Red Tomb: A Village Study in Northern Thailand. Thailand: The Prince Royal's College.

Kitching, Gavin. 1982. Development and Underdevelopment in Historical Perspective. London: Methuen.

Krauze, Tadeusz and Kazimierz M. Slomczynski. 1985. "How Far to Meritocracy? Empirical Tests of a Controversial Thesis." Social Forces, Vol.63, No.3.

Kuhn, Thomas. 1970. The Structure of Scientific Revolutions. 2nd ed. Chicago: University of Chicago Press.

Laclau, Ernesto. 1971. "Feudalism and Capitalism in Latin America." New Left Review, No.67 (May-June).

Ladoo, Harold "Sonny." 1974. Yesterdays. Toronto: Anansi.

Lane, Arthur. 1971. Greek Pottery. 3rd. ed. London: Farber.

Lee, Shu-Ching. 1951. "Agrarian and Social Upheaval in China." American Journal of Sociology, Vol.56 (May).

Lemarchand, Réné and Keith Legg. 1972. "Political Clientilism and Development: A Preliminary Analysis." Comparative Politics, Vol.4 (January).

Lenin, V.I. 1966. Imperialism, the Highest Stage of Capitalism. Moscow: Progress Publishers.

------. 1969. What Is to Be Done? Moscow: Progress Publishers.

Lerner, Daniel. 1965. The Passing of Traditional Society. New York: The Free Press.

Levitt, Kari. 1970. Silent Surrender: The Multinational Corporation in Canada. Toronto: Macmillan of Canada.

Lewis, Oscar, Ruth M. Lewis and Susan M. Rigdon. 1977. Four Women: Living the Revolution. An Oral History of Contemporary Cuba. Vol.II. Chicago: University of Illinois Press.

Lewis, W. Arthur. 1983. Selected Economic Writings of W. Arthur Lewis, ed. Mark Gersovitz. New York: New York University Press.

Leys, Colin. 1977. "Underdevelopment and Dependency: Critical Notes." Journal of Contemporary Asia, Vol.7, No.1.

Lipset, Seymour Martin. 1967. "Values, Education and Entrepreneurship." In Elites in Latin America, ed. S.M. Lipset and Aldo Solari. New York: Oxford University Press.

------. 1985. "Canada and the United States: The Cultural Dimension." In Canada and the United States, ed. Charles F. Doran and John H. Sigler. Toronto: Prentice-Hall.

Long, Norman. 1977. An Introduction to the Sociology of Rural Development. London: Tavistock Publications.

Lorber, Judith. 1990. "Editor's Note." Gender and Society, Vol.4, No.3.

Lucas, Rex. 1971. Minetown, Milltown, Railtown. Toronto: University of Toronto Press.

Macpherson, C.B. 1965. The Real World of Democracy. Toronto: CBC Publishing Co.

Magdoff, Harry. 1966. "Economic Aspects of U.S. Imperialism." Monthly Review, Vol.18, No.6 (November).

Maine, Sir Henry Sumner. 1907 [1885]. Ancient Law. New York: Henry Holt.

Mamdani, Mahmood. 1976. Politics and Class Formation in Uganda. New York: Monthly Review Press.

Mannheim, Karl. 1936. Ideology and Utopia. New York: Harcourt, Brace and Company.

Manuel, Frank Edward. 1956. The New World of Henri Saint Simon. Cambridge, Mass.: Harvard University Press.

Marx, Karl. 1963. The Eighteenth Brumaire of Louis Bonaparte. New York: International Publishers.

------. 1970. A Contribution to the Critique of Political Economy. Moscow: Progress Publishers.

------. 1972a. The Class Struggles in France 1848-1850. New York: International Publishers.

------. 1972b. On Colonialism. New York: International Publishers.

------ . n.d. Capital. Vol.1. New York: International Publishers.

------ and Friedrich Engels. 1955. The Communist Manifesto. New York: Appleton-Century-Crofts.

------ and Friedrich Engels. 1969. The German Ideology. New York: International Publishers.

------ and Frederick Engels. 1975. "The Holy Family." In Collected Works. Vol.IV. New York: International Publishers.

Matthews, Ralph. 1982. "Regional Differences in Canada: Social Versus Economic Interpretations." In Social Issues: Sociological Views of Canada, ed. D. Forcese and S. Richer. Toronto: Prentice-Hall.

McAlister, John and Paul Mus. 1970. The Vietnamese and Their Revolution. New York: Harper and Row.

McCain, Garvin and Erwin M. Segal. 1969. The Game of Science. Belmont, Cal.: Brooks/Cole Publishing Co.

McClelland, David. 1963. "Motivation Patterns in Southeast Asia." Journal of Social Issues, Vol.29, No.17 (January).

------. 1964. "The Achievement Motivation in Economic Growth." In Development and Society: The Dynamics of Economic Change, ed. David Novack and Robert Lekachman. New York: St. Martin's Press.

McGinnis, Robert. 1965. Mathematical Foundations for Social Analysis. New York: Bobbs-Merrill.

Mead, George Herbert. 1934. Mind, Self and Society: From the Standpoint of a Social Behaviourist. Chicago: University of Chicago Press.

Meltzer, Bernard, John W. Petras and Larry T. Reynolds. 1975. Symbolic Interactionism: Genesis, Varieties and Criticism. Boston: Routledge and Kegan Paul.

Menzies, Ken. 1982. Sociological Theory in Use. Boston: Routledge and Kegan Paul.

Merkx, Gilbert and Nelsón Valdés. 1972. "Revolution, Consciousness and Class: Cuba and Argentina." In Cuba in Revolution, ed. R. Bonachea and N. Valdés. New York: Doubleday and Co.

Merton, Robert K. 1957. Social Theory and Social Structure. New York: The Free Press.

Mies, María, Veronika Bennholdt-Thomsen, and Claudia von Werlhof. 1988. Women: The Last Colony. London: Zed Books.

Migdal, Joel. 1974. Peasants, Politics and Revolution. Princeton, N.J.: Princeton University Press.

Miles, Robert. 1989. Racism. London: Routledge.

Millikan, Max and Walt W. Rostow. 1957. A Proposal Key to an Effective Foreign Policy. New York: Harper and Brothers.

Mills, C. Wright. 1982. The Sociological Imagination. London: Oxford University Press.

Mintz, Sidney. 1953. "The Folk-Urban Continuum and the Rural Proletarian Community." American Journal of Sociology, Vol.59.

———. 1974. "The Rural Proletariat and the Problem of Rural Proletarian Consciousness." Journal of Peasant Studies, Vol.1, No.3.

Molyneux, Maxine. 1986. "Mobilization Without Emancipation? Women's Interests, State, and Revolution." In Transition and Development: Problems of Socialism in the Third World, ed. Richard R. Fagen, Carmen Diana Deere, and José Luis Coraggio. New York: Monthly Review Press.

Moore, Wilbert E. 1964. "Predicting Discontinuities in Social Change." American Sociological Review, Vol.29, No.3 (June).

Moore, Barrington Jr. 1966. Social Origins of Dictatorship and Democracy. Boston: Beacon Press.

Moore, Wilbert E. 1963. Social Change. Englewood Cliffs, N.J.: Prentice-Hall.

Moreno Fraginals, Manuel. 1976. The Sugarmill: The Socio-Economic Complex of Sugar in Cuba. New York: Monthly Review Press.

Morgan, Lewis Henry. 1963. Ancient Society. New York: The World Publishing Co.

Morrissey, Marietta. 1989. Slave Women in the New World: Gender Stratification in the Caribbean. Lawrence: University of Kansas Press.

Mulkay, M. 1979. Science and the Sociology of Knowledge. London: Allen and Unwin.

Munck, Ronaldo. 1984. Politics and Dependency in the Third World: The Case of Latin America. London: Zed Books.

Myrdal, Gunnar. 1968. Asian Drama. 3 vols. London: Penguin Press.

Nash, June. 1990. "Latin American Women in the World Capitalist Crisis." Gender and Society, Vol.4, No.3.

Nash, Manning and Robert Chin. 1963. "Psycho-Cultural Factors in Asian Economic Growth." Journal of Social Issues, Vol.29, No.1 (January).

Niosi, Jorge. 1985. Canadian Multinationals. Toronto: Garamond Press.

Nisbet, Robert A. 1966. The Sociological Tradition. New York: Basic Books, 1966.

Nisbet, Robert A. and Robert G. Perrin. 1977. The Social Bond. 2nd ed. New York: Alfred A. Knopf.

Nun, José. 1991. "Democracy and Modernization Thirty Years After." Paper presented at the XV World Congress of International Political Science Association, Buenos Aires, Argentina, July 21-26.

O'Connor, James. 1970. The Origins of Socialism in Cuba. Ithaca, N.Y.: Cornell University Press.

------. 1972. "Cuba: Its Political Economy." In Cuba in Revolution, ed. R. Bonachea and N. Valdés. New York: Doubleday and Co.

Ojeda, Tomás Thayer. 1929. "Francisco de Aguirre." Revista Chilena de Historia y Geografía, No.64.

Osgood, Charles E., P.H. Tannenbaum, and G.J. Suci. 1957. The Measurement of Meaning. Urbana: University of Illinois Press.

Oxaal, Ivar, Tony Barnett, and David Booth. 1975. Beyond the Sociology of Development. London: Routledge and Kegan Paul.

Parkin, Frank. 1982. Max Weber. New York: Tavistock Publications.

Parsons, Talcott. 1954. Essays in Sociological Theory. Glencoe, Ill.: The Free Press.

------. 1964. "Evolutionary Universals in Society." American Sociological Review, Vol.29, No.3 (June).

Pearse, Andrew. 1972. "Peasants and Revolution: The Case of Bolivia." Economy and Society, Vol.1, Nos.3-4.

Petras, James. 1975. "New Perspectives on Imperialism and Social Classes in the Periphery." Journal of Contemporary Asia, Vol.5, No.3.

Plange, Nii-k. 1984. Science and Social Theory. Suva, Fiji: South Pacific Review Press.

------. 1980. "Underdevelopment in Northern Ghana: Natural Causes or Colonial Capitalism." Review of African Political Economy, Nos.15/16.

Portes, Alejandro. 1976. "On the Sociology of National Development: Theories and Issues." American Journal of Sociology, Vol.82, No.1 (July).

Powell, John. 1970. "Peasant Society and Clientilist Politics." American Political Science Review, Vol.LXIV.

Quijano, Aníbal. 1967. "Contemporary Peasant Movements." In Elites in Latin America, ed. S.M. Lipset and A. Solari. New York: Oxford University Press.

------. 1974. "Imperialism and International Relations in Latin America." In Latin America and the United States: The Changing Political Realities, ed. J. Cotler and J. Fagen. Stanford, Cal.: Stanford University Press.

Ramsaran, Ramesh. 1989. The Commonwealth Caribbean in the World Economy. London: Macmillan Publishers.

Randall, Margaret. 1974. Cuban Women Now. Toronto: The Women's Press.

------. 1981. Women in Cuba: Twenty Years Later. New York: Smyrna Press.

Redclift, Michael. 1975. "Peasants and Revolutionaries." Journal of Latin America Studies, Vol.7, Part 1.

Redfield, Robert. 1941. The Folk Culture of the Yucatan. Chicago: University of Chicago Press.

------. 1947. "The Folk Society." American Journal of Sociology, Vol.52.

------. 1956. Peasant Society and Culture. Chicago: University of Chicago Press.

Rejai, M. 1971. "Political Ideology: Theoretical and Comparative Perspectives." In Decline of Ideology, ed. M. Rejai. Chicago: Aldine and Atherton.

Ríos, Palmira N. 1990. "Export Oriented Industrialization and the Demand for Female Labour: Puerto Rican Women in the Manufacturing Sector, 1952 1980." Gender and Society, Vol.4, No.3.

Ritzer, George. 1992. Classical Sociological Theory. New York: McGraw-Hill.

Rodney, Walter. 1972. How Europe Underdeveloped Africa. Surrey, England: Love and Malcolmson.

Ropers, R. 1973. "Mead, Marx and Social Psychology." Catalyst, Vol.7 (Winter).

Rosenblat, Angel. 1954. La Población Indigena y el Mestizaje en América. 2 vols. Buenos Aires.

Rostow, W.W. 1962. The Stages of Economic Growth: A Non-Communist Manifesto. Cambridge: Cambridge University Press.

Rudra, Ashok. 1976. "Hiring of Labour by Poor Peasants." Economic and Political Weekly, Vol.XI, Nos.1-2.

Safa, Helen Icken. 1990. "Women's Social Movements in Latin America." Gender and Society, Vol.4, No.3.

Sanders, R. 1978. Lost Times and Promised Lands: The Origins of American Racism. Boston: Little, Brown and Co.

Sansom, Robert. 1970. The Economics of Insurgency in the Mekong Delta of Vietnam. Cambridge, Mass.: MIT Press.

Sartre, Jean-Paul. 1961. Sartre on Cuba. New York: Ballantine Books.

Scott, James. 1970. "Patron-Client Politics and Political Change." Paper presented at APSA meetings, September.

Seidman, Stephen. 1983. Liberalism and the Origins of European Social Theory. Berkeley: University of California Press.

Seltman, C.T. 1920. "Two Heads of Negresses." American Journal of Archaeology, Vol.24.

Shanin, Teodor. 1970. "Class and Revolution." Journal of Contemporary Asia, Vol.1, No.2.

———. 1971a. "The Peasantry as a Political Factor." In Shanin 1971b.

———. 1971b. Peasants and Peasant Societies. Baltimore: Penguin Books.

Shils, Edward. 1968. "Color, the Universal Intellectual Community, and the Afro-Asian Intellectual." In Color and Race, ed. J.H. Franklin. Boston: Houghton Mifflin.

Skinner, B.F. 1972. Beyond Freedom and Dignity. New York: Bantam Books.

Smelser, Neil J. 1967. Sociology: An Introduction. New York: John Wiley

———. 1968. Essays in Sociological Explanation. Englewood Cliffs, N.J.: Prentice-Hall.

Smucker, Joseph. 1980. Industrialization in Canada. Toronto: Prentice-Hall.

Snowden, Frank M. Jr. 1970. Blacks in Antiquity: Ethiopians in the Greco-Roman Experience. Cambridge, Mass.: Harvard University Press.

———. 1983. Before Color Prejudice: The Ancient View of Blacks. Cambridge, Mass.: Harvard University Press.

Sorokin, Pitrim A. 1969. Society, Culture and Personality: Their Structure and Dynamics. New York: Cooper Square Publications.

Spencer, Herbert. 1897. The Principles of Sociology. Vol.1. New York: D. Appleton and Company.

Stavenhagen, Rodolfo. 1970. Agrarian Problems and Peasant Movements in Latin America. New York: Doubleday and Co.

Stepanov, L. 1970. "The Problem of Economic Independence." In The Third World, ed. Zhukov et al. Moscow: Progress Publishers.

Stevenson, Michael. 1992. "Columbus and the War on Indigenous Peoples." Race and Class, Vol.33, No.3.

Sunkel, Osvaldo and Pedro Paz. 1970. El Subdesarrollo Latinoamericano y la Teoría del Desarrollo. Mexico: Siglo Veintiuno.

Sutherland, Elizabeth. 1969. The Youngest Revolution: A Personal Report on Cuba. New York: The Dial Press

Sweezy, Paul. 1968. "The Proletariat in Today's World." Tricontinental, No.9

Talib, B.D. and A. Majid. 1976. "The Small Farmers of Punjab." Economic and Political Weekly, Vol.XI, No.26.

Thomas, Hugh. 1971. Cuba: Or the Pursuit of Freedom. London: Eyre and Spottiswoode.

Thomas, W.I. and Dorothy S. Thomas. 1928. The Child in America. New York: Alfred Knopf.

Thompson, Edgar T. 1959. "The Plantation as a Social System." In Plantation Systems of the New World. Washington, D.C.: Pan American Union, Social Science Monographs, Vol.VII.

Thomson, Charles. 1935. "The Cuban Revolution: Fall of Machado." Foreign Policy Reports, No.21 (December).

Tilly, Charles. 1981. As Sociology Meets History. New York: Academic Press.

Toennies, Ferdinand. 1957. Community and Society. East Lansing: Michigan State University Press.

Turner, Bryan S. 1986. Equality. New York: Tavistock Publications.

Turner, Jonathan H. 1985. Sociology: A Student Handbook. New York: Random House.

United Nations Development Program (UNDP). 1993. Human Development Report 1993. New York: Oxford University Press.

Utley, Francis Lee. 1941. "Noah's Ham and Jansen Enikel." Germanic Review, No.16.

Valdés, Teresa and Marisa Weinstein. 1989. "Organizaciones de Pobladoras y Construcción en Chile." Working Paper No.434. Santiago: FLACSO-Chile.

Veltmeyer, Henry. 1978. "The Underdevelopment of Atlantic Canada." Review of Radical Political Economics, Vol.10, No.2.

Von Bothmer, D. 1961-62. "A Gold Libation Bowl." Bulletin of the Metropolitan Museum of Art, No.21.

Wagner, Henry Raup. 1967. The Life and Writings of Bartolomé de las Casas. Albuquerque: University of New Mexico Press.

Wallace, Ruth A. and Alison Wolf. 1986. Contemporary Sociological Theory: Continuing the Classical Tradition. 2nd ed. Englewood Cliffs, N.J.: Prentice-Hall.

Wallerstein, Emmanuel. 1974. The Modern World System: Capitalist Agriculture and the Origins of the Modern World Economy in the Sixteenth Century. New York: Academic Press.

Warren, Bill. 1973. "Imperialism and Capitalist Industrialization." New Left Review, No.81.

------. 1980. Imperialism: Pioneer of Capitalism. London: New Left Books.

Watson, Robert I. 1971. The Great Psychologists. Philadelphia: J.B. Lippincott.

Weber, Max. 1949. The Methodology of the Social Sciences. New York: The Free Press.

------. 1958. The Protestant Ethic and the Spirit of Capitalism. Trans. Talcott Parsons. New York: Charles Scribner's Sons.

------. 1964. The Theory of Social and Economic Organization. New York: Oxford University Press.

------. 1978. Economy and Society, ed. Guenther Roth and Claus Wittich. 2 vols. Berkeley: University of California Press.

Weiner, Myron. 1966. Modernization: The Dynamics of Growth. New York: Basic Books.

Westby, David L. 1991. The Growth of Sociological Theory: Human Nature, Knowledge, and Social Change. Englewood Cliffs, N.J.: Prentice-Hall.

White, H. 1972. "The Forms of Wildness: Archaeology of an Idea." In The Wild Man Within: An Image in Western Thought from Renaissance to Romanticism. Pittsburg: University of Pittsburg Press.

Williams, Eric. 1966. Capitalism and Slavery. New York: G.P. Putnam's Sons.

Wilson, John. 1983. Social Theory. Englewood Cliffs, N.J.: Prentice-Hall.

Wolf, Eric. 1969. Peasant Wars of the Twentieth Century. New York: Harper and Row Publishers.

--------. 1971a, "On Peasant Rebellions." In Shanin 1971b.

--------. 1971b. "Peasant Rebellion and Revolution." In National Liberation, Revolution in the Third World, ed. Miller and Aya. New York: The Free Press.

Wolpe, Harold. 1975. "The Theory of Internal Colonialism: The South African Case." In Oxaal, Barnett, and Booth 1975.

Worrell, Delisle, Compton Bourne, and Dinesh Dodhia, eds. 1991. Financing Development in the Commonwealth Caribbean. London: Macmillan Education Limited.

Zeitlin, Irving M. 1981 & 1987. Ideology and the Development of Sociological Theory. 2nd & 3rd eds. Englewood Cliffs, N.J.: Prentice-Hall.

--------. 1972. Capitalism and Imperialism. Chicago: Markham Publishing Co.

Zhukov, Y. 1970. "Driving Forces of the National Liberation Revolutions." In The Third World, ed. Zhukov et al. Moscow: Progress Publishers.

INDEX

A

Abercrombie, N. et al. 19, 20
absolute truth 24
accumulation of capital 85, 94, 156
Acosta-Belen, E. and C. Bose 127, 192
African as 'Other' 176
African as inferior being 171-172; 185
agrarian capitalism 159
Aguilar, L. 163
ahistoricism 12
Alavi, H. 93, 131, 134, 137, 148-150,
    153-154
Alexander the Great 174
alienation 10, 160
Allahar, A.L. 85, 91, 96, 111, 122, 181
American Revolution 88
American sociology 16-17, 34
Amin, S. 137
anarchical party 34
ancient slavery 172
androcentrism 45
Angola 78
anti-Enlightenment sentiments,
    Comte and 34
apartheid in South Africa 169-170, 174
Arabs 177
Arafat 97
Aristotle 173
Aron, R. 16-17, 34
Ashley, D. 80-81
Assad 97
attitudinal traits and development 82-83
Ayatollah Khomeini 98

B

backwardness and underdevelopment 86
Ballantine, J. 84-85
Banaji, J. 131, 134, 136
Baran, P. 93, 102-103
Barbalet, J.M. 131, 134
Barratt-Brown, M. 141
Barry, T. et al. 93-94
Bastide, R. 179, 181, 185
Becker, H. 73
Beckford, G. 56, 131, 132
behaviourism: 12, 39, 43; and positivism
    36- 38
belief systems: 10; as self confirming theories
    18
beliefs vs facts 21
Bell, D. 22
Bengelsdorf, C. 193-194
Benton, T. 35
Berger, I. 187, 190
Bergmann, G. 21
Best, L. 131, 133
biological determinism: 40; evolution 61,
    196; sciences 76;
Blackburn, R. 163
blackness: as comical caricature 173; as
    evil 172, 174, 178, 180; as inferiority
    174; as monstrousity 174-175; as
    punishment from God 174, 178,
    180; as sinful 172, 174; as
    sinister 179; as ugly 173
blacks as lacking the capacity for freedom
    and democracy 185
blacks in antiquity 172-173
Blau, P. 150
Blumberg, A. 59, 62
Blumer, H. 40, 43; critique of positivism 43

220   Sociology and the Periphery

Bodemann, Y.M. 91
Boeke, J. 70
Boorstein, E. 163
Bottomore, T.B. 32
bourgeois feminism 194
bourgeoisie: comprador 127, 144;
  nationalist vs anti-nationalist 131, 163
Bourque, S. 158
branch plant economy 122
Britain and Canada 123
Britain and India 103, 130
Bryant, J. 105
Burke, P. 31
Bush, G. 97, 99

C

Caldwell, M. 142, 145
Campbell, G. 103
Canada and Britain 123
Canada and the US compared 88-89
Canada's public enterprise system 88
Canadian economy, external control of 122
Canadian capitalist class 124-125
Canadian MNCs 125, in the Caribbean
  112, 126-127
Canadian conservatism 88
capital accumulation 111
capitalism: and democracy 17; and
  underdevelopment 115
capitalism, revolution against 198
capitalism, imperialism, and patriarchy 195
capitalist accumulation 50, 111, 142, 198
capitalist penetration of the country-
  side 149, 160; and revolution 17, 160
Cardoso, F.H. 105
Caribbean, direction of trade 114; US
  investments 93-94
Caribbean dependency 113
Caribbean Basin Initiative (CBI) 126
CARIBCAN 126
Carpenter, T. 116-117
Carroll, T. 147
Casal, L. 193
cash cropping 158
Cashmore, E. 27, 37, 59, 63, 65

Castro, F. 163, 164
Catholic Church 87
Catholic Church and slavery 180
Catholic priests: and the woman of colour
  184-185; and sexual activity 184-185
cause-effect relationships 20, 35, 62-63
Central America, trade deficit 93
centre and periphery 123
chain of dependency 108-109, 123, 125
change: and conflict 64;
  and development 10
Che Guevara 155, 164
Chilcote, R. and J. Edelstein 105, 116,
  131
Chile 78
Chinchilla, N. 191-192, 195
Chirot, D. 93, 96, 108, 143
Chodak, S. 73, 81
Chodorow, N. 46
Chomsky, N. 22, 23, 116
Christianity and racism 179-182, 186

Christianity vs Islam 172, 176-177
CIA 116
class: analysis 12-13, 124, 154, 198; conflict
  19; consciousness 47, 51; struggle 50,
  165; inequality 96
class consciousness 121-122, 141, 166; and
  imperialism 164
class: and revolution 142, 149; and leadership
  162, 164
class in itself and for itself 141
Clement, W. 123, 124, 125
Cohen, R. 144, 149
Cold War 94-95
collective conscience 69; 73
Collier, S. 183-185
Collins, R. and C. Markowsky 28-29
colonial development, patterns of 133
colonial mode of production 131, 134-139;
  and capitalism 137; elements of 136
colonialism: 111; and imperialism 10, 61, 66,
  77, 82, 98, 102, 105, 109, 129, 130-134,
  197; and racism 182
colonies: of conquest 131-133, 136; of
  exploitation 131-133, 136; of settlement
  131-132, 136

colour and morality 174
colour and race as social markers 170
colour symbolisms and Old Testament
    Christianity 171, 179-182, 186
commercialization of agriculture 158
communism: as attractive to poor
    countries 96; and socialism 78
communist scare in the US 95-96
Comte, A. 32-34, 57-62; as a conserva-
    tive 34; as sexist 169
Comte's evolutionary theory 34
conditioning 36-37
conflict, individuals vs groups 15
consciousness: 37; and will 25; rural
    proletarian 159
conservatism 16, 22, 165; definition of 15
conservative science 18
constant capital 51, 136
contradiction 50
Cooley, C.H. 73
core and periphery 108
Côté, J. 85
Coulson, M. 26
covering law 35
creationism 177-178
Cuba 78, 98, 155, 180, 183,
Cuba, antecedents of the revolution 163
Cuba, imperialism and class
    consciousness 164
cultural symbols 39
cultural chauvinism 82
culture: 39, 81, 98; and progress 99; and
    social values 85; transmission of 39
Curtin, P. 176

D

Daniel, N. 177
Darwin, C. 77
Davidson, B. 154
Davis, A.K. 123
de Armas, R. 131
de Aguirre, Francisco 183
Deal, D. 148, 155
Debray, R. 155
debt and dependency 187

debunking social myths 28
declining terms of trade 111, 133
deconstructionism 46
deep social structure 26, 49, 106
Deere, C. et al 126, 187-190
Demas, W. 131, 133
democracy at home, dictatorship abroad
    99-100
democracy: 12, 121; and class 101-102;
    and ideology 98-101, 117; as a form of
    government, 100; as illusion 101;
    and inequality 101-102; and social
    control 23
democratic liberalism 101-102
democratic institutions 17
demonstration elections 116
depeasantization 144, 149
dependence: definition of 109-111; and
    underdevelopment 119; and distorted
    development 131; political solutions
    127-128
dependency and regionalism in Canada
    122-127
dependency theory 12-13, 105, 107-115;
    123, 127-129 139; and colonialism
    123; and Marxism 115-122; Marxist
    critique of 129; and nationalism 129
dependency theory as critique of
    modernization 115
dependency theory, ideology of 197
dependent: industrialization 122;
    development 123
Descartes 36
description vs analysis 79, 82, 115
determinism and positivism 107
Deutchman, I. 45
development as unilinear 66
development and underdevelopment: 9;
    internal causes 82, 98; external
    causes 82
development of underdevelopment 94, 109
development and underdevelopment as
    relational 9, 113, 199
development and technology 119-120
development as uneven process see uneven
    development
development decade 94

Dewey, J. 41
dialectical method 48
dictators, US installed and supported 100
differentiation and integration 67
diffusionism: 89, 92, 113; criticisms of 93; as tautology 93
divine law 21
divine right 29
division of labour 62, 69-70, 94; international 136
dominant ideology thesis 20
Dominica 117
Dominican Republic 78
Dos Santos T. 105, 109, 111, 129
dualism 89-92, 113, 92
Duggett, M. 143, 147-148, 154
Dulles, J.F. 102
Durkheim, E. 10, 58, 62, 66, 72-73, 68-69; and morality 69-70

E

early colonization 132
East-West 94
Eastern Europe 84
economic polarization and revolution 91-92
economic: backwardness 72; blackmail 95; dependence 10-12; development 11, 56; enclaves 113; growth 9, 55-56, 66; rape 113; stages of 75; take-off 75
Economic Commission for Latin America (ECLA) 128
Eisenstadt, S. 66, 70, 71
El Salvador 78
elective affinity 20
Eliot, T.S. 31
empirical research 29, 33, 35
empiricism, a definition 106
Engels 141, to Kautsky 142
Enlightenment: 11, 28-29, 33-34, 44; attack on religion 60
entrepreneurship 83, 102-103
epistemology: 11-12, 23-24, 32, 36, 44, 47, 196; feminist-constructivist 45-46

Espín, V. 193-195
ethnicity 10
ethnocentrism 11, 85
Evans, P. 80, 99
evolution, definition of 72
evolutionary progress 57; stages 57; theory 66; universals, 71, 72
evolutionism: 79; and functionalism 66; ideology of 197; politics of 75-76
expanded reproduction 137
exploitation: 13, 50, 51, 119, 159-160, 172, 197; in the periphery 186
export orientation 127

F

factory work in early capitalism 145
facts as subjective interpretations 21
Faletto, E. 105
false consciousness 121
Fancher, E. 27
Fanon, F. 145
Feder, E. 143
Federation of Cuban Women (FMC) 193
female unemployment 186-187
feminism: 12, 21-22, 43; bourgeois 194; constructivist critique of 46; and class 195; and reformism 195; liberal 195; and positivism 45, 47; post-modernist 44, 46; radical 195; and subjectivism44; and socialism 192-195; in Cuba 192-195; vs the Cuban women's movement 194
feminist: critique of science 18; revolution 191; feminist consciousness 191; interests 191
feudal society 60, 100
Firth, R. 148, 149
Flax, J. 44, 47
forces of production 134, 141
foreign aid 127; hidden agenda 96-97, 103-104
foreign debt, Third World 133; Latin America 134

foreign capital 56, 115, 127, 129
forerunners of sociology 28-29
Forman, S. and J. Riegelhaupt 159
Foster, G.M. 148
Foster-Carter, A. 134
Frederiksen, H. 156
free enterprise 39, 86
free trade 15
free will 43; and determinism 106-107
freedom and unfreedom 107
freedom of speech 23
freedom vs equality 101
French Davis, R. 93
French Revolution 11, 28, 34, 60, 88
Freud and the unconscious 139
Freyre, G. 184-185
Friedman, J.B. 173-175, 178-179
Fromm, E. 48
Frondizi, S. 93
Fryer, P. 176
Fuentes, C. 86, 102
functionalism: 12, 79; ideology of 72; as conservative ideology 64
functions and dysfunctions 65
Furtado, C. 105, 145, 147

G

Gadhafi 97
Galeano, E. 86, 108
Galjart, B. 152-153
Galtung, J. 123
Geertz, C. 156-157
gender division of labour 13, 28
gender: 186; as socially constructed 46-47
gender, ethnicity and class 190-192
gender interests 191; practical 190-191, 195; strategic 191, 195
generalized others 42
geographical determinism 99
Gerth, H. 19
Giddens, A. 28, 32, 35, 36, 38, 141
Gilligan, C. 46
golden triangle 124
Goldthorpe, J. 62

González Casanova, P. 109
Grabb, E. 63
Great Depression 197
Greco-Roman society 172, 175, 178
Grenada 78, 117
Griffin, K. 93
Guatemala 78
guerrilla warfare 165
Gunder Frank, A. 76, 93-94, 103, 105, 115, 123, 129, 142

H

Hagopian, M. 18, 21
Hallas, D. 161
Haralambos, M. 40, 43
Harding, S. 44-45
Hare-Mustin, R. and J. Marecek 46
Harrison, L. 98-99, 101
hedonistic principle 37
hegemony, US 95
Herman, E. 116
Hill-Collins, P. 194
Hiller, H. 122, 123
Hindess, B. 18
historical sociology 31
historical materialism 48
Hobsbawm, E. 143, 148, 152, 154, 160-161
Hoetink, H. 183
Holy Wars or Crusades 177
Homer 174
Hooks, B. 194
Hoselitz, B. 73, 75
Hsiao-Tung, F. 159
Huberman, L. and P. Sweezy 163, 165
human agency: 12, 55, 60, 66, 196-197; and social change 77
human rights 22
humans as active 83
humans as passive 37, 43
Hunter, A. 48
Hunter, G. 92
Huntington, S. 158
Hutchinson, B. 157
Hutton, C. and R. Cohen 148

I

idea of progress 33
ideal type: 62, 75, 90, 134; definition of 72
ideas and material interests 19-20; and
social location 21; as autonomous
forces 19; as effective forces in history
19, 80
ideological superstructure 134
ideological: conservatism and radicalism
12; conflicts 167
ideology: 12-13, 18, 20, 103, 180, 198;
a broad definition 21-22; and belief 18-
19; and class structure 19-20, 121; of
democracy 95-96, 99, 104; and dogma
21; and domination 19; and emotion 22;
functions of 22; Marx's definition of 19;
and male science 45; as mobilized
belief 22; and modernization 86; as
propaganda 22-23; and racism 176-177,
181; and religion 33; social base of 22;
and social change 18; and social control
22, 96-97, 121; of social evolutionism
77-78; and social reality 196; and
science 18, 21; of sexism; and theory
196; and truth 21-24, 196-197; and
utopia 20
idiographic knowledge 9
IMF 86, 103, 186-187
imperialism: 11, 96, 98, 113-115, 136,
166; as capitalism overseas 142; and
class structure in the periphery 144; and
the countryside 156; economic and
political dimensions 120; and the
peasantry 156-158; politics of 115, 131;
and social class 119-120; and class
consciousness in Cuba 164; in the work
of Marx and Engels 141-142; and
nationalism 121; theory of 141; and
underdevelopment 133; and the working
class 142
imperialist exploitation 139
import substitution industrialization 129,
197
indentured servants 132

independent peasants 152
individual as unit of analysis 16
individual uniqueness 25-26
individualism: 88; and rise of the personal
conscience 69
industrial Canada 124
Industrial Revolution 145
industrialization 34, 49, 55-56, 79, 81-82
Inkeles, A. 84
inner states of mind 37
instincts 38
intellectuals and revolutionary leadership
161-163;
interactionism: 16, 38-39, 55; and feminism,
43; and structuralism 40; and
voluntarism 40
internal colonialism 109, 123
internal economic disarticulation
137-139
interpretation of symbols 39
interpretive understanding 40
Islam vs Christianity 172, 176-177

J

Jacoby, E. 156
Jalée, P. 93, 142
James, W. 41
Jordan, W. 176
Joshi, P.C. 159

K

Keat, R. 47, 48
Keen, M. 28
Kemp, T. 56
Kingshill, K. 157
Kitching, G. 93
knowledge, sources of 24
Krauze, T. 84-85
Kuhn, T. 18

L

labour intensive methods of work 111
Laclau, E. 130
Ladoo, H. 181
landlord-government alliance 151
Lane, A. 173
Latin America: colonial conquest 87;
  culture and values 85-88; feudal or
  capitalist 130
law: of gravity 35; of progress 59; of three
  stages 59; and religion, 69
laws: of behaviour 37; of history 16; of
  capitalist development 131
leadership and revolution 160-167
learned behaviour, 38
Lee, S. 157
Lemarchand, R. and K. Legg 151
Lenin 130-131, 161
Lerner, D. 83-84
Levitt, K. 122, 125
Lewis, W.A. 91
Lewis, G.K. 172
Lewis, O. et al 195
Leys, C. 129
liberal freedoms 100-101; as ideological 23
liberal democracy 12, 95; contradictions
  of 102
liberal democratic society 23, 100-102;
  traditions of 88
Lipset, S.M. 85-89, 98, 102, 123
local markets 113
Long, N. 90
lopsided development see also
  uneven development
lopsided development 119, 122, 136
Lorber, J. 186, 190
lord-peasant relations 150, 152-153
Lucas, R. 125

M

Macpherson, C.B. 95, 100
Magdoff, H. 93

Maine, H. 57, 73
male science 21, 44
Mamdani, M. 157
manifest and latent 65
Mannheim, K. 19, 20; and Marx 20
Manuel, F. 169
manufacturing truth 23
market: competition 50; demand 113;
  economy 156; society 84, 100-101,
  166; transactions 67
Marx the humanist 49
Marx, K. 10, 18, 19, 48, 62, 103, 130-131,
  141, 199
Marx and Engels 20, 49-51, 143, 145,
  160, 162
Marx on peasants 147
Marx's model of revolution 13
Marxism: 12, 198; and revolution 107, 143-
  146; orthodox and non-orthodox views
  143- 144; and dependency 115-122; and
  ideology 20; and positivism 130-131; and
  social change 129; and underdevelopment
  116
Marxist methodology 12, 13; sociology 16
Marxist-feminists 191
Marxist-Leninist doctrine 98
masking truth 22
Matthews, R. 123, 124
McAlister, J. and P. Mus 159
McCain, G. 21
McClelland, D. 82-85, 89, 98, 102
McGinnis, R. 106
Mead, G.H. 40, 41, 43
means of production 49, 50, 51
measurement of meaning 36
mechanical solidarity 69, 73
media and propaganda 23
Menzies, K. 39
meritocratic society 79, 84
Merton, R. 64, 65
metaphysics 35
metropolis and hinterland 123; and
  satellite 123
Mies, M. et al 192
Migdal, J. 149-151, 156-157

226   Sociology and the Periphery

migration from rural to urban 90-91
Miles 170-171, 175, 177
Millikan, M. 95
Mills, C.W. 19, 31
mind as blank slate 41
mind and self 41
mining and manufacturing 125
mining colonies 111
Mintz, S. 144, 149, 159
miscegenation 182-183
MNCs: 109, 119-120, 122, 124, 129, 133, 198; in the Caribbean 109-110, 112; and host economies 119; and underdevelopment 109
mobile personality 86
mode of production 50, 129, 154, 198; capitalist 134, 136; feudal 134
modern man 81, 83-84, 86
modern society 80-81, 84; transition to 91; definition of 79
modernization: 71, 79, 98, 127-129, 196-197; challenge of 89; criticisms of 84; and development 77; and Latin America 85; politics and ideology of 94, 98, 104, 197; promises of 96; and social control 102; and social evolution 91, 103
modernization theory, a critique 115
modernization: values and attitudes 197; and beliefs 199
Molyneux, M. 190-191; as liberal feminist 192
money and credit 67
monocrop economies 137
Monroe Doctrine 96
monstra 175
monstrous races 175, 178
Montesquieu 29
Moore, W. 65, 66, 87, 91-92
Moore Jr., B. 159
morality 73
Moreno Fraginals, M. 172, 180, 184
Morgan, L. 57
Moslems and Jews 87
Mozambique 78
Mulkay, M. 34
Mullan, B. 27, 37, 59, 63, 65
multinational corporations see MNCs

multinational corporations 78, 93-94
Munck, R. 130
Myrdal, G. 158-159

N

Nash, M. 92
Nash, J. 190
national consciousness 136
nationalism 9, 22, 131, 171; and imperialism 121
nativism 36
natural science 24, 32, 35-36, 58
natural selection 72
natural laws 58-59, 130; natural social laws 32
necessary labour 52-54
need for belonging 107
need for achievement 83, 102
negative criticism 33-34, 60
negative philosophy 34
negotiated social meaning 42
new revolutionary classes 144
New World 182-183
New World Order 78, 116
Nicaragua 78, 117
Niosi, J. 122-125
Nisbet, R. and R. Perrin 25, 26, 28
nomothetic knowledge 9
non-socialist societies 16
Noriega, M. 116
North-South 94, 117
Nun, J. 85, 101

O

O'Connor, J. 163-164
objective knowledge 17, 38, 44,
objectivity: and scientific methodology 17, 18; and data 18
Ojeda, T. 183

Old Testament 180; colour symbolisms 171
Old Testament and racism *see* racism in the Old Testament
ontology, positivist 105; realist 105
ontology 11, 23, 24, 32, 45, 47, 196
order 33-34; and progress 60-61
Orenstein, D. 80-81
organic solidarity 69-71, 73
organic intellectuals 162-163, 167
organismic analogy 58, 62, 63, 67, 68, 76, 80
Orwell, G. 23
Osgood, C.E. et al. 36
Oxaal, I. 93

P

Panamá 78
Parkin, F. 17
Parsons, T. 63, 66, 71-74, 85
patron-client relations 87, 134, 151, 156, 157-158
pattern variables 73-75, 85, 88-89
Patterson, O. 9
Paz, P. 120
Pearse, A. 157
peasant communities: demographic changes 156-157; transformation of 149; differentiation within 149-152, differentiation vs stratification 153
peasant revolutionary mobilization 152-154, 155-156
peasant households: pressures on 158-159; social relations among 152
peasant inward orientation *see* peasant insularity
peasant insularity 150-151, 153, 157-158, 166
peasant social organization 149-151
peasantry: 13; as a class 147-149; and class struggle 148
peasants: and revolution 13, 147, 159-160; and the Cuban revolution 163-165; and rural guerilla warfare 155; and imperialism 156-158; and revolutionaries 164

peasants, two conceptions 148
periphery, lack of autonomous development 111, 115, 131, 136
personality traits and development 81
Petras, J. 144, 149, 160
phallic critique 45
Philosophes 28-29, 60
Plange, N. 91, 106
plantation colonies 111, 136; economy 109, 159; system 10, 132;
play stage and game stage 42
Pliny the Elder 174
political: independence 9; ideology 22; consciousness 165
politics of race 172
portenta 175
Portes, A. 40, 73, 75-77, 80, 120
positive philosophy 33-34
positivism: 12, 32-38, 43-44, 59-61, 79, 82; aims of 35; and constructivism 46; and determinism 107; as male science 45; feminist critique of 45; and interactionism 38; and behaviourism 36-38; and prediction 35; and immutable laws 61; and empiricism 62, 199; and social evolution 57; essential tenets 32; and social meaning 39; and empiricism 36, 43; and Marxism 36
positivistic method 36, 61
post-Cold War era 12, 78, 97
poverty: 9, 17, 91, 93, 113, 120, 125, 145, 160, 165; and imperialism 94; and misery 145; and revolution 141; and underdevelopment 105; and the woman of colour 186; and single mothers 186-187
Powell, J. 151
pragmatism 41
pre-modern society 80
Prebisch, R. 129
predestination 179
prediction and accuracy 25, 26
primary social attachments 73
primitive societies 71
primitive accumulation 50, 171
process of production 49, 141
productive forces 50, 52, 198
profit 52-53; maximization 90; pursuit of 50

progress 33-34, 57
proletarian revolution, a modification of Marx's theory 145
proletarianization 144, 149, 157, 159, 166
proletariat: 50-51; industrial 145, 160; as non-revolutionary 146; rural 144, 149, 159-160, 164, 166, 198; Third World living conditions of 142, 145-146; urban 146
proxy wars 116
psychological dimensions of development 81, 83; of change 81
Puerto Rico 78

Q

Quijano, A. 152, 155, 160

R

race and the European mentality 176; *see also* racism
race relations 109
race, biological and social definitions 185
race as justification for sexual exploitation 185
race as a relation of production 171
race, colour, and Christianity 177-182, 186
racism: 9, 13, 17, 22, 121, 169-172; before slavery 172; and colonialism 182; definition of 171; historical roots 173-174, 185; as ideology 171; and religious doctrine 182; and slavery 172; in the Old Testament 178
racism in classical antiquity 175
radical, definition of 15
radical: science 18; sociologists 17
Rafsanjani 97
Ramsaran, R. 126
rate of exploitation 52
rational market orientation 90
rationality: 61, 79-80; and irrationality 29; instrumental and value 81; and religion 29

Reagan, R. 97, 99, 126
realism: 12-13, 47, 55, 105, 139; and empiricism 47, 106-107; and historical materialism 48-51; and positivism 47
reality as socially constructed 46
reason 29, 33
Redfield, R. 73, 90
Reformation 34
reformism 16-17,
regionalism 122-123
reinforcement: positive and negative 37
relations of production 134, 144, 150, 154
religion: as irrationality 29; as source of human bondage 29; and economics 20; and social solidarity 62
religion and ideology 121
Renaissance 60
representative government 101
resource based economies 124
retrograde party 34
revolution: subjective and objective dimensions 121
revolution: 12-13, 50, 51, 77, 92, 120, 139; and leadership 160-167; Marx's theory of 141; and peasants 13; in the periphery 166-167; as social pathology 58; of rising expectations 91-92
revolution vs revolt and rebellion 154-155, 160, 166
revolutionary consciousness 152; leadership and ideology 161
revolutions in the 20th century 144
Riddell, C. 26
Ritzer G. 33, 60-62, 68, 72
Rodney, W. 113
role taking 41
Rosenblat, A. 182
Rostow, W. W. 75-77, 92, 95
Rousseau, J.J. 29
Rudra, A. 152
ruling ideas 20
rural labour shortage 90

S

Saddam Hussein 97
Safa, H. 187, 190-192, 195
Sanders, R. 176
Sandinistas 117
Sansom, R. 151
Sartre, J.P. 109
science: aims of 24; as a way of knowing 24; and the game of objectivity 17, 44; and dogma 21; and ideology 11, 18, 21; and objectivity 18; subject matter of 24
science and religion, role of 33
science and behaviour 37; and industry, principles of 34;
scientific: method 24; rationality 79; revolutions 18; truth 21, 33-34, 36
scientists as moral and intellectual leaders 61; as opinion makers 18; as priests, 61
Scott, J. 158
seasonal unemployment 142
secondary social attachments 73
secular religion 79
secularization 34
Segal, E. 21
Seidman, S. 28, 34
self and social interaction 42
self-identity 42
self-understanding 47
Seltman, C.T. 173
sensory experience 35
separation of church and state 88
sexism: 9, 13, 121, 169; and morality 183; and socialism 192
sexual division of labour 191
Shanin, T. 142, 145, 147, 148, 150, 154-155, 162
shared symbols and meanings 39, 41
Shils, E. 172
significant others 42
single industry towns 124, 125
situationally transcendent ideas 20-21

Skinner, B.F. 36, 38, 44
slavery 109, 132; and colonialism 171; and economics 181; and racism 172
slavery as an economic institution 172; 181
slavery as redemption for black sinners 180-181
Slomcyznski, K. 84-85
small economies 133
Smelser, N. 65, 66, 68, 70-71
Smucker, J. 124
Snowden Jr., F. 172-173, 174, 179
social revolution see revolution
social science: subject matter of 25; and natural science contrasted 25, 32
social: complexity 66-67, 111; consciousness 49, 161; control 13; control in liberal society 22-23; Darwinism 57, 72; differentiation 70-71, 73; dynamics 34, 58; engineering 37; evolutionism 12, 107, 127-129; equilibrium 65, 67; exchange 150-151; forecasting 25; inequality 13; integration 64, 66, 70; meaning 40, 43, 79-80, 170-172, 199; needs 63, 80; order 10, 39, 62, 65, 68; psychology 16, 41, 81; reality 80; solidarity 68-69; statics 33; structure 11, 27, 43, 62, 106-107, 139, 161; system 67-68, 70
social and natural science compared 25, 32
social banditry 152, 166
social behaviour as patterned 26-27, 38, 48
social change 34, 38, 55, 57, 65; sources of 66; metaphysical view 60; theological view 59-60; and development 48, 80
social change and Marxism 129
social evolutionism see also evolutionism
social evolutionism: conservative ideology of 61; functionalist aspects of 62
social revolution, context of 167
socialism as answer to dependent capitalism 129
socialist revolution 130
societal evolution 196
society as integrated whole 58; as a system 63

sociological generalization 9, 25
sociological imagination 31
sociology: and common sense 27; and
   criticism 26, 28; of development 73, 75;
   and the individual 26; and prediction 25;
   as a science 23, 36; as subversion 28
Sorokin, P. 25, 26
Soviet Union 16, 94, 96
Soviet sociology as State ideology 16
Spain 87
specialization of functions 67, 69
specialization and complexity 70, 71
Spencer H. 58, 62, 66, 70, 72; as
   conservative 68; as evolutionist 66-68
spiritual unity 33
St. Simon 32, 33, 59; as racist 169, 178
stages of economic growth, criticisms
   of 76
standpoint epistemology 44, 47
Stavenhagen, R. 143
Stepanov, L. 142
Stephens, J. 80, 99
Stevenson, M. 176
stimulus and response 36-37
structural features of society 47-48
structural functionalism 62-72, 92, 107;
   see also functionalism
structural: adjustment 186-187; inequalities 102; thinking 26, 80
structure of dependence 105, 139
structures as patterned relationships 64
subjective meaning 15, 40, 44, 46-47,
   80; truth and proof 21, 24, 25
subjective component of revolutionary
   consciousness 141
subjectivity and bias 17, 38; and individuals 15; and knowledge 17; and
   science 18; and values 18
subsistence peasants 158
substructure 19
Sunkel, O. 120, 129
superpowers and the Third World 95
superstructure 19; ideological 134
surplus labour 52-54
surplus value: 51-54, absolute 53;
   relative 54
survival of the fittest 77

Sutherland, E. 193
Sweezy, P. 144
symbolic interactionism 39-41; see also
   interactionism
symbolic meaning 43
system survival 64, 65
system regulation 67
systemic sexism 45
systems and sub-systems 63-64

T

Talib, B. and A. Majid 144, 149
targets of sociological inquiry 29
tautology 62-63
teleology 62-63
theological world view 29, 34
theoretical realism see realism
theory and ideology 196
Third World: is also capitalist 115; living
   conditions 55, 142; intellectuals and
   revolutionary leadership 163
Third World: external debt 133, 135;
   long term debt 135
Thomas, H. 163
Thomas, W.I. and D. Thomas 179
Thompson, E. 131, 132
Thompson, C. 164
threats to objectivity 17
Tilly, C. 31
Toennies, F. 72, 73
totalitarian society 23
traditional man 83
traditional society 84, 86, 91; source of
   change 92
traditional intellectuals 162-164, 167
tribalism 171
Trinidad-Tobago 117
truth: pre-scientific sources 29; subjective
   and objective 24; and fact 21, 23, 24; and
   evidence 18
Turner, J. 28
Turner, B. 180

U

underdevelopment: 10, 12, 139; as original state 108; blaming the victim 197; class explanation 116; capitalist causes 108, 115; as ideology 115; making of 77; politics of 116
undeveloped and underdeveloped, a distinction 77, 108
uneven development *see also* lopsided development
uneven development 9, 57, 111, 115, 122, 161; in Canada 123, 125, 127
United States *see* US
universal stages of change and development 66
universal intellectual order and unity 33, 61
universal law 35
Urry, J. 47, 48
US and LA compared 86
US: 94; business interests in Canada 122-123; as enemy of democracy 117; foreign capital in Cuba 163; interference in the Third World 95-96; and invasions in the Third World 116-117;and military assistance to the Caribbean 118; and military support for Third World dictators 116; opposition to revolution in the Third World 78; Supreme Court and kidnapping 116
US liberalism 88
USSR 78, 84
Utley, F. 178

V

Valdés T. and M. Weinstein 190
value judgements 22; as ideology 17
value orientations 80, 81; theory 73
values and attitudes: 89-90, 99, 102; and development 81-84, 86-87
variable capital 51-52
Veltmeyer, H. 123, 124
verstehen 40
Vietnam 23, 78, 98
Virgil 174
vital system needs 63
voluntarism 43
von Bothmer, D. 173

W

wage relationship 51-54, 132
Wagner, H.R. 174
Wallace, R. 39
Wallerstein, E. 113
Warren B. 119
watch analogy 27
Watson, J.B. 36, 44
Weber M. 10, 17, 18-20, 40, 61-62, 80-81, 180; ideas and class 19; and interactionism 40; and subjectivity 19
Weber on Marx 19
Weiner, M. 81, 94
Westby, D. 58
Western Europe 85
White, H. 176
Williams, E. 172
Wilson, J. 35, 47, 48, 65, 105
Wolf, A. 39
Wolf, E. 143, 149, 154-156, 160, 164
women in development 13
women and poverty, responses 190
women and development: 186-189; Jamaica 187; Dominican Republic 187-189
women and socialism 192-193; and patriarchy 192-193
women of colour 183-185
women in Cuba, revolutionary demands on 192-193
women: contribution to household finances 190; interests of 191; political mobilization 190-191
working class families 187
world capitalist system 13, 111, 108, 127
world market 137
World Bank 103, 187
World War II 197
Worrell, D. et al 127

X

xenophobia 174-175

Z

Zeitlin, I. 19, 28-29, 33-34, 115, 131, 169
Zhukov, Y. 142